EGYPTIAN MAGIC

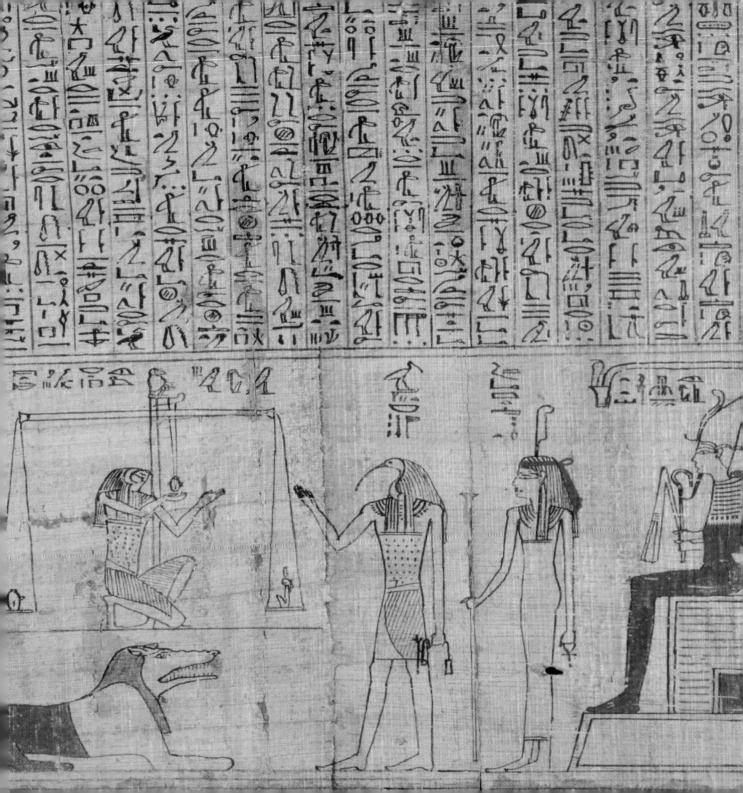

EGYPTIAN MAGIC

THE QUEST FOR THOTH'S BOOK OF SECRETS

MAARTEN J. RAVEN

THE AMERICAN UNIVERSITY IN CAIRO PRESS

CAIRO   NEW YORK

The following extracts from published translations are reproduced by permission:

Pages 7–8 *(Go into the library . . . 'The Book of Magic.')*, page 11 *(Well tended . . . by night.)*, page 33 *(The Majesty of the King . . . of their festivals.)*, pages 40–41 *(The priest said to . . . what had been in it.)*, page 55 *(he had a sheet . . . had been in it.)*, page 75 *(I will have you taken . . . form of rising.)*, page 127 *(Furnish your . . . ready too.)*, and page 128 *(The* ba *comes . . . give it water)* from M. Lichtheim, *Ancient Egyptian Literature I–III* (Berkeley: University of California Press, 1975–80); page 12 *(Everybody trembles . . . over the other gods.)* and page 47 *([Re speaks:] . . . the entire land)* from J.K. Ritner *The Mechanics of Ancient Egyptian Magical Practices* (Chicago: Oriental Institute of the University of Chicago, 1993); page 59 *(Words to be said . . . festival of Renenutet.)*, page 79 *(murderers . . . from afar.)*, page 91 *(Backwards . . . accordingly!)*, and page 105 *(Hail to you, . . . Renenuet-festival.)* from J.F. Borghouts, *Ancient Egyptian Magical Texts* (Leiden: Brill, 1978); page 86 *(The method of . . . Hurry, hurry!)* from H.D. Betz, *The Greek Magical Papyri* (The University of Chicago Press, London © 1986, 1992 by the University of Chicago); pages 173–74 *(Kouchos, Trochos . . . Quickly! Quickly!)* from J. Drescher, *Annales du Service des Antiquités de l'Égypte* 48 (1948).

Illustration, page 2: From The Book of the Dead (detail), see page 155.
Illustration, page 6: Seal of Moses (detail), see page 186.

This paperback edition published in 2019 by
The American University in Cairo Press
113 Sharia Kasr el Aini, Cairo, Egypt
200 Park Ave., Suite 1700, New York, NY 10166
www.aucpress.com

Copyright © 2010, 2012, 2019 by Maarten J. Raven
First published in Dutch in 2012 as Egyptische Magie. Translated into English by arrangement with Rijkmuseum van Oudheden, p/a Ultgeversmaatschappij Walburg Pers, Zutphen

Dar el Kutub No. 26360/18
ISBN 978 977 416 933 5

Dar el Kutub Cataloging-in-Publication Data

Raven, Maarten J.
    Egyptian Magic: The Quest for Thoth's Book of Secrets / Maarten J. Raven.—Cairo: The American University in Cairo Press, 2019.
        p.   cm.
        ISBN: 978 977 416 933 5
        1- Egypt – Antiquities
        2- Magic, Egyptian
        932

1 2 3 4 5   23 22 21 20 19

Designed by Andre Klijsen
Printed in China

CONTENTS

PREFACE

This spell was found in Hermopolis beneath the feet of the majesty of this august god, on a block of Upper Egyptian quartzite [inscribed] by the hand of the god himself, at the time of the King of Upper and Lower Egypt Menkaura, by Prince Hordedef who found it when he came to inspect the temples.

These words conclude a number of spells from the ancient Egyptian Book of the Dead (chapters 30B, 64, 137, and 148), the best known of Egypt's funerary texts. The 'august god' concerned can only be Thoth, god of wisdom, whose sacred town of Khemenu lies in central Egypt (modern name: al-Ashmunayn). The town later acquired the name Hermopolis, because Greek visitors to Egypt considered Thoth to be identical to their own god Hermes. What made the Egyptians believe that a god had put magic spells at their disposal? And why would they identify him as Thoth, the god of writing, who was usually depicted as an ibis or as a man with an ibis head?

No invention exerted as much influence on life in ancient Egypt as did writing. Its introduction dates back to about 3000 BC, the period when Egypt was united by the first pharaohs. Without a writing system the rulers could never have controlled this enormous kingdom—which measured roughly a thousand kilometers from north to south—from a single capital. Without writing, the entire fascinating culture of ancient Egypt would not have been possible. We know the Egyptian script under a Greek name: *hieroglyphs*, which means 'sacred inscribed signs.'

This designation is adequate insofar as it expresses the Egyptians' conviction that their script had a supernatural origin. They believed the god Thoth had personally invented it so as to serve as secretary to the other gods. Later, he also granted it to the Egyptians.

At first, the hieroglyphic script was only employed by a select number of the pharaoh's officials. Later its use became slightly more common, although 99 percent of the Egyptian population remained illiterate. This explains how the title 'scribe' became a mark of distinction. Those who were able to write were regarded by the majority as persons with eerie supernatural powers: sages, wizards, sorcerers. The scribes themselves made sure that this image was maintained by making the writing system extraordinarily complicated and inaccessible.

As a result Thoth was also seen as the god of wisdom and magic, *guardian of the great book with the divine words*, as he is called in another spell from the Book of the Dead (chapter 167). The Second Story of the magician Khaemwas says of Thoth: *It is you who put magic in writing, it is you who suspended the sky, who founded the earth and the netherworld, and who assigned the gods to their constellations.* And the same text shows that very occasionally, the god answered the invocations of his faithful servants, the magicians: *Go into the library of the temple of Khemenu. You will find a chamber that is locked and sealed. Open it and you will find a chest in this chamber, and in it a papyrus scroll which I wrote with my own hand. Take it out, make a copy of it, and put it back in its place. Its name is 'The Book of Magic.'*

Modern readers of these stories may find all this difficult to believe. For the ancient Egyptians, however, the existence of magic offered the most plausible explanation for the layout of the cosmos. How else to explain that sun and moon do not drop out of the sky, that day and night alternate, that people fall ill and recover, and that (as the Egyptians firmly believed) a new life follows after death? Magicians were neither idiots nor impostors, but rather the indispensable guardians of the god-given cosmic order *(ma'at)*, learned scholars who were always searching for the magic book of Thoth which could explain the wonders of nature. Magic was a gift the gods gave mankind to help them in the struggle for life.

This belief in the divine origin of supernatural wisdom and potential mastery over the cosmos survived for thousands of years, throughout the entire pharaonic period, and beyond. Trust in magic grew as Egyptian political power weakened. During the last millennium before the Christian era, the country witnessed several economic crises and periods of anarchy or foreign occupation. The invasion by Alexander the Great in 332 BC and the foundation of the new capital of Alexandria gave rise to a new blend of cultures: Hellenism. The

new immigrants marveled at the architectural and intellectual wonders that had been realized along the banks of the Nile. Those ingenious creations were clear evidence of the exceptional wisdom of the Egyptians, and nobody doubted that the origin of such genius was of a supernatural and magic character.

The scholars of the famous Alexandrian library made a thorough study of Egyptian traditions. Numerous old stories were put in writing for the first time and translated into Greek. Among these were the ancient Egyptian books of magic, which were treated with the same awe that nowadays is reserved for the publications of important scientists. Books of magic were believed to provide the key to understanding the universe, since through them gods such as Thoth-Hermes had allowed mankind to glimpse this superior reality. Such ideas were in perfect accordance with Greek philosophical concepts, especially those of Plato and Pythagoras.

The outcome of this quest for knowledge was codified in the so-called Hermetic treatises, which survived not just the pharaonic era but also classical antiquity. They were rediscovered during the Renaissance and exerted a profound influence on the rise of new esoteric societies, such as Freemasons, Rosicrucians, theosophists, and spiritualists. Alchemy and the varied European subculture of magicians, medicine men, fortune-tellers, and witches have likewise derived part of their inspiration from oral and written traditions ultimately originating in ancient Egypt. The same is true of more modern fantasies concerning pyramid power and the curse of the pharaohs, the popularity of mediums and alternative healers, and even the success of the Harry Potter books.

Seen in this light, Egyptian magic is still very much alive today. In the field of Egyptology, a fair number of publications have been devoted to the theory and practice of magic, justified by the fact that a study of this phenomenon is essential for a clear understanding of pharaonic culture. None of these publications is still readily available. The opportunity to write this book arose in 2010, when the National Museum of Antiquities (Rijksmuseum van Oudheden) in Leiden, the Netherlands, decided to organize a major exhibition on this fascinating theme (15 October 2010–13 March 2011). The search for the magic book of Thoth will lead us to the remotest corners of human fantasy, and I hope the readers will enjoy it as much as the author.

Part of the pleasure for me lay in my travel companions on this journey. I would like to thank José Bouman, Rob Demarée, Marc Etienne, Willem van Haarlem, Cisca Hoogendijk, Eline Kevenaar, Nozomu Kawai, Marieke Meijers, Sigrid van Roode, John Taylor, Lucie Wassink, Ton Wiechmann, and Carolien van Zoest, without whom both the book and the exhibition would definitely have had a different character. I am most grateful to Peter Jan Bomhof and Anneke de Kemp, the photographers of the Leiden Museum, for their enormous dedication in producing most of the illustrations. The attractive layout of this book is due to the designer Andre Klijsen and to the Walburg Pers (Zutphen, the Netherlands). A special word of thanks is due to Neil Hewison and Randi Danforth of the American University in Cairo Press, who immediately embraced the idea of publishing an English edition, to Salima Ikram for supporting these efforts and checking the translation, and to my wife Nienke for her sound advice on both the language and contents of this edition.

A PRESENT OF THE GODS

Well tended is mankind—god's cattle.
He made sky and earth for their sake.
[...]
He made for them plants and cattle,
Fowl and fish to feed them.
[...]
He made for them magic as weapons,
To ward off the blow of events,
Guarding them by day and by night.

(INSTRUCTION FOR KING MERIKARE, 130–37)

FIG. 1. The sun god Re sails over the waters of the netherworld, protected by a serpent and accompanied by Sia (in front) and Heka (behind). Unfinished painting in the tomb of Pharaoh Horemheb, Thebes. Photograph: RMO.

COSMIC WISDOM OR BLACK ART?

in the modern world, magic no longer plays a part in contemporary life. At least, that is what many like to believe. In the western world, magic is generally dismissed as something backward, as a superstition that may still be common among representatives of 'exotic' religions or non-western cultures, but of course not with modern people. Magic is often seen as something discreditable, 'black art' or 'voodoo practices' which primitive people used to make each other's lives miserable. Magic and religion are seen as two quite separate matters. Moreover, in the western world even the influence of religion is diminishing, and many people do not appear to mind at all.

But is this picture correct? Perhaps, in the west, people attend religious services less frequently, but it seems as if there has never been a greater interest in paranormal phenomena such as astrology, transcendent meditation, alternative treatments, 'healing,' mysticism, and other forms of spirituality. Often these should in fact be regarded as superstition: attitudes which do not fit into a coherent world view, irrespective of whether the latter is based on religion or not (although magic concepts fit harmoniously within other coherent religions or world views, and then we cannot call them superstition). Even western nonbelievers may have superstitious feelings about the number thirteen, they touch wood (preferably oak) in order to avert bad luck, or they place a book under their pillow the night before they have to pass an exam. Christian practice includes rituals and traditions which cannot be explained in a rational way and which do not always allow a clear distinction between belief, superstition, and magic. And we are all very attached to ritual on the occasion of special events such as birth, marriage, or death, although we often do not understand their original significance.

Matters were completely different for the ancient Egyptians. Magic was an indispensable element of a well-ordered life, and it was impossible to draw a border between religion and magic. Magic was nothing to be ashamed of, it was not illegal, and the moral distinction between 'white' and 'black' magic did not yet exist. All gods could be invoked for the purposes of sorcery, and even threatened if they appeared reluctant to do what was demanded of them. Only those who used magic to endanger the life of the pharaoh (and thereby jeopardized Egypt itself) were accused of high treason and condemned to death. Magic was practiced not just by herdsmen reciting charms or old women with a knowledge of herbs, but also by the high priests of the most important gods and other representatives of the intellectual elite. It was a science studied by the greatest minds of their time, a discipline intimately linked with astronomy, medicine, chemistry, philosophy, and other fields of knowledge in which the Egyptians were a long way ahead of other contemporary cultures.

Magic was an important means to help the weakest members of society: pregnant women and young children, the ill and the elderly, and of course the dead (for whom it meant that they could continue to be members of the community). According to the Instruction for King Merikare (a book of wisdom that became one of the classics of Egyptian literature), the Creator granted magic power to humans as a special favor that privileged them over other creatures. But even the Egyptian gods themselves were subject to magic. A hymn to the gods states: *Everybody trembles when he manifests himself, Magic who has power over the other gods.* Magic was older than most of the gods and was sometimes regarded as the firstborn son of the Creator.

The word 'magic' is derived from Greek, which gave it to Latin in its turn. It refers to a tribe in ancient Persia, the Magi, who provided the Persian court with priests who specialized in the presentation of offerings to the gods, the explanation of dreams and omens, and the prediction of the future. In the course of time they acquired the reputation of 'the wise men from the east,' so that the term Magi is also used by the author of the well-known biblical story of the birth of Christ (Matthew 2:1). In Rome the Magi did not enjoy such a favorable reputation. On several occasions these oriental soothsayers and their adherents were accused of subversive activities against the state and removed from the city. The history of the Magi alone addresses two questions that have always been associated with magic: does it denote superior wisdom or is it a black art?

A STRUGGLE FOR LIFE AND DEATH

Magic can be defined as a body of spells and actions that seek to affect fate by supernatural means. How one defines 'fate' is largely determined by the cultural context, and in ancient Egypt this would have been radically different from what it is today. Prior to the development of the modern sciences, people assumed the existence of connections within the cosmos that most of us no longer acknowledge. Much of what ancient Egyptians thought about magic arose directly from their religious beliefs about the creation of the world and the relationship between gods and men. Consequently, any modern understanding of how Egyptian magicians worked requires a basic knowledge about Egyptian religion and mythology.

Most Egyptian myths of creation recount how the earth was once covered by an enormous sea: the primeval water. The Creator manifested himself in the water and caused a well-organized world to emerge from the shapeless protoplasm by neatly separating the opposites: dark and light, wet and dry, male and female, good and evil, order and chaos. Thus from the water rose a primeval hill on which the first forms of life could develop. In this ordered world, the Creator lived in the midst of his creatures in perfect harmony. He is usually called Atum or identified with the god Re, whose brilliant eye is the sun. He engendered the first divine couple, Shu and Tefnut, the ancestors of all other gods. Next, he created humans, animals, and plants. According to one version of the myth, the Creator simply spoke the names of all the creatures that he wanted to bring into being. First he contrived them with his intellect *(sia)* or in his heart, and then he gave them life with his utterance *(hu)* or his tongue. His magical powers *(heka)* also played an essential part in the process. The three concepts Sia, Hu, and Heka were regularly regarded as independent gods, a kind of hypostasis of the Creator and forming his permanent escort (fig. 1).

As in all creation myths, this paradisiacal world was not to last long. Man rebelled against King Re, who therefore sent out his solar eye against them in the guise of the bloodthirsty lion goddess Sekhmet ('the Mighty One,' fig. 2). Many people perished, and the carnage would have been much worse if Re had not mixed the spilled blood with beer so that Sekhmet, who lapped up the brew, became drunk and fell asleep. From then on, death and disease have been prevalent on earth to keep humanity under control.

Even so, Re did not feel secure so he separated heaven (the goddess Nut) and earth (the god Geb) in order to

FIG. 2. The goddess Sekhmet is usually depicted as a woman with the head of a lioness. As daughter of Re she carries a sun disk on her head. Photograph: RMO (acc.no. F 1953/5.2).

FIG. 3. The god of the air, Shu, separates heaven and earth. To the right and left, the bark of the sun god sails through the sky. Painting from the funerary papyrus of Paser. Photograph: RMO (acc.no. AMS 34).

FIG. 4. The fight between Re and Apophis, depicted as tomcat and serpent respectively. From the Book of the Dead of Kenna. Photograph: RMO (acc.no. SR).

control the situation from above (fig. 3). He also created a netherworld *(duat)*, where he could recover after a long day's work. This became the abode of the dead who, like the sun, could arise again at daybreak. The reddish hue of the sky at dawn and dusk reminded the Egyptians that the forces of chaos had not yet been eliminated, and that each day another bloody battle had to be fought to preserve the world order *(ma'at)*. Re's chief opponent was the gruesome serpent Apophis, who could manifest himself as a cloud blocking the sun's rays or as a sandbank in the river of the netherworld obstructing the free passage of the solar

FIG. 5. This bronze triad shows the mummiform Osiris flanked by his wife Isis and their son Horus. Photograph: RMO (acc.no. CI 83).

FIG. 6. A wooden figure of Seth shows him with the head of a mythical creature resembling a donkey. It was made during the time when the god was still worshiped in his own temples. Photograph: RMO (acc.no. AH 213).

bark. The sun god tried to overcome these dangers by continuously assuming other forms himself, like a tomcat or a mongoose attacking the serpent (fig. 4).

The next generations of gods were not spared from bloodshed. The children of the first divine couple (Shu and Tefnut) were Geb and Nut, who produced four children: Osiris, Isis, Seth, and Nephthys (figs. 5–6). With them the family of primeval gods was complete (usually called the Ennead, Greek for 'the Nine'), but this was no guarantee of harmony. Osiris became king on earth, only to be murdered by his jealous brother Seth. Isis reassembled his dismembered body and brought him to life again, but Osiris was unable to continue his earthly rule and instead became king of the netherworld.

Seth had assumed his path to the throne would be clear, but to his dismay he discovered that Isis had miraculously become pregnant by her deceased spouse and had given birth to a son, Horus. Seth set out to find and kill mother and son, but Isis had found refuge in the marshes of the Delta and she possessed so much magic power that she succeeded in warding off all attacks.

When Horus reached adulthood, he entered into battle with his murderous uncle (fig. 7). The ensuing fight was terrible; it cost Seth his testicles and Horus one of his eyes. Subsequently, however, a divine court of justice declared Horus to be his father's rightful heir and the new king of Egypt. Bit by bit the gods restored his injured eye, a phenomenon we can still observe in the sky as the moon waxes until it is whole *(wedja)* again. Seth, now sterile, was banished to the infertile deserts, from where he continued to threaten the ordered world of the Nile valley.

FIG. 7. Horus the Elder is falcon-headed and wears the crowns of Upper and Lower Egypt. He is represented as standing on an antelope, a manifestation of the vanquished Seth. Photograph: RMO (acc.no. AB 163).

This was the hard world that faced the Egyptian magicians. Life in Egypt was precarious, even for its kings. Although as Horus's earthly manifestation the pharaoh maintained order and quiet, he was also a mere mortal. After his death, he was supposed to unite with Osiris and continue his rule in the netherworld, and his son would inherit the earthly throne as the new Horus. But Seth was always lying in wait, for instance in the guise of foreign enemies who threatened the country.

In the meantime, the Egyptian population was prone to suffer from plagues and other physical hardships, especially during the hot summer months when the Nile was low and the granaries were empty. That was the season when the messengers of Sekhmet roamed the country and shot their arrows at men. Many would perish, but who would guarantee they would live on in the netherworld? Egypt as a whole depended on the Nile floods, but what if time stopped between one flood cycle and the next, during the five intercalary days at the end of the year? What if Apophis disrupted the cycle of day and night? The consequences might have been extremely grave, were it not for the Creator's gift of magic.

THE LEADING ACTORS

The mythological stories demonstrate how indispensable magic was, even to the gods, for preserving creation. There was no shame in the practice of magic. On the contrary, magicians possessed an utterly legitimate gift, and the gods demonstrated how to deploy it in the battle between good and evil. That is why spells usually refer to situations in a mythical past: if god X found benefit in a certain spell or action then this will also be beneficial now to patient Y. This connection underlines the importance of being familiar with Egyptian mythology in order to understand magical practice in ancient Egypt. Certain principal actors recur time and again.

In the first place we should mention the god Heka. He remains a somewhat indistinct character, an abstract being rather than one of flesh and blood. The word *heka* is sometimes interpreted as 'who propels the *ka* *(hu-ka)*, where *ka* is the vitality or energy of life that moves all creatures. That Heka himself is a driving force is also expressed by the special hieroglyph used to write his name: it depicts the rear part of a lion, in ancient Egyptian script the symbol for 'power.' Accordingly, Heka is often represented as a man carrying this symbol on his head (fig. 8). Sometimes he holds serpents in his hands, creatures crawling from the earth and so forming a connection with the mysterious netherworld. Moreover, snakes regularly shed their old skins, thus becoming a symbol of new life after death.

The importance of Thoth as a god of magic has already been mentioned (fig. 9). He was also considered a moon god, and consequently deputy of the sun god Re. This explains the part he played in restoring the *wedjat* eye (fig. 71), which symbolizes the moon. Thoth serves as secretary to the divine court of justice, which determines the fate of every human being in the hereafter (fig. 127) and which also issued the verdict on the battle between Horus and Seth. He preserves all the gods' records—including the scrolls of magic—and determines the passing of time. His sacred animals were the ibis and the baboon (fig. 133).

The goddess Isis, who restored her murdered husband Osiris to life and saved her child Horus from Seth's assaults, was also very important. But how did Isis acquire her magical power? This is recounted in an amusing story, which tells how Isis used all her guile to discover the secret name of the sun god Re. In the end, she succeeded in getting hold of some of the god's spittle, mixing it with clay, and modeling it into a serpent, which she laid on the

path Re usually followed. The serpent bit the god, who cried out in pain and called to all the gods for help—to no avail. Finally Isis came toward Re and said that she could cure him, but only if he revealed his secret name. After offering a number of false names, Re finally gave in. He told Isis the name that contained all his magic (as did the spittle she had collected earlier), and so she was able to cure him and became foremost among the gods in the field of sorcery.

Being the child of Isis, Horus likewise wielded extraordinary magic powers. Even as a child (Harpocrates or 'Horus the Child') he contrived to vanquish the serpents and scorpions that Seth sent to him. This explains why the naked child with his side-lock (a hairstyle worn by all children in ancient Egypt) is often represented with these dangerous animals in his hands, or even restraining lions and antelopes (frightening creatures from the desert, Seth's domain) and standing on crocodiles (fig. 73). Sick patients were often identified with Harpocrates by the attendant doctors and magicians to mobilize the healing powers of the child and its mother, Isis. Horus was associated with his sacred animal, the falcon.

A less well-known manifestation of the same god was Horus of Three-hundred Town (Horus *imy-shenut*), a cult center probably situated near Sohag in central Egypt. Usually this god was depicted as a falcon-headed crocodile (fig. 95). He was the patron of physicians and is often represented holding knives which he uses to ward off enemies. As 'lord of words' and 'prince of books' he was closely associated with the god Thoth.

Doctors also worshiped the god Imhotep, who is rendered in the guise of a seated man with shaved skull,

How Isis got to know the secret name of Re

The goddess had conceived in her heart to get to know the name of the august god. Every day Re appeared at the head of his crew seated on the throne of the horizon. The god was old, his mouth was weak, and he let his saliva drip on the ground. The spittle had fallen on the ground, and Isis kneaded it with her hands, together with the soil adhering to it. She modeled it into a sacred snake and made it look like a pointed object. It did not move, even though it had come to life in her presence. She left it behind on a road crossing which the god usually passed in order to make his heart abide with his Two Lands.

The august god came out of the palace with the gods in his following and strode forth as he did every day. Then the sacred snake bit him: the living fire burst forth from him and even caused a devastation among the trees. The august god shouted out and the voice of His Majesty even reached heaven. And the Ennead said, "What is the matter? What is the matter?" And his gods said, "What is happening?" But he could not use his mouth in order to answer. His lips trembled and all his limbs were shaking. The poison had taken possession of his body, just as the inundation takes possession of everything behind it. . . .

Then Isis said to Re, "Tell me your name, divine father! A person can only relive if one speaks a conjuration using his name!" "I am he who created heaven and earth, who knotted together the mountains, who created everything which is on them. I am he who made the water, so that the Great Swimmer [the primeval cow goddess, source of all life] came into being. I am Khepri in the morning, Re in the afternoon, and Atum in the evening."

But the poison was not hindered in its spreading, and the great god did not feel relieved. Then Isis said to Re, "Your name did not occur among what you said. You have to tell it to me, then the poison will disappear. A person only relives if one speaks a conjuration using his name!"

The poison stung with a biting pain. It had become more powerful than flames, than fire. And the Majesty of Re said, "Lend me your ear, daughter of mine. Let my name be transferred from my body to yours . . . . And the great god told Isis his name, she of great magic.

(PAPYRUS TURIN 1993, VERSO 6.11–9.5)

FIG. 10. The sage Imhotep is represented as a shaven-headed priest reading from a scroll. Photograph: RMO (acc.no. F 1954/5.12).

reading from a scroll (fig. 10). Imhotep was an actual historic personality, the architect of the famous Step Pyramid of King Djoser near the capital Memphis. Since this was the earliest stone architectural monument in Egypt (and even in the world), the architect was believed to have supernatural talents. Because of his reputation as an exceedingly wise man, Imhotep was gradually deified by posterity. The Egyptians chiefly regarded him as the god of medicine, a profession dominated by wise and literate persons.

Physicians also had to face another divine being: the redoubtable goddess Sekhmet ('the Mighty One') who in primeval times almost destroyed humanity and still periodically manifested herself (fig. 2). The hot summer months in particular, when the Egyptian population was already weakened by lack of food and water, frequently brought on 'the plague of the year.' Then death and disease roamed the country as if the lioness had been loosed again. The goddess was also identified with the eye of the sun, daughter of Re, who scorches the fields in summer. Sekhmet presided over the seven knife-bearers, and she could also conscript the thirty-six gods of the decades (the periods of ten days each into which the year was divided; see fig. 83). Man had no defense against their arrows, so people did their utmost to pacify the angry goddess. To this end, they invoked her by numerous different names in the course of extensive rituals. If these succeeded, Sekhmet would transform herself into her alternative forms of the peaceful cat Bastet, the cow goddess Hathor, or the mother goddess Mut of Thebes. In order to control plagues, more than seven hundred statues of Sekhmet were erected in the temple of Mut at Karnak (fig. 103). Others graced the mortuary temple of Pharaoh Amenhotep III on the opposite bank of the Nile. The priests of Sekhmet were expert magicians, and they were the only ones who could cure the diseases caused by the goddess. They became, as a result, Egypt's first specialized physicians.

In Sekhmet, we come across a phenomenon that is characteristic of the Egyptian pantheon. The gods were neither good nor evil, but often very ambiguous. It was necessary to please them or they might become hostile. This accounts for the hippopotamus goddess Taweret ('the Great One'). Hippopotami could be extremely dangerous if inadvertently encountered in the marshes. They were not really popular with the farmers either, as they used to destroy the crops. Because they spent their lives in the fertile waters of the Nile, however, they were regarded as a source of new life themselves (fig. 42). Taweret is represented as a pregnant hippopotamus, often with human breasts or the tail of a crocodile (fig. 11). She was considered to be the protector of expectant mothers and young children.

Hearth and home also enjoyed the protection of a god having the appearance of a dwarf with crippled arms and legs and a large head, often provided with a lion's mane or tail. Today we know that dwarfism is caused by hormonal defects, but according to the ancient Egyptians a dwarf was a supernatural creature wielding specific magical powers. Dwarf gods were known by various names: In the Middle Kingdom they were often called Aha, 'the Warrior,' and carried knives and swords to ward off evil (fig. 12). Later they were usually designated as Bes and connected with all kinds of activities that make life enjoyable, such as song, dance, music, cosmetics, drunkenness, and sex. Although to modern eyes his appearance may seem comical, Bes lay always in wait to avert demons that might try to harm helpless human beings.

A relatively late development is the introduction of the god Tutu. He did not become known before the third century BC, when Egypt was already dominated by the Greeks. As a rule he was depicted as a sphinx, a mythical

FIG. 12. This image of the dwarf god Bes shows him with sword raised and wearing a frightening lion's mask, in the company of his wife Beset. Photograph: Allard Pierson Museum, Amsterdam (acc.no. 07762).

FIG. 13. The sphinx-shaped Tutu wields knives for eliminating his enemies. His tail ends in a frightful cobra. Photograph: RMO (acc.no. F 1959/5.1).

creature combining the physical strength of a lion's body and the intelligence of a human head (fig. 13). In Egypt, the image of the sphinx had a long history; it is the representation of a king in his aggressive aspect, or of the sun god himself. Tutu is easily distinguished from standard sphinxes by his serpent-shaped tail and extra heads, of a crocodile, ram, falcon, or ibis. These indicate that he incorporates the power of many other gods, for Tutu is regarded as the captain of Sekhmet's demons. He holds knives or axes in his claws for fighting the enemies of men and gods. Tutu is the god of magic *par excellence*. The Greco-Roman Period saw several such gods (especially dwarf gods) who combined the attributes of other powers

in a single body. Such images reflect a trend toward pantheism in contemporary religion: the notion that all deities are mere manifestations of a single god. The time had come for the rise of the great monotheistic religions that would dominate the succeeding period.

All these beneficial and apotropaic (evil-averting) gods were opposed by a number of notorious wrongdoers. After all, evil cannot be wiped out forever, and it has already been noted that even friendly gods could be dangerous. Real villains were Apophis and (at least in later periods of Egyptian history) Seth. Apophis, who is generally depicted as a large serpent, does not really have any positive attributes. As the opponent of the sun god, he endangers the survival of the cosmos. Still, some funerary books acknowledge that even Apophis plays a part in the universe as the embodiment of chaos.

Much more ambivalent is the character of Seth. Usually, he is represented as a mythical creature with a head like a donkey, erect ears, and a forked tail, or as a man with the head of such an animal (fig. 67). Horus and Seth were dual gods who both delegated their power to the pharaoh. Seth had his own domain as lord of the desert and the foreign territories. Until the end of the New Kingdom, Seth possessed his own temples, priests, and statues. He was especially worshiped in the eastern Nile delta because he was identified with the supreme deity of the immigrants from Palestine who made up part of the local population (a god usually called Baal), and in the western desert. Two pharaohs of this period even called themselves 'man of Seth' (Seti).

Later such a thing became impossible: Seth was increasingly demonized and cursed, and destructive rituals involving images of Seth were performed in the temples (fig. 92). A single exception survived. Because one evil can wipe out another, Seth is occasionally depicted in the prow of the solar bark, fighting Apophis (fig. 14). Like the serpent Apophis, Seth possesses the 'evil eye,' a hypnotizing glance that cuts like a knife and paralyzes men and gods alike. This belief in the evil eye is still widespread in the modern Near East.

FIG. 14. This stela of a man named Takyana was erected in honor of Re and Seth. The main scene shows a fight between Seth and the serpent Apophis. Photograph: RMO (acc.no. AP 60).

FIG. 15. A herdsman recites a charm against crocodiles, while his anxious cows cross a canal. One of his arms is extended in a commanding gesture; his stick serves as a magic wand. Photograph: RMO (acc.no. F 1939/2.7).

THE MAGICIANS OF EGYPT

WITCHES AND MEDICINE MEN

With so many principal actors on the stage, it is evident that a good education was essential for whoever wanted to practice magic professionally. At the same time, magic was so closely connected with all aspects of life that there were illiterate sorcerers. We may even assume that every Egyptian man and woman knew a number of charms for everyday use and had a vague notion of the concomitant gestures and rituals. These will have included quick prayers to alleviate certain complaints or inconveniences, simple domestic remedies for curing injuries, protective formulas to be recited at special occasions, and so on. Such traditions are the equivalent of what was known as 'natural' or 'white' magic in Europe during the Middle Ages and later. Even devout Christians considered this to be relatively innocuous because it made use of principles which God himself had put at humanity's disposal: the employment of medicinal herbs and plants, the healing power of certain stones and minerals, and the application of astrological concepts. A substantial body of knowledge of this kind dates back to age-old traditions, mostly deriving from late antiquity. Since the Greeks and Romans borrowed a fair proportion of their learning from the wonderland of the pharaohs, this means that in fact many ancient Egyptian ideas have survived in this way. Although modern science has demonstrated that many of these concepts cannot bear the test of criticism, alternative therapies seem to be more popular than ever before.

FIG. 16. This scorpion depicting the goddess Selkit has a human body and arms restraining serpents. The figurine once topped a staff carried in processions. Photograph: RMO (acc.no. F 1953/10.4).

In Europe this type of natural magic used to be especially associated with people whose lifestyles were more attuned to nature, such as herdsmen, fisherfolk, or collectors of medicinal herbs. From ancient Egypt, too, we have several depictions of herdsmen using magic to protect their flocks. When a herd of cattle is represented entering the water to cross a canal, a herdsman often stands ready with one arm extended to charm away the crocodiles (fig. 15). We may assume that this gesture was accompanied by the recitation of a protective formula. Indeed, one hieroglyphic caption specifies that it made the crocodiles go blind. A similar commanding gesture with fingers outstretched is made by herdsmen watching the birth of a calf. In that case it was probably done to ward off invisible forces that might bring bad luck or disease, and presumably the herdsmen invoked the help of supernatural powers or demons. Thereby they entered the domain which in medieval Europe was labeled 'black' magic, a term reflecting the belief that these practices were diabolical and anti-Christian. In ancient Egypt, however, 'black' magic was a legitimate practice within the religious system, reflecting the greater flexibility in religious thought in pre-monotheistic religions.

For more complicated problems every village must have had a local sage or medicine man (or woman). Life was hard and most people did not get very old. Those who did live to an advanced age automatically became the oracle of the inhabitants of their village. Thus some texts refer to a 'wise woman' *(rekhet)* who could give advice on diseases or predict the future. Often she also served as the local midwife. In (post-)medieval Europe such women would have run the risk of being persecuted as witches, but in ancient Egypt they were treated with the respect they deserved. For a society in which proper medical expertise was still in its infancy, their magical abilities generated reassurance and social cohesion. Male medicine men were often designated as 'protectors' *(sa)*, and their field of action likewise included both soothsaying and the healing of body and mind.

Everybody sooner or later was confronted with the unwanted presence of vermin in the house or storeroom or on the fields. In modern Egypt snakes and scorpions are still a real nuisance (fig. 16). Even today there are certain families that specialize in the capture and eradication of such animals, and in ancient Egypt it was no different. Such specialists were called 'masters of Selkit,' after the scorpion goddess with whom they had such an unusual relationship (fig. 17). We may dismiss scorpion charming as mere trickery, but according to the ancient Egyptians it clearly belonged to the domain of magic. The most able scorpion charmers were given the opportunity to advance in the eyes of the king: they were selected to accompany the royal expeditions to the quarries in the eastern desert, where they had to supervise the welfare of the workmen. Some 'masters of Selkit' combined their office with other titles in the magical-medical sphere, which indicates that they must have had some kind of formal education.

HIGH SCHOOL FOR MAGICIANS

Individuals who could read and write (fig. 18) earned far more respect than these simple village doctors. They belonged to an elite comprising no more than one percent of the population and possessed the education with which they were able to organize the work of the other 99 percent. A well-known school text states: *The scribe is the only one to control the work of all. Be resolved to become a scribe, a nice profession . . . which gives you the command of others.* This explains why those who had been initiated in this art liked to be a bit mysterious about it.

The Egyptian writing system, of which the principles dated back to about 3100 BC, is notoriously difficult. It consists of a mixture of phonograms (identifying one, two, three, or more sound values), rebus signs or ideograms, and determinatives indicating the general meaning of the preceding word. Spelling reform could have led to a

FIG. 17. This stela was erected in honor of the deities Ptah and Hathor by a group of workmen. Among them is the scorpion charmer Amenmose (lower row, second from the left). Photograph: British Museum (acc.no. EA 265).

major improvement, but the scribes would then have lost their privileged position. At the same time, they really believed that writing was a divine gift which should not be altered in any respect. Thus the literati easily acquired the reputation that they 'knew things' *(rekh-khet)* which remained a secret to others; in other words, they possessed occult knowledge.

One became a scribe by taking lessons from an early age, most frequently at a private school run by a retired official. Here one mastered the principles of the writing system (both the complicated hieroglyphs and the cursive writing known as hieratic) by copying isolated signs or words, and later complete texts dictated by the teacher. After a basic education of about four years the boys were allowed to call themselves 'scribe' (hardly any girls went to school). They continued their education by working for some public institution, an additional training period which lasted some ten years. After that, they were qualified as independent civil servants in any position which the state saw fit to assign them, because whoever was able to write could fill any post. Many officials combined a wide variety of duties in the course of their careers: at the treasury or in the barracks, as expedition leader or army officer, or perhaps as priest, sorcerer, or physician.

Of course, the latter jobs required very specific knowledge. This could be acquired in the House of Life, an institution that has been compared to modern universities and was connected with the country's major temples. This comparison is not altogether accurate, because the House of Life was first and foremost a place where magical rituals were performed for the preservation of life in Egypt. However, it included a library and archives where the sacred 'books of the gods' were kept: scrolls of papyrus about astronomy, geography, history, and mythology, hymns and prayers, texts for use in the daily cult or for special festivities, Books of the Dead and other funerary compositions, and magical-medical

treatises. There were also model books for instructing artists, people who had a special relationship with the Creator (in this context usually identified as Ptah or Khnum) because they, too, created things which had not existed before. Artists notably produced statues and reliefs for temples and tombs, which had to be brought to life by means of a special ritual in order to function. This so-called Ritual of Opening the Mouth was performed by priests likewise connected with the House of Life, who thereby completed the artists' creative acts (fig. 19). No wonder that sculptors were called 'life-givers' *(sankh)* and that their work was checked meticulously; it was quite literally of vital importance.

There is no clearer text about the significance of the House of Life than the autobiography of the chief physician Wedjahorresnet. He lived during the Persian occupation around 500 BC, when numerous Egyptian monuments and institutions had already suffered from years of war and neglect. He writes: *The Majesty of the King Darius commanded me to return to Egypt . . . to restore the establishment of the House of Life, after it had decayed. . . . I did as His Majesty had commanded me. I furnished them with all their staffs consisting of the wellborn, no lowborn among them. I placed them in the charge of every learned man* (rekh-khet) *in order to teach them all their crafts. His Majesty had commanded to give them every good thing, in order that they might carry out all their crafts. I supplied them with everything useful to them, with all their equipment that was on record, as they had been before. His Majesty did this because he knew the worth of this guild in making live all that are sick, in making endure forever the names of all the gods, their temples, their offerings, and the conduct of their festivals.* This clearly demonstrates the connection that existed between bookish knowledge, religion, magic, and medicine, and the state's interest in holding on to the ancient traditions. It was the scholars of the House of Life who guaranteed the survival of ancient Egyptian civilization for almost three thousand years.

FIG. 19. A group of priests performs the Ritual of Opening the Mouth on a tomb statue. The man standing in front has the title *sem*; his colleagues are characterized as lector priests by the stola crossing their chest. From the tomb of Meryneith, Saqqara. Drawing: Dorothea Schulz, RMO.

FIG. 18. Even the highest officials of ancient Egypt liked to be portrayed as a scribe holding a papyrus scroll: a scribe was a person possessing mysterious power and wisdom rather than a humble clerk. Photograph: RMO (acc.no. AST 31).

Scribes who had finished their advanced training at this honorable institution regularly feature in Egyptian texts and representations. Usually they bear the title of 'lector priest,' or more literally 'carrier of the feast scroll' *(khery-heb)*. They are depicted holding a papyrus scroll and wearing a sash diagonally over one shoulder. These scrolls contained the correct text for every ritual and were copied from the originals kept in the library of the House of Life. This means that the institution must have included a writing room or scriptorium, much like the monasteries of medieval Europe.

The 'chief lector priests' in particular *(khery-heb hery-tep)* had the reputation of being redoubtable sorcerers. Special rituals, such as the 'Opening of the Mouth,' also involved other priests, such as the *sem*, who usually wears

FIG. 20. A *sem* priest wearing a leopard skin and a lector priest holding a scroll direct
the funeral of Meryneith at Saqqara. From the tomb of Meryneith, Saqqara. Photograph: RMO.

a plaited side-lock to his wig and a panther skin knotted around his shoulders (fig. 20). Physicians and magicians frequently stressed their relationship with the House of Life. The gods Thoth, Isis, and Horus of Three-hundred Town were called master or mistress of the House of Life. To the illiterate population, all the wisdom recorded there must have seemed like pure magic.

THE MAJOR LEAGUE

Although the majority of the sorcerers and witch-doctors of ancient Egypt are no longer known by name, the greatest magicians of their time have never been forgotten as their exploits have been recorded on papyrus for the instruction and amusement of future generations. Nowadays we would regard these texts as nothing more than exciting fairy tales, but in ancient Egypt the audience must have shivered with awe when stories about Imhotep or Hordedef were told. When the Egyptians wanted to stress the world's transitory nature, they liked to contrast it with the enduring memory of such great names: *Those who built themselves houses, their abodes do not exist anymore. What has happened to them? I have heard the words of the sages Imhotep and Hordedef, whose sayings are in everybody's mouth. Where are their tombs?*

This statement about sayings being in everybody's mouth is quite true. Several spells from the Egyptian Book of the Dead (chapters 30B, 64, 137, and 148) recount how they were discovered by the illustrious Hordedef during the reign of King Menkaura (2490–2472 BC), about a thousand years before the texts themselves were written down. And Imhotep, the famous architect of the Step Pyramid of King Djoser, was reputed to be the composer of a 'book of wisdom' that was still copied for centuries after his death. He was even believed to have been the author of part of the so-called Hermetic treatises, the books of wisdom connected with the god Thoth-Hermes, which

themselves date to the period around the beginning of the Christian era. By then, Imhotep had already long been deified as the patron of medical science (fig. 10). Until the nineteenth century AD his memory was even honored by the Muslims of Egypt, who confused him with the patriarch Joseph. But who was Hordedef?

In order to answer that question we must turn to a popular story set in the court of Pharaoh Khufu, the grandfather of Menkaura and the builder of the Great Pyramid at Giza. According to the Papyrus Westcar, one day Khufu asks his sons to tell him fairy tales. The first three princes choose stories from the past. Unfortunately the fragile papyrus scroll has not preserved the first story, but the second one is told by Prince Khafra. It deals with a chief lector-priest Webaoner who punished his wife's lover by modeling a wax crocodile seven hand-breadths long (fig. 21). When thrown into the pond where the lover used to swim, the figurine turned into a live crocodile seven cubits long, which seized the man and disappeared with its prey. Next, Prince Rabauef gets up to tell the third story about a lector-priest Djadjaemankh, who once organized a diversion for Pharaoh Snefru, Khufu's own father. He made twenty pretty, half-naked girls paddle a boat along the lake of the royal palace. The pharaoh had just begun to enjoy it when suddenly the girls stopped rowing. It turned out that one had dropped a hair ornament in the water and refused to go on. Djadjaemankh was summoned; he raised one half of the lake above the other, plucked the ornament from the bottom, and put the water back in its place.

After these stories are told Hordedef rises and proposes another entertainment. Is not Khufu aware of the fact that there are still famous sorcerers around? Why do not they invite Djedi, an old man of 110 who can work all kinds of miracles? The proposal is accepted, and Djedi arrives at the palace to show his tricks. At first he demonstrates how he can rejoin the severed head of a goose to its body so the animal lives again; he repeats this with an ox. Then he tames a wild lion so that it follows him as meekly as a lamb. Finally, to test whether he is a true magician rather than a trickster, Khufu asks him to reveal a piece of information known only to the initiates: how many chambers are in the sanctuary of Thoth? Djedi says that although he does not know the answer himself, he knows where to find it: in a secret chest in the temple of Heliopolis (the city close to Memphis where the great sun temple was located). The chest, however, can only be opened by the as yet unborn child that Re has begotten by the wife of a sun priest.

The story continues with a lengthy description of the birth of this child, and then the papyrus breaks off. We will never know the number of secret chambers in the temple of Thoth, but we can assume that Prince Hordedef played a prominent part in their discovery. This is in perfect accordance with the aforementioned spells from the Book of the Dead, where he is also credited

with many discoveries in temples. Incidentally, Hordedef is a real historical figure whose tomb was discovered at Giza. The location of Imhotep's tomb, on the other hand, is unknown, although many archaeologists have been searching for it at Saqqara near the Step Pyramid of his patron, King Djoser.

More than a millennium after Imhotep and Hordedef lived, a prince with magical powers was born, a son of Pharaoh Ramesses II (1290–1224 BC), who was called Khaemwas (fig. 22). He was destined to succeed his father on the royal throne, but died prematurely. He spent years of his life in Memphis acting as both high priest of the god Ptah and as a *sem* priest. Khaemwas constructed subterranean burial vaults in the Memphite cemeteries of Saqqara for Ptah's sacred animals, the Apis bulls. Recently, archaeologists have found a temple-shaped monument bearing his name on a nearby hilltop (fig. 64). Khaemwas

FIG. 21. Wax figurines depicting crocodiles actually existed in Ancient Egypt. This crocodile carries a mummy on its back, a reference to a mythological tale about the corpse of Osiris being thrown into the Nile by Seth. Photograph: RMO (acc.no. F 1969/2.10).

carved a series of very curious inscriptions on a large number of pyramids, such as that of King Unas at Saqqara. Even in his time, these monuments were already ages old. The inscriptions indicate that Khaemwas identified the original owners of these pyramids and had the pyramids restored. Obviously Khaemwas was interested in antiquities, and ordinary people knew what to think of his nosing around the ancient cemeteries: the prince was searching for occult wisdom.

This search, at least, forms the theme of two stories recorded on papyrus scrolls more than a thousand years after his death. The first dates back to the last few centuries before the Christian era, the second to the Roman imperial period. Both feature Prince Khaemwas, also known as Setne (a garbled version of his title *sem*, see fig. 23).

Papyrus Setne I tells how in his wanderings over the necropolis of Memphis the prince encounters a number of ghosts in an ancient tomb. They tell him the story of their lives, and it turns out that they are the wandering souls of a Prince Naneferkaptah, his wife Ahure, and their little son Merib. In his lifetime, Naneferkaptah had been as intent on acquiring magical charms as was Khaemwas. When he discovered that, in a secret and well-guarded chest at the bottom of a lake at Coptos, there was a book written by the god Thoth with his own hand, he had to have it. Thanks to his great magical powers he succeeded, but the book brought him nothing but bad luck. Thoth was furious about the theft and caused Naneferkaptah, his wife, and their child to drown in the Nile. Ahure and Merib were buried in Coptos, but the prince was interred in Memphis, together with the book.

FIG. 22. Khaemwas put up this statue of himself in a temple at Abydos. The prince here holds two standards, the one on his right terminating in a triad of Osiris, Isis, and Horus, the one on the left surmounted by the reliquary of Abydos, which contains the head of Osiris. Photograph: British Museum (acc.no. EA 947).

Fig. 23. Khaemwas liked to be portrayed with the side-lock of a *sem* priest, as in this funerary figurine. His later name Setne is a garbled version of the title. Photograph: © 2003 Musée du Louvre/ Georges Poncet (acc. no. N.478).

From the Papyrus Setne I

Naneferkaptah asks an old priest where the magic book of Thoth may be found:

The priest said to Naneferkaptah:"The book in question is in the middle of the water of Coptos in a box of iron. In the box of iron is a box of copper. In the box of copper is a box of juniper wood. In the box of juniper wood is a box of ivory and ebony. In the box of ivory and ebony is a box of silver. In the box of silver is a box of gold, and in it is the book. There are six miles of serpents, scorpions, and all kinds of reptiles around the box in which the book is, and there is an eternal serpent around this same box."

[Immediately Naneferkaptah left for Coptos]

When the morning of our fifth day came, Naneferkaptah had much pure wax brought to him. He made a boat filled with its rowers and sailors. He recited a spell to them, he made them live, he gave them breath, he put them on the water. He filled the ship

FIG. 24. Part of the Papyrus Setne II, written in demotic during the Roman imperial period. Photograph: British Museum (acc.no. EA 10822, sheet 2).

of Pharaoh with sand, he tied it to the other boat. He went on board, . . . and said to the rowers: "Row me to the place where that book is!" They rowed him by night as by day. In three days he reached it. He cast sand before him, and a gap formed in the river. He found six miles of serpents, scorpions, and all kinds of reptiles around the place where the book was. He found an eternal serpent around this same box. He recited a spell to the six miles of serpents, scorpions, and all kinds of reptiles that were around the box and did not let them come up. He went to the place where the eternal serpent was. He fought it and killed it. It came to life again and resumed its shape. He fought it again, a second time, and killed it; it came to life again. He fought it again, a third time, cut it in two pieces, and put sand between one piece and the other. It died and no longer resumed its shape.

Naneferkaptah went to the place where the box was. He found it was a box of iron. He opened it and found a box of copper. He opened it and found a box of juniper wood. He opened it and found a box of ivory and ebony. He opened it and found a box of silver. He opened it and found a box of gold. He opened it and found the book in it. He brought the book up out of the box of gold.

He recited a spell from it; he charmed the sky, the earth, the netherworld, the mountains, the waters. He discovered what all the birds of the sky and the fish of the deep and the beasts of the desert were saying. He recited another spell; he saw Re appearing in the sky with his Ennead, and the moon rising, and the stars in their forms. He saw the fish of the deep, though there were twenty-one divine cubits of water over them. . . .

He had a sheet of new papyrus brought to him. He wrote on it every word that was in the book before him. He soaked it in beer, he dissolved it in water. When he knew it had dissolved, he drank it and knew what had been in it.

(PAPYRUS SETNE I, III.17–IV.4)

41

When Setne hears the story, he simply has to obtain the book in his turn. Naneferkaptah proposes they play a game of chess to decide, and thanks to his superior magical powers Setne wins and takes the book with him, despite Naneferkaptah's dire warnings. Immediately he is struck by all kinds of calamities, and the story ends with him returning the book to Naneferkaptah and having the mortal remains of Ahure and Merib transferred from Coptos to the tomb in Memphis. Thus Setne and Naneferkaptah and his family finally know peace.

The story of Papyrus Setne II deals with the miracles performed by Setne's son Siosir (fig. 24). While still a child, he descends with his father into the netherworld, where it is discovered that he already has a surprising foreknowledge of everything they see there. At the age of twelve, he becomes involved in a strange contest. A Nubian sorcerer has come to the court of Ramesses II, carrying a scroll and challenging the Egyptians to read it without opening it. Even Setne with all his magical experience does not succeed, but Siosir just laughs and surprises the whole court the next day by effortlessly reading the whole papyrus.

It contains the story of a contest between two sorcerers, the Nubian Horus-son-of-the-Nubian-woman and the Egyptian Horus-son-of-Panesh. According to the papyrus, long ago the Nubian modeled a carrying-chair and its four carriers from beeswax and magically used this to abduct the Egyptian pharaoh and give him a good thrashing. The Egyptians were incensed. After a long search the Egyptian sorcerer found a magic book personally written by Thoth that contained a spell to repay this humiliation in kind. Thereupon the Nubian came to the Egyptian court, where in the middle of the throne hall a duel was fought between the two magicians which makes even the most frightening scenes from the adventures of Harry Potter seem dull by comparison. In the end Horus-the-son-of-the-Nubian-woman acknowledged defeat and promised to leave Egypt in peace for fifteen hundred years.

This concludes the story contained in the papyrus—but Siosir then reveals that the fifteen hundred years have now passed, and the quarrelsome Nubian facing him is none other than Horus-son-of-the-Nubian-woman, who has returned intent on resuming the battle. An even greater surprise is that Siosir himself turns out to be Horus-son-of-Panesh: he had heard in the netherworld that this was going to happen and therefore caused himself to be reborn as Setne's son. Immediately Siosir causes fire to beat down on the treacherous Nubian and then disappears, to the astonishment of everyone present. And thus the tale ends.

Setne Khaemwas was clearly a historical figure who stirred the imagination for many centuries. One more person we must mention in this respect is none other than Egypt's last indigenous pharaoh, Nectanebo II (360–343 BC; fig. 25). During his reign Egypt witnessed a cultural revival, so that temple remains bearing the king's name can still be seen across the country. The entire period was dominated by the ultimately ineffective struggle against the Persians, who conquered Egypt for a second time during Nectanebo's reign, only to lose it eleven years later to the Macedonian Alexander the Great.

Nectanebo's sustained resistance against the Persian oppression was much admired by his contemporaries, who soon whispered that he made use of magical practices to succeed where others had failed. Whenever the invaders approached by sea, Nectanebo would withdraw to a room of his palace, armed with his wand and a bowl of water containing wax figures of both the Egyptian and the foreign ships and marines. He would recite magical formulas over the wax figures and prompt them in a mock battle: the Egyptian figures always won, and this decided the outcome of the real battle. One day, however, Nectanebo observed to his dismay that the enemy's wax ships were being steered to victory by the Egyptian gods (fig. 26), and he realized that the fall of Egypt was inevitable. He disguised himself, sneaked out of the palace,

FIG. 25. Presumably this royal head is a portrait
of Pharaoh ectanebo II. Photograph: RMO
(acc.no. F 1996/7.1).

FIG. 26. Wax figure of the goddess Neith in a boat, almost literally what was revealed
to Pharaoh Nectanebo in the Romance of Alexander. Photograph: RMO (acc.no. F 1969/2.8).

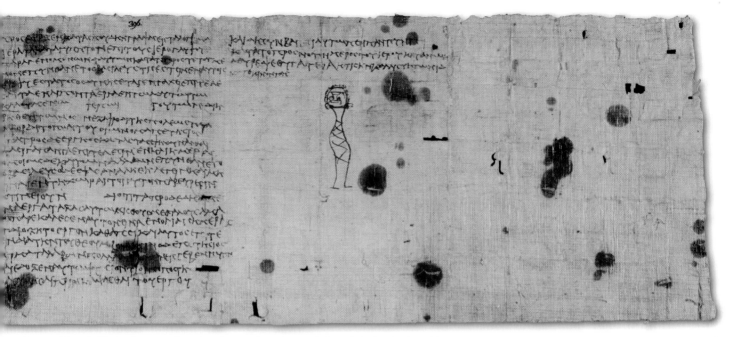

FIG. 27. The end of the Greek papyrus about Pharaoh Nectanebo. Unfortunately the scribe broke off in the middle of his story, doodled a funny figure, and left the rest to our imagination. Photograph: RMO (acc.no. AMS 67).

and fled to Pella in Macedonia where he settled as a magician. Again he employed wax figures to send a dream to the Macedonian king and queen, Philip and Olympias, which predicted that a child would be born to them whose true father was the Egyptian god Amun. Actually, the story implies, it was Nectanebo himself who fathered Olympias's child, a son who would conquer half the known world under the name Alexander the Great. One of the countries he conquered was Egypt, and thus Nectanebo wreaked his revenge on the Persians.

This legend has been preserved in Greek tales about the life of Alexander: the so-called Romance of Alexander. The text was originally attributed to Alexander's court poet, Callisthenes, although its source has since been disputed. In the Middle Ages the Romance of Alexander was translated into numerous European languages, and so the magician Nectanebo was also remembered. Although the text was not recorded in writing before the third century AD, many centuries after Callisthenes, these attractive legends seem to be based on folk stories that are much older. One indication for this is a Greek papyrus kept in the Leiden Museum and dated to about 150 BC (fig. 27), which describes a dream Nectanebo had a few days before the fatal Persian invasion: the town god Onuris of the contemporary Egyptian capital Sebennytos complained that the construction of his temple had still not been finished. Nectanebo awoke in panic and immediately gave money to a sculptor, ordering him to complete the job. The sculptor, however, spent the first portion on drink and then was distracted by a beautiful girl. The papyrus breaks off, but it suggests that all the magic in the world is no match for wine and women. Nectanebo ultimately lost his country.

SURFING THROUGH THE UNIVERSE

[Re speaks:] I am the one who made heaven and who established it in order to place the bas *of the gods within it. I shall be with them for eternity which time begets. My ba is Magic, it is older than [time]. The* ba *of Re is in Magic throughout the entire land.*

(BOOK OF THE COW OF HEAVEN, 218–20)

FIG. 28. The *ba* was usually depicted as a human-headed bird to suggest the soul's transience and mobility, which enabled it to contact all levels of the cosmos. Photograph: RMO (acc.no. L.IX.30).

THE COSMIC INTERNET

Colorful stories about famous magicians of the past give us an impression of the methods employed by Egyptian sorcerers: the use of wands, charms, and models of beeswax, the taming of wild animals, and the manipulation of nature. To understand why they believed this to be possible, though, we must study the underlying theories. The Egyptians believed magic was as old as creation. That is why Heka is sometimes called the Creator's eldest son. One of his epithets is 'lord of the *ka*s,' where *ka* was the Egyptian equivalent of 'vitality.' By means of magic this divine energy of life can diffuse across the created universe, as if passing through the invisible wires of a cosmic Internet.

According to Egyptian mythology the created world became increasingly complex. After the earth, the heaven and netherworld came into being. The three domains were connected by Heka. *Whatever is below, is just as that which is above*, as it is formulated by a Hermetic text. The connection between these three worlds was maintained by various means. The invisible gods of heaven and the netherworld could manifest themselves in a visible shape on earth by sending their soul (*ba*, fig. 28) to inhabit an earthly body (for instance, that of a sacred animal), a tree, a well, or anything else.

FIG. 29. The deceased worships his own *ka*, represented as a pair of arms framing an offering table provided with food and drink. Vignette of chapter 105 from the Book of the Dead of Djedhor. Photograph: RMO (acc.no. AMS 47a).

Gods could be invoked, or their manifestations *(bau)* could occur spontaneously.

Contact between gods and men could also be established through intermediaries: demons who haunted men's dreams or spread disease, or the dead, who were not 'departed' but still very much belonged to the community of the living. Their bodies lay well mummified in their tombs, their vitality (*ka*, fig. 29) had to be nourished there with food and drink and resided in the tomb statues, and their souls *(ba)* flew in the bright sunlight

by day and returned to the mummies by night. The dead were also thought to live on with the god Osiris in the netherworld, somewhere beyond the western horizon where the sun sets. That is why a false door made of stone (fig. 30) was installed in the west wall of the tomb chapel, a portal through which the living and dead could still communicate, like a computer screen which enabled the dead and the living to continue chatting with each other.

As long as the dead were well provisioned by their surviving relatives, they could hope to acquire the status of a privileged one *(akh)* with the sun god in heaven. The term *akh* connotes the magical power that these spirits shared with the gods themselves, and *akhu* could be used as a synonym of *heka* (magic). Meanwhile, the ghosts of those who died violently or prematurely could haunt the earth and spite the living, trying to kill children or tormenting adults with nightmares and psychological troubles. Witch doctors could try to exorcise the patients' obsessions, but sorcerers also invoked these malicious spirits to work evil against others.

Contact with the heavenly domain could be established through any flying thing. That is why the *ba* is represented as a human-headed bird, the *akh* has the appearance of a heron, and the phoenix (a symbol of the solar cycle) is depicted as some kind of egret (fig. 31). The falcon and vulture were the sacred animals of celestial

FIG. 30. False door of a man Fefi, the slit-shaped door surmounted by a window-shaped representation of the deceased before an offering table. Photograph: RMO (acc.no. F 1970/5.1).

FIG. 31. Limestone mold for casting a wax figure of a phoenix. Photograph: RMO (acc.no. AAL 153a-b).

gods Horus and Mut, whereas Isis, Nephthys, and Nut are examples of winged goddesses. Male gods with wings were rarer but appeared regularly during the period of growing pantheism. The dung beetle or scarab (a symbol of resurrection) naturally possesses wings, but the Egyptians had no objection to representing the sun disk, the *wedjat* eye, or the uraeus serpent (cobra) with wings as well. And the smell of the burnt offerings and incense sacrificed in the temple cult rose up to heaven.

It was more complicated to establish contact with the netherworld. Alongside the deceased, all kinds of serpents here played an important role. As the inhabitants of mysterious underground caves, they were seen to have a connection with the subterranean realm of the dead. Sanctuaries were sometimes installed in caves and caverns so that priests could be closer to the gods of the underworld. Libations and animal sacrifices were offered to the gods and the dead alike, and the water, wine, or blood allowed to drain into the soil.

IN QUEST OF THE LAWS OF NATURE

Apart from the various messengers between 'above' and 'below,' there were other means to mobilize the forces of nature (which were thought to include witchcraft). Magical power was regarded as being inherent to stones, metals, and minerals; astral bodies (although astrology did not play an important part in ancient Egypt); and plants, animals, and the products thereof. To harness the magic of these diverse tools, one had to be familiar with their respective properties. Therefore, sorcerers had to be natural scientists, and indeed modern science originates

FIG. 32. A *sem* priest purifies the mummy of Merymery, as part of the ritual of Opening the Mouth. The god Anubis (or another priest wearing a jackal mask) holds the mummy in an upright position. Photograph: RMO (acc.no. AP 6-b).

in the observations and experiments of these ancient magicians. Their investigations, however, focused on establishing similarities of color, smell, brilliance, form, or sound—in other words, identifying any kind of sensory attribute that recalled something else. To us, such fleeting associations may seem purely accidental and meaningless, but to the prescientific mind any similarity was indicative of a deeper magical identity. According to the principle of 'sympathy,' anything experienced by one element of a magic pair would be felt by the other. Complex mythological tales, often seeming to have been made up for the occasion, were offered to explain the relationship between such elemental twins.

The notion that similarity breeds sympathy had far-reaching consequences. When humanity received the gift of magic, this included creative powers. Making two- or three-dimensional representations of divinities, demons, human beings, animals, or plants gave us power over these creatures, because similarity in form forged a sympathetic bond. It was even better if the magical model contained part of the creature it represented. It has already been mentioned how Isis used the spittle of Re to make a serpent that could bite the sun god. Similarly, sorcerers tried to obtain the hair, nails, sweat, sperm, urine, or feces of all kinds of animals, or of the humans who were the intended victims of their black arts. If these were not available, a shred of clothing worn by the person concerned or any possession once belonging to him would have the same effect, because magical identity could rub off on lifeless objects through direct contact.

However true to nature a depiction or magical model might be, it could not be alive. This problem was solved by the Ritual of Opening the Mouth (fig. 32): a series of spells and magical acts which caused a spark of life to jump from the creature represented to its representation. Or, continuing the metaphor used previously, we might say it provided the software which bootstraps the computer. The ritual was performed on the statues of deities, kings,

and private persons in the large sculptors' workshops. It was also performed on mummies at the funeral. The soul of the deceased had been banned from the body during mummification so it did not have to witness the gruesome process. At the moment the body was interred in the tomb, however, it was essential that life be returned to the corpse. To this end, the mortuary priest touched the mouth, nose, eyes, and hands of the mummy with various implements, so that the deceased would again be able to eat, breathe, see, and take the food offerings. The same ritual was enacted on magical models and representations.

KNOWLEDGE GIVES POWER

Alongside magic, the gods gave humanity another precious gift that distinguishes us from animals: our power of speech. ancient Egyptians believed that as the Creator (and especially the god Ptah, fig. 33) made everything in the universe by pronouncing its name, so, too, could humans adopt the same technique. The name was believed to encompass the whole magical identity of any living thing, including supernatural beings. He or she whose name was pronounced had no choice but to obey. That is why in spells from the Book of the Dead and other magical formulas the deceased repeats to all the gods and demons that confront him: *I know you and I know your names.*

Even more powerful was the secret name that should be revealed to no one. We have seen how mighty Isis became as soon as she had obtained the secret name of Re. All Egyptians also had such a name, bestowed upon them by their mother at birth and which they did not tell to anybody. One reason why the mother's name rather

FIG. 33. The creator god Ptah is depicted mummiform and wearing a close-fitting cap. In his hands he holds the symbols of omnipotence and durability. The silver base is not ancient. Photograph: RMO (acc.no. AED 10).

than the father's is used in spells for patients or the dead is that only maternity is certain, and giving the wrong name would make the whole spell utterly useless. Various spells were meant to guarantee the survival of the name of the deceased. Chapter 25 of the Book of the Dead is even entitled: *Spell for preventing a deceased from forgetting his own name.* A person's name was a crucial part of his identity; to forget it would risk his very existence.

Numerous spells summon deities and demons to assist the magician. To be quite sure that the gods will listen, they are frequently invoked using a whole array of different names: at least one is bound to elicit a reaction. Some of these names are pure 'abracadabra': magic words made up of unusual syllables with no underlying meaning. Thus chapter 165 of the Book of the Dead contains an invocation to the god Amun, whose name means 'the hidden one' and whose true identity was the subject of much speculation: *Amun Netkeret, Amun hidden of form and secret of appearances, lord of the two horns, greatest one of heaven, Kerky is your name, Keska is your name, Ruty is your name, Kesbek is your name, Amun Ninkektekesher Amun Ruty is your name.* Occasionally such nonsensical words were derived from other languages, such as Nubian or Hebrew. This served the dual function of letting the magician show off his linguistic skills and harnessing the power of the witchcraft of Egypt's traditional enemies, which might very well be more powerful than Egypt's own. Nubian sorcerers in particular were much feared by the Egyptians, as the Second Story of Setne makes clear.

Some magic names may have possessed a more occult significance. It is well known that at least in the Greco-Roman period letters also had a numerical value. A god of magic who was popular at the time was called Abrasax or Abraxas (fig. 34). If one adds up the numerical value of the Greek letters of his name (A = 1, B = 2, X = 60, R = 100, S = 200), the outcome is 365, the number of days of the calendar year. Abrasax was thus regarded as the god of time or eternity. It is unknown whether similar

principles were valued in the pharaonic period, although the magic of numbers did play an important role. One was the number of the single Creator; two often symbolized the disunity of opposites that was established during creation; and three signified the multiplicity of everything created. Four referred to the four directions of the sky (fig. 131), and therefore charms were often repeated four times while the sorcerer turned to the north, south, east,

FIG. 34. The god Abrasax has the head of a rooster, a human body wearing armor, and legs terminating in snakes. In his hands he carries a shield and a whip. On this seal his image is surrounded by a combination of Greek vowels (partly inspired by the name of the Jewish god, Iao or Jahweh) and magic signs. Photograph: RMO (acc.no. H+ 20b).

and west. The theory of the four elements (earth, water, fire, and air) and the four vital juices or humors (blood, phlegm, yellow bile, and black bile) is not Egyptian, but originated in Greek antiquity. Seven is the number of the orifices in the head (eyes, ears, nose, and mouth), of the vowels of the Greek alphabet, and of the seven 'planets' of the ancient astronomers (sun, moon, Mercury, Venus, Mars, Jupiter, and Saturn), and therefore a sacred number. For this reason, many spells had to be recited seven times. Nine to the Egyptians referred to the nine primeval gods (the Ennead, fig. 35); it is also the square of three, hence innumerable. All these numbers occur in Egyptian spells, especially four and seven. This kind of numerology certainly influenced the development of Kabbala, the occult interpretation of sacred Jewish writings which was first introduced in the Hellenistic circles at Alexandria.

The use of language also provided access to all kinds of magical formulas, so that the sorcerer now could share in the authoritative utterances *(hu)* of the gods themselves. Language has a central position in the Ritual of Opening the Mouth, and language gave magical models and representations their identity and purpose. The wording and grammar of charms differ from everyday speech. In that sense they are not unlike other religious texts: sorcerers expressed themselves in a somewhat solemn and antiquated manner, using language that had already been obsolete for many centuries (comparable to the use of Latin in Catholic mass). Many formulas are a mixture of short hymns to the gods, mythological tales, invocations or outright threats addressed to gods and demons, recipes for preparing medicines, and practical stage directions for the benefit of the magicians themselves. The frequent use

FIG. 35. Magic bowl representing the Ennead in a bark. From right to left: Atum, Shu, Tefnut, Nut, Geb, and Osiris, with Isis and Nephthys squatting behind and the falcon of Horus perched on the prow. Photograph: RMO (acc.no. AT 98.B1).

FIG 36. Without the captions, the awkwardly drawn figures on this linen amulet would hardly be identifiable, and would thereby be devoid of power. It should be noted that evil forces such as the god Seth have been drawn in red ink. Photograph: RMO (acc.no. AMS 59a).

of puns is not intended to be funny, but rather expresses the conviction that sympathetic connections exist even in language and can be exploited by the sorcerer.

SACRED INCISIONS

In the same way that man has learned to depict creation in two- or three-dimensional art, he also possesses the ability to record his own language. For this purpose the ancient Egyptians used hieroglyphs, a Greek term which literally means 'sacred incisions.' It was the god Thoth himself who allowed mankind to share in the invention of writing. Pictorial representations could thus be provided with written commentary (fig. 36) and magical figures identified by name (fig. 104). Spells such as those in the Book of the Dead gain their power from texts and illustrations together. Magical formulas could be collated to form complete handbooks for sorcerers. These served to record supernatural wisdom for posterity, though of course for initiates only. This becomes clear from the warnings at the end of many spells: *Take good care! Do not use this spell for whomsoever, but only for yourself, your father or your son, for it is a great secret of the west, an initiation into the mysteries of the netherworld.* Or: *Employ this spell in such a manner that no eye perceives it!*

Another way to prevent a text from becoming public is to learn it by heart and then destroy the original copy. A related measure that unfortunately only works for

real magicians is described in the Papyrus Setne I: when Setne had appropriated the magic book of Thoth, *he had a sheet of new papyrus brought to him. He wrote on it every word that was in the book before him. He soaked it in beer and dissolved it in water. when he knew it had dissolved, he drank it and knew what had been in it.* In a similar vein, other sorcerers occasionally wrote a spell or vignette on their palm and licked it off. Charms were also inscribed on drinking bowls or so-called healing statues (fig. 37). Water or another liquid poured into or over them was thought to absorb the power of the charm and thereby to become an effective medicine—a conviction again based on the principle that magic can 'rub off' through direct contact with a powerful creature or object. Protective charms were also written on strips of papyrus which were then tightly rolled up and suspended around the neck as a talisman (fig. 38). Numerous texts explicitly prescribe that a new piece of papyrus be used. Papyrus was an expensive writing material, so sheets were often reused by washing off the existing texts. This practice, however, could well be fatal for the outcome of a spell: parts of the earlier text might still be legible and obstruct the efficacy of the charm.

Hieroglyphs—which are after all miniature depictions of human beings, animals,

FIG. 37. This statue of a priest carrying a so-called Horus stela is covered with magical spells. The hard stone figure once stood in a temple where visitors could pour water over it in order to cure their injuries. Photograph: Louvre (acc.no. E.10777).

FIG. 38. Wooden tube for containing a rolled-up papyrus amulet. The gold leaf covering the edge for the sliding lid is stamped with a few life symbols *(ankh)*.
Photograph: RMO (acc.no. F 1963/2.3).

plants, and inanimate objects—were always regarded as representations of a portion of reality. They therefore had the potential to possess a frightening magical force independent of the words they spelled out, and might transform into living creatures. This explains why hieroglyphs remained in use as the favorite script for magical texts (like the Book of the Dead), even after they were replaced in everyday use by more practical writing systems such as hieratic and demotic. When demotic was introduced in the seventh century BC, however, hieratic began to appear suitable for use in sorcery; the same happened to demotic when Greek was introduced after Alexander the Great conquered Egypt. Employing hieroglyphs could also be risky: on some objects from Egyptian tombs those signs depicting dangerous animals such as serpents or lions have been cut in two, while birds and other animals have been rendered without legs (fig. 39). Obviously, the Egyptians were wary of locking the deceased in a sealed tomb together with such ferocious creatures.

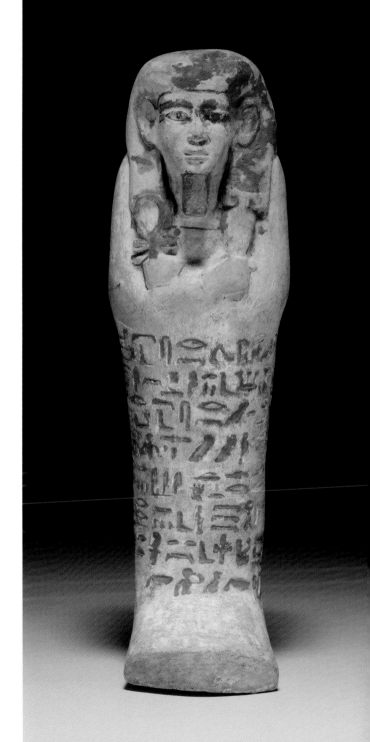

FIG. 39. Hieroglyphs depicting humans or animals on this funerary figurine have consistently been depicted without legs, so that they will not be able to harm the deceased. Photograph: British Museum (acc.no. EA 49343).

FIG. 41. Amulets in the shape of a papyrus column (or rather a papyrus stalk ending in a flower umbel) symbolize new life, fertility, and prosperity. They are always made of green materials such as feldspar or green faience. Photograph: RMO (acc.no. EG-ZM1231).

FIG. 40. This pendant in the shape of a so-called Isis knot has been made of two magical materials: gold and carnelian. Photograph: RMO (acc.no. AO 7b).

THE PRACTICE OF MAGIC

Words to be said over a piece of fine linen. These gods are to be drawn on it, and it is to be fitted with twelve knots. To offer to them bread, beer, and burning incense. To be applied to a man's throat. A means to save a man from the plague of the year. An enemy will have no power over him. A means to placate the gods in the retinue of Sekhmet and Thoth. Words to be said by a man from the last day till New Year's Day, on the Wag festival, and at daybreak on the festival of Renenutet.

(Papyrus Leiden AMS 23a, 2.3–5)

SHOWING ONE'S COLORS

Alongside texts, representations in two or three dimensions played an equal role in Egyptian magic. In the margins of his magic books, on separate sheets of papyrus, and on strips of linen, the sorcerer drew figures of deities, demons, men, or animals, or scenes depicting certain actions or events. He also modeled, cast, or cut figurines and amulets representing such creatures and combined them to form composite models. He always made a careful selection of the materials to be used because stones, minerals, and other substances were believed to possess their own magical power. His choices were usually based on the presumed presence of sympathetic bonds, as described above, and color symbolism played a major part in his considerations.

Specific red stones, such as jasper or carnelian, were thought to help against bleeding, wounds, and miscarriages. They were commonly used for carving *wedjat* eyes (fig. 71) and other amulets, and especially to depict the so-called knot of Isis, which may have represented the cloth women used while menstruating or some kind of protective belt for pregnant women (fig. 40). Red is also the color of the rising and setting sun and of fire; it referred to celestial battle but also to resurrection and new life. In other words, it was a very ambiguous color. It was likewise the color of hostile powers such as Seth, and red-haired people were regarded as most suspicious. In writing, red ink was selected for recording the names of Seth and Apophis (fig. 36), and sometimes for extensive curses.

Green, on the other hand, is the color of vegetation, fertility, and new life. Green stones such as nephrite or green feldspar were used for making so-called heart scarabs and papyrus column amulets (fig. 41). Green-veined stone such as serpentine (whose modern name still refers to the stone's snake-skin pattern) was considered to be very suitable for carving Horus stelae *(cippi)*, which offered protection against snake bites and scorpion stings by means of their magical texts and pictures. The Egyptians were also able to make artificial green and blue pigments by mixing copper compounds with lime, sand, and soda. This material, which is known as Egyptian faience, was widely used in the production of all kinds of amulets and ornaments. Feldspar, meanwhile, was ground to make the green ink used for writing certain charms.

Blue is the color of heaven and water. The hair of the gods was thought to consist of lapis lazuli, an exotic material from Afghanistan from which ancient Egyptians cut small figurines representing deities connected with the four directions of heaven, such as the goddesses Isis, Nephthys, Neith, and Selkit. Blue faience was considered an appropriate material for magical water bowls (fig. 129) because it was the color of the primeval water, the source of all life. Since they lived in the primeval water, the well-known funerary figures of hippopotami were also made of this material (fig. 42). Meanwhile, the nets of blue beads that were draped over mummies referred to heaven and the goddess Nut, who wraps her wings around the dead.

Black is the color of the fertile soil and therefore of new life. At the same time it was a symbol of night, death, and the netherworld, and so possessed both positive and negative connotations. Heart scarabs and abdominal scarabs were usually made of black stone, whereas the black, shiny hematite was used to make headrest amulets (fig. 43). Magical prescriptions frequently prescribe the ritual slaughter of animals with black fur or feathers, and in this context black represented hostile forces.

White was the color of purity, a precondition for all kinds of magical rituals. This explains the explicit prescriptions that the sorcerer be dressed in white linen, his feet in white sandals, and that charms be written on new linen or new sheets of papyrus (still having their original white color). Other magic inscriptions or vignettes, for instance those on a ground of ceramic or wood, were applied in white ink, a preparation containing a kind of pipe clay from Nubia (fig. 35). White was also the color of natron, a mixture of salt and soda used by the ancient Egyptians for washing their bodies and clothes, rinsing their mouths, or cleaning the floor on which a ritual was going to take place (see also Chapter 8). Another white substance is milk, the first food given to babies and therefore a liquid that was poured out during funerals in order to promote rebirth.

KNOWLEDGE OF COMMODITIES

In some rituals the use of metals was taboo. This was true for instance in embalming, during which priests opened the abdominal cavity using a flint knife (according to the report by the Greek historian Herodotus). The Ritual of Opening the Mouth likewise prescribed the use of stone blades (fig. 56). This suggests that the taboo originated when metal was still a new and relatively unknown commodity, and therefore regarded as suspect by the magicians. Some metals, however, soon became favorite materials in the sorcerers' toolbox. This applies especially to gold.

Because of its brilliant appearance, gold was connected with the sun god Re, the source of all life. The ancient Egyptians were convinced that the gods' flesh consisted of gold, their bones of silver, and their hair of lapis lazuli. The celestial god Horus was known as the 'falcon of gold'

FIG. 42. The hippopotamus lives in the water, source of all life. Therefore this figure has a blue skin painted with floral motifs. The animal's legs have intentionally been damaged so that it cannot harm the deceased. Photograph: RMO (acc.no. AED 170).

FIG. 43. Amulets in the shape of a headrest are always made of shiny black hematite, a stone associated with night, earth, and the netherworld as the sources of new life. Photograph: RMO (acc.no. F 1950/12.14).

or the 'child of gold,' and one of the names of the pharaoh was preceded by the epithet 'golden Horus.' It was believed that interring the dead with golden masks (fig. 44) and sheathing their fingers and toes in gold would make them live forever, because gold is not subject to decay. Both the sculptors' ateliers connected with the large temples and the embalmers' workshops were known as the Mansions of Gold. A Late Period funerary papyrus addresses the deceased as follows: *May you be adorned with gold, covered with electrum* [an alloy of silver and gold], *may your fingers be shiny in the House of Osiris, the embalming place of Horus himself. May the gold come to you which originates from the mountains, the perfect protection of the gods in their domain. It will illuminate your face in the netherworld. May you breathe by means of the gold, may you leave your tomb due to the pure gold.* Because gold was so precious, the Egyptians also looked for substitutes. One was a rather rare gold-colored pigment called orpiment (sulphite of arsenic), but as a rule they were satisfied with the cheaper yellow ocher.

Another metal often used by magicians was lead. Clearly it was not the metal's (rather unattractive) appearance which appealed but rather its remarkable heaviness. To the ancient Egyptians this could only mean one thing: that lead possessed a very special magical quality by which it was pulled down to the netherworld. Curses were therefore often engraved on lead tablets, a tradition which the Greeks and Romans

FIG. 44. Funerary masks are preferably made of gold, indicating that the deceased has acquired divine status by conquering death. Photograph: RMO (acc.no. F 1948/10.1).

FIG. 45. A lead falcon with extended wings has sometimes been laid on the mummy's chest. Presumably this is a symbol of the sun god, although it is unclear why lead has been used for this purpose. Photograph: RMO (acc.no. AB 158c).

later adopted. Some items of jewelry found on mummies were made of lead (fig. 45). And because lead has an extremely low melting point, it was very suitable for making magical figurines that could easily be destroyed in the fire. It was the only metal for which no complicated ovens were needed.

Another material, however, was the absolute favorite for making such figurines: beeswax. As we have already seen above, beeswax was used by magicians such as Webaoner, Horus-son-of the-Nubian-woman, Horus-son-of-Panesh, and Nectanebo. The key characteristics of wax were its low melting point and great malleability, as well as its striking resemblance to human skin, a property still exploited nowadays by Madame Tussaud's. Wax could thus serve to make figurines that looked scarily lifelike (fig. 46) but were easily destroyed. Such figurines were used to gain power over people, make them ill, or even kill

them. In one famous account of a conspiracy at the court of Pharaoh Ramesses III (1194–1163 BC) wax figurines were created for the purpose of eliminating the palace guards. Ancient Egyptians believed that wax was created by the tears Re wept when he discovered the treason of mankind. It was therefore regarded as a primeval material which contained a portion of the Creator's magical power, making it extremely suitable for use in rituals of life and death. It was much used in mummification to close apertures or cover skin. Bees use wax (or propolis) in a similar way when they want to block off areas of the hive, for instance if a mouse or another animal has made its way in. Some scholars have suggested that in this way bees may have taught man the art of mummification!

Propolis is in fact a mixture of wax (produced by bees in special glands) and resin (which they collect, just like nectar and pollen). The ancient Egyptians, too, collected all

kinds of resin for magical and medical purposes. Various figurines depicting gods and funerary amulets were made from resin (fig. 47), and beads and wig rings of this material have also been found. The material's gloss and warm golden color were probably associated with the sun, and one should not forget that it is the sun which causes tear-shaped drops of resin to ooze from trees. A creation myth identifies resins as primeval materials: *Horus cried and the water from his eye fell on the ground, it ran out and thus myrrh came into being. Geb did not feel well and blood from his nose fell on the ground, it ran out and became fir trees, and thus resin came into being from their sap. Shu and Tefnut wept bitterly and the water from their eyes fell on the ground, ran out, and thus incense came into being.* The Egyptians used to burn myrrh and incense for their fragrant smell, which was believed to dispel evil spirits. These resins were therefore also employed as a binding agent in the ink used for writing charms. When rubbed with a cloth, objects made of resin or amber can become charged with static electricity, causing them to attract dust and small objects. Our word electricity is in fact derived from the Greek word *electron*, meaning 'amber.' This miraculous property explains the use of resin and amber for jewelry and amulets: it was believed to attract evil and thereby to protect the wearer.

Similar magical figures were occasionally made of bread dough, another malleable substance that resembles the whitish skin of human corpses (though of course not all ancient Egyptians were equally pale-skinned). It could be baked for better preservation, but even without baking it was remarkably durable. More important still was the fact that it could be dissolved in water to annihilate an enemy. In this it was not unlike clay, which is another substance frequently used in magic.

FIG. 46. Possibly this wax image of a naked woman once played a part in a love charm. Photograph: RMO (acc.no. F 1992/7.2).

Numerous myths recount how the Creator made man from clay; in Egypt this is said of the god Khnum, who used a potter's wheel for the purpose. Modeling figurines of humans or animals is one of humanity's earliest creative arts, and the magical aspect must have played some part in this. A surprising number of magical objects made by ancient Egyptians were made of unbaked clay, a fragile material preserved thanks to Egypt's dry climate. Other statuettes were fired in a kiln or on the hearth; these may have possessed the same magical faculties.

So many substances of animal or vegetable origin were employed by Egyptian sorcerers that not all can be listed here. Numerous species of animals had a close connection with specific deities because it was believed that the *ba* of a god could temporarily be incarnated in the body of an animal. Sometimes this meant that the species was held sacred and each individual was sacrosanct. In other cases, however, a magician could use the animal's fur, bone, blood, or dung to give his potions and medicines supernatural potency. All kinds of plants, flowers, fruit, and seed were used for a similar purpose because they, too, were thought to possess sympathetic connections with superior powers. Unfortunately, many of the plant names are unintelligible to us: what are 'sedge of Nemti,' 'Syrian reed,' and 'cyperus grass of the Oasis'? Some of these names are essentially in code, and a Greek book of magic (now in the Leiden Museum) contains a table of such words and their translations. Thus 'mouse-tails' proves to be mallow, and 'seed of Hermes' was a designation for dill. Sometimes even common plant names are difficult to fathom, much like foxglove today, which takes its name from its flowers' similarity to fox paws rather than to any real association with foxes. Easier to understand is the symbolism of the lotus (fig. 77), the first flower to float on the primeval water and which opened to give birth to the sun god. Equally clear is the use of the papyrus plant, which offers a guarantee of wellbeing and prosperity because of its green color and luxuriant vegetation (fig. 41).

A wide variety of properties were probably valued for the numerous herbal mixtures, ointments, and potions used in ancient Egypt. Some were fragrant, soothing, and relaxing to benefit the patient, especially those that contained honey or vegetable extracts which have been proved to possess healing powers; others were made from disgusting ingredients, such as crocodile dung, a dead shrew, or a billy goat's gall, and meant to chase away the demons that had caused infection and would hopefully loathe the medicine as much as the poor patient who had to swallow it. Saying that modern science has shown such medicines to be ineffective neglects the important psychological factor of the patient's renewed confidence in his own recovery as a result of the treatment. Indeed, the placebo effect is well known in modern medicine.

Reference has already been made to the sympathetic use of human hair, nails, blood, sweat, or sperm in magical concoctions. Such ingredients regularly appear in love potions. Special mention must be made of magical and medicinal properties believed to inhere in the milk of a woman with a newborn son. Mother and child would have been associated with Isis and Horus, and the patient who drank this mother's milk would therefore recover as easily as Horus the child. Special flasks in the shape of a mother and child were made to contain this ingredient (fig. 48).

THE RIGHT TIME AND PLACE

The magic of language and material is strengthened by that of concomitant actions. During the recitation of charms and the manipulation of magical representations, figurines, or recipes, the sorcerer performed certain

FIG. 48. Vessel depicting a mother and child; it probably contained mother's milk, an ingredient mentioned in several medical recipes. Photograph: RMO (acc.no. AT 69).

rituals to achieve the desired result. Much depended on timing. Thus some rituals had to be enacted during the night, others at sunrise or sunset (fig. 49). It should come as no surprise that several spells from the Book of the Dead had to be recited on the day of the funeral. Others state explicitly that only a full-moon night will do, or else the new moon that coincides with the first day of the month. Special rituals existed for Osiris's birthday or for New Year's Day. The former was one of the so-called epagomenal days, the five intercalary days added at the end of each year (itself consisting of twelve months of thirty days each). Because these did not fit into the regular pattern, ancient Egyptians feared that during that liminal time the whole cycle of the cosmos might simply stop, and particular spells and rituals existed in order to prevent that. To find on New Year's Day that the world had not ended was a source of much relief, akin to that experienced on New Year's Day 2000 when the Y2K computing problem did not cause the chaos that many had predicted. Ancient Egyptians celebrated each new

beginning by giving each other special New Year's presents (fig. 85).

Usually there was no precise description of where a particular magical act or ritual should take place. Some certainly had to be performed at the tomb or in the temple, but it appears that otherwise a magician was free to work at home, provided he worked in a clean and pure place. The floor had to be sprinkled with water and natron or a layer of clean sand laid down (for instance for the Ritual of Opening the Mouth) to purify the area. As a rule, incense was burned to purify the air. No goats or pigs should have walked over the floor. Some materials used in rituals were not allowed to touch the unclean soil and were instead raised on new bricks (often three, four, or seven in number). To invoke gods and demons, the sorcerer would withdraw to a dark spot and there light his magic lamp. In the flame he often burned various herbs or

FIG. 49. The deceased worships the sun on the horizon. Vignette from the Book of the Dead of Kenna. Photograph: RMO (acc.no. SR).

other ingredients, and sometimes also a strip of papyrus inscribed with his magical formulas or with the question he wanted to put to the gods. Another favorite location for sorcery was the roof, either of the magician's house or of a temple, where rituals were performed in the sun's first rays. The sun at dawn had just risen from death and was believed to be much more vigorous with the power of life than the weary sun of evening.

PULLING THE STRINGS

The surrounding circumstances dictated the kind of actions performed in a ritual. Because reciting a spell takes no more than a moment, the sorcerer was looking for ways to make its effects last longer. In this light, simply writing a text may be regarded as a magical act. A charm could also be read over or inscribed onto an amulet, statue, or other magical figurine, which would preserve the spoken word as long as it remained intact. A physician would recite a healing formula over his patient or fix an amulet around his or her neck. One particular method consisted in tying a knot in a piece of string or a linen bandage as soon as a charm had been recited so the magic formula would be fixed inside it. The hieroglyph for 'protection' *(sa)* is thus usually a knotted string. Actual strings often show seven knots because many charms had to be repeated seven times (fig. 50). The string, frequently hung with a number of amulets, was then fixed around the patient's neck. The Egyptian word for knot can also signify 'vertebra,' and it cannot be a coincidence that human beings have seven cervical vertebrae. Moreover, the head has seven orifices

FIG. 50. Linen cord with seven knots, forming part of an amulet. Photograph: © 2010 Musée du Louvre/ Georges Poncet (without acc. no.).

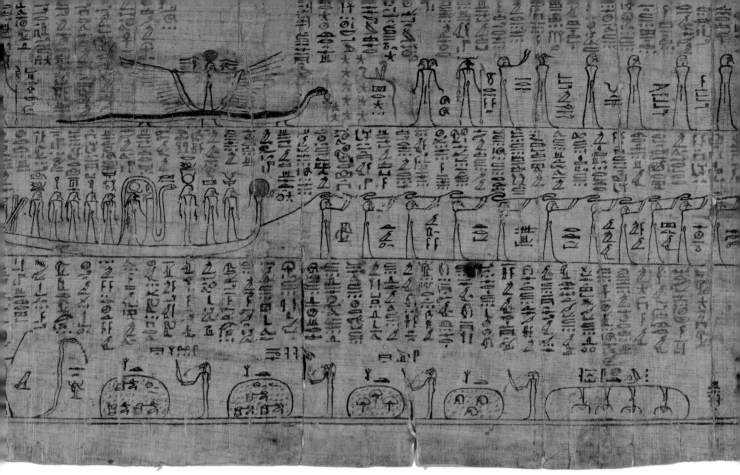

FIG. 51. The elimination of the damned in the hereafter. Lion-headed goddesses spitting fire and wielding long knives guard several flame-filled pits. These contain bound prisoners, their corpses, their spirits, their shadows, and their decapitated heads. From the eleventh hour of the book *Amduat*. Photograph: RMO (acc.no. L.I.1).

which serve as access routes for pathogenic germs, and the result of such invasions often becomes manifest in swollen glands in the neck and a sore throat. It is therefore not such a strange idea that the Egyptians believed the neck was the weakest spot, where head and body were 'knotted' together.

This belief made decapitation a favorite method for dispatching an enemy, whether man or beast. Capital punishment was not often performed in ancient Egypt, and beheading was not the usual method. It was, however, sporadically performed on foreign enemies. The famous palette of King Narmer (c. 3100 BC) shows rows of beheaded opponents lying on the battlefield. Also notorious is the magical deposit discovered near the Nubian border fortress of Mirgissa (c. 1850 BC), where a human skeleton with detached skull was found. Figurines of enemies have been recovered from many sites, made of unbaked clay or terracotta and ritually decapitated. Tomb walls and funerary books show the enemies of Re or Osiris with their heads severed or being cooked in large cauldrons (fig. 51). Apophis and other powers of evil

are depicted with huge knives at their throats. Magical rituals and offering ceremonies occasionally involve the beheading of animals, especially when they can be interpreted as the confederates of Seth or Apophis.

There were several other magical acts of destruction, usually performed on figurines of bound prisoners made of beeswax, clay, lead, bread dough, and so on. Statuettes of hippopotami (here representing the god Seth) were harpooned (fig. 91), and in vignettes from the Book of the Dead the same weapon is wielded by the deceased against all kinds of dangerous animals (fig. 122). Wax figures were burned, as demonstrated by the presence of five crucibles and the remains of ashes in the Mirgissa deposit. Enemy figures were trampled or pierced (fig. 52), and clay tablets inscribed with their names were broken. During an Egyptian funeral the participants used to smash red pottery vessels to dispel evil forces. Sorcerers also used to spit on figurines depicting Seth or Apophis: the spittle was supposed to transfer the power of the words from the magician's mouth.

Figurines pierced by pins or nails rather stir our imagination because we tend to associate them with voodoo rituals. In ancient Egypt, however, there is hardly any evidence of their existence. There is one famous set consisting of a clay figure and a lead tablet, found together inside a pottery vessel and now in the Louvre in Paris (fig. 53). The figure depicts a naked woman whose hands and feet have been tied behind her back. Her body has been pierced by thirteen bronze pins; yet these are not meant to torture her but to subject her, from top to toe, to the will of the man who scratched the love charm on the accompanying lead tablet. This 'fixative' use of pins can be compared to that of the knots in a string. Using

FIG. 52. This figurine of unbaked clay represents a prisoner whose arms are tied behind his back. The body is inscribed in red ink with curses mentioning the names of indigenous or foreign enemies. The figure has been decapitated and the knees have likewise been cut off during a ritual of destruction. Photograph: RMO (acc.no. F 1941/8.1).

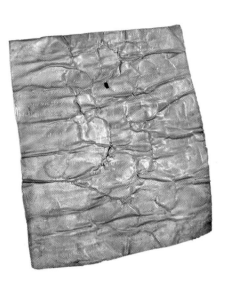

FIG. 53. A love charm dating to the Roman period consists of a ceramic jar containing a lead tablet with a magic inscription and a female figure of unbaked clay, pierced with thirteen needles. Photograph: © 2010 Musée du Louvre/Georges Poncet (acc. no. E.27145 A-C).

pins in this manner is prescribed a number of times in magical texts dating to the Greco-Roman period, always in a context more innocent than it seems. The opposite is the case with an apparently rather innocuous spell from the so-called Coffin Texts (c. 2000 BC) involving a charm to be recited over the figure of an enemy made of beeswax, with on its chest an inscription with the name of this enemy, incised by means of the fishbone of a *Synodontis*. The sting is, quite literally, in the tail: *Synodontis* has a venomous fin spine (figs. 54–55) and whoever is stung by it will suffer excruciating pain.

Encircling or embracing was seen as an effective means of spreading protective magic over something or someone. For this reason Egyptian gods are often represented with their arms outstretched: Horus embracing the King, Isis wrapping her wings around Osiris, or Nut extending her winged arms above the deceased. Therefore, the Egyptians used to say that protection is wielded 'around' something or somebody. Similarly, a funeral cortège walked four times around the tomb, and the images of the gods were carried around the temple or the city walls during annual processions. Ordinary citizens might walk around their houses with a staff to safeguard it against contagion. And thus 'to encircle' *(pekher)* became the normal word for 'to enchant,' and the word for medicine *(pekhert)* was derived from it.

Apart from all the actions the magician performed, there were others he had to avoid for a spell to be successful. Many texts stress the need to be 'pure,' which refers primarily to purity of the body. Like priests, magicians also had to wash themselves, to rinse their mouths with natron, and to dress in clean linen. Wearing

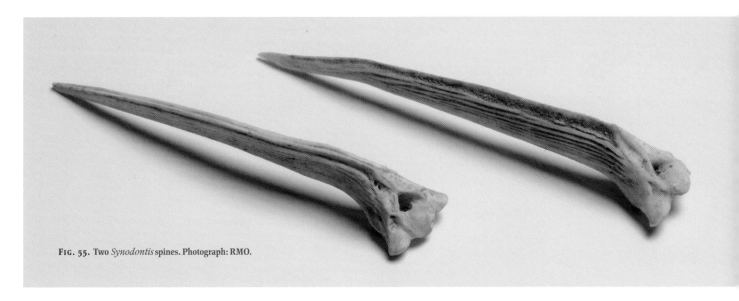

FIG. 55. Two *Synodontis* spines. Photograph: RMO.

wool was considered taboo because it could not be washed as easily as linen and attracted vermin. Priests also had to shave both their heads and their bodies, and of course they had to be circumcised like all Egyptian males. Occasionally the use of unguent and eye make-up was prescribed. Purity also implied that a magician should abstain from contact with unclean creatures and substances. A frequently mentioned taboo forbade the consumption of fish or the meat of goats and sheep, probably in view of the pungent smell of these foods in a hot climate. Women likewise were considered to be (potentially) impure, so the magician had to avoid having sex for a number of days. Presumably this was mainly connected with the fear of contact with blood, though parallels from other cultures suggest that it was also to prevent the sorcerer from being 'contaminated' with too many 'female' qualities. To predict the future, magicians preferred to employ as their mediums young boys who had not yet known women. After all, one could not be too careful when associating with gods and other supreme powers lest the magic turn on the magician.

FIG. 54. A fisherman removes the poisonous spine of a *Synodontis* to prevent injuries. Scene from the tomb chapel of Hetepherakhet. Photograph: RMO (acc.no. F 1904/3.1).

FIG. 56. This tool kit for the Ritual of Opening the Mouth comprises a number of stone knives and vessels. Photograph: © 2004 Musée du Louvre/ Christian Décamps (acc. no. E.11140).

BOOKS OF MAGIC

I will have you taken to the place where that book is that Thoth wrote with his own hand . . . . Two spells are written in it. When you [recite the first spell, you will] charm the sky, the earth, the netherworld, the mountains, and the waters. You will discover what all the birds of the sky and all the reptiles are saying. You will see the fish of the deep [though there are twenty-one divine cubits of water] over [them]. When you recite the second spell, it will happen that, whether you are in the netherworld or in your form on earth, you will see Re appearing in the sky with his Ennead, and the moon in its form of rising.

(PAPYRUS SETNE I, 12–14)

FIG. 57. This ebony wand is shaped like a ram-headed serpent. Photograph: RMO (acc.no. L.IX.28).

A MAGICAL TOOLBOX

Practicing magic was not easy. Years of preparation schooled apprentices in the proper way of thinking and the ready knowledge they would need for their work. All kinds of exotic ingredients not easily available in Egypt were required to produce magical models and prepare medicines. Some of these had to come all the way from Nubia, Syria, or the oases. Was there an ancient Egyptian equivalent of Harry Potter's Diagon Alley where all such things could be bought? The texts inform us that there were also particular tools used in many rituals. It is often quite difficult to picture them because they are only rarely represented, for instance in the vignettes of the Book of the Dead or on tomb walls. Often these representations concern well-known acts, such as those from the Ritual of Opening the Mouth. Fortunately in some rare cases the actual toolboxes of magicians have been found, or at least the places where they performed their magic (such as the aforementioned deposit at Mirgissa). Unviolated tombs can also be regarded as intact magical stockpiles to ensure the deceased's survival. Such finds are rare, though, and as a rule we must be content with isolated discoveries that have been removed from their archaeological context.

Basic sets of magicians' tools include, for example, the stone tablets with instruments used in the Ritual of Opening the Mouth. This ritual was performed on tomb and temple statues at the moment they left the workshop, but also on mummies before they were buried in underground tomb chambers (fig. 32). The funerary priest employed a

FIG. 58. Two alabaster bricks, possibly identifiable as the polishing stones used in the Ritual of Opening the Mouth. Photograph: RMO (acc.no. AAL 155a-b).

whole array of instruments with which he symbolically touched the face and hands of the deceased. The tradition of depositing a kit of tools in the tomb so that the dead could repeat the ritual at will developed in the Old Kingdom. Such kits consist of rectangular slabs of limestone with recesses for the various implements made of harder stone (fig. 56). Generally these comprise two water jars and four cups for natron (to perform a purification), two flint blades, and a third knife shaped like a fishtail: the *peseshkef* (for 'opening' the mouth and eyes). During the New Kingdom the tombs occasionally contained four rectangular pieces of alabaster (fig. 58), which may have been the polishing stones mentioned in the ritual text.

The Ritual of Opening the Mouth also involved the use of various carpentry tools, as if the tomb statue still had to be carved from wood. These include several distinct types of adze: an instrument with a razor-sharp bronze blade lashed to a curved handle and used as a plane. The priests also employed a staff shaped like a writhing snake. In texts this is called the 'great one of magic' *(weret-hekau)* and it can be regarded as a proper magic wand. Such wands were found in tombs dating to the Late Period; they are made

of ebony and terminate in a ram's head (fig. 57). Elsewhere there have been rare finds of large bronze wands shaped like serpents (fig. 59). The Bible relates how Egyptian sorcerers were able to change their wands into live serpents and how Moses and Aaron also mastered that art (Exodus 7). It has already been explained that in ancient Egypt snakes were considered to be mysterious creatures connected with both the netherworld and celestial forces. The god Heka himself is often depicted holding serpent wands. A ram's head was a well-known symbol for the notions 'majesty' and 'soul' *(ba)*.

A similar serpent wand made of bronze was found in 1896 by James Quibell in a shaft tomb dating to the end of the Middle Kingdom (c. 1800–1700 BC) and located under the later mortuary temple of Ramesses II in Thebes (the Ramesseum). At the bottom of the shaft were the remains of the tools of an Egyptian sorcerer, probably once contained in a basket or bag which had decayed (fig. 60). These comprised the figurine of a naked lion-headed woman holding two snakes, presumably depicting a female form of the god Aha (or Bes). Next, there were three 'magic knives' carved from hippopotamus tusks and incised with figures of apotropaic creatures, including the same lion-masked woman wielding snakes. As we will see below, these objects served for the protection of young children. A clapper, a fragment of a wand with a rectangular section and decorated with two lions, an amulet symbolizing 'duration,' and the figurine of a boy carrying a calf on his shoulders had also been carved from (hippopotamus?) ivory. Four statuettes of nude women in faience, wood, or limestone served for stimulating fertility. There were also faience amulets of a lion and two baboons (the sacred animal of the god Thoth). Otherwise the deposit contained a quantity of human hair, several seeds and fruits, a lotus-shaped cup, the faience model of a cucumber, and a number of beads in semi-precious stones and faience. However, the most important item in this magician's burial was a wooden box of about 45 x 30 x 30 cm, whitewashed and with a jackal drawn on the lid in black ink. To any Egyptian, this was a clear message: the box contained the magician's greatest secrets, for the jackal hieroglyph can be read as 'keeper of secrets.'

When the box was opened, the excavator lost heart. It was found to be one third full of papyrus scrolls in extremely bad condition, inscribed in hieratic. Roughly three quarters of the texts had already been lost, and the rest crumbled as soon as they were touched. Even so, Quibell decided to take the papyri to England, hoping that the able papyrologist F.Ll. Griffith of the British Museum would be able to reconstruct at least some of them. This was a good idea, for it proved possible to save the remains of over twenty different texts. Together they offer an excellent

impression of the private library of an Egyptian magician. As was to be expected, the majority consists of magic books for various purposes. Four of these are medical handbooks. Another text was devoted to the protection of women and babies and so matched the figurines and magic knives in the cache. Another charm serves to protect during the dangerous intercalary days at the end of the year, and there is also a scroll containing nothing but invocations to various demons. That our magician also executed other activities is proved by the copy of a funerary ritual. This suggests that the owner of the box also served as a priest, a hypothesis supported by the presence of copies of hymns to the crocodile god Sobek and of the ritual for the coronation of Pharaoh Senwosret I (1971–1926 BC). The latter text is known as the Ramesseum Dramatic Papyrus and is the oldest known illustrated Egyptian manuscript. The magician was likewise interested in literature and possessed copies of contemporary classics, such as the *Story of the Eloquent Peasant* and the *Story of Sinuhe*. We may even regard him as a scholar, because he owned two papyri with so-called books of wisdom and an encyclopedia containing the names of birds, plants, mammals, and towns. It is noteworthy that many texts were written on the reverse of discarded administrative documents: papyrus was an expensive writing material, and therefore the scrolls were often used on both sides.

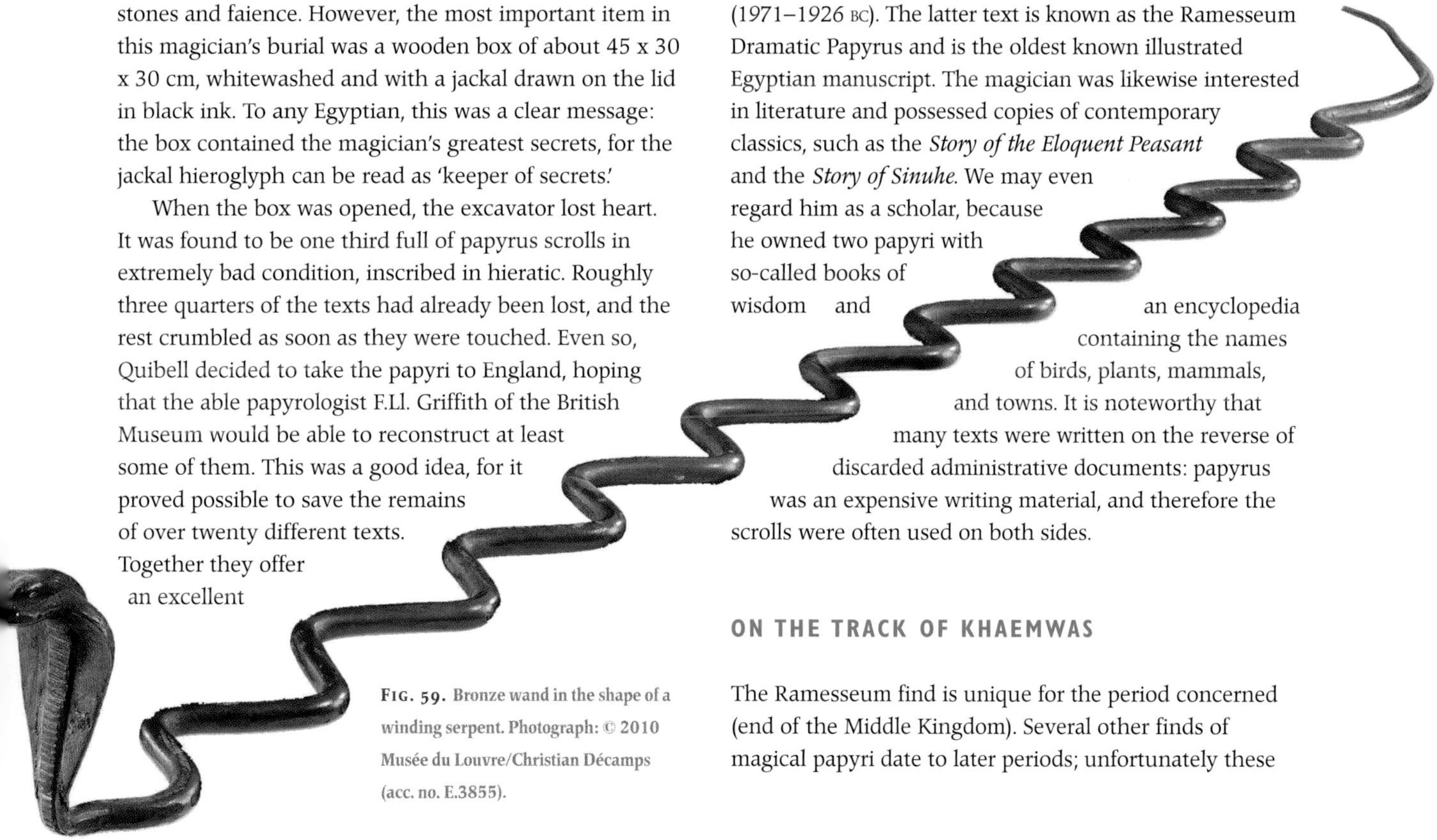

FIG. 59. Bronze wand in the shape of a winding serpent. Photograph: © 2010 Musée du Louvre/Christian Décamps (acc. no. E.3855).

ON THE TRACK OF KHAEMWAS

The Ramesseum find is unique for the period concerned (end of the Middle Kingdom). Several other finds of magical papyri date to later periods; unfortunately these

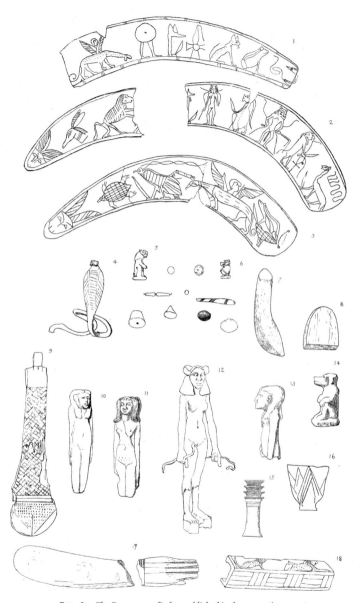

FIG. 60. The Ramesseum find as published in the excavation report.
Reproduced after Quibell, *Ramesseum*, pl. iii.

were not as well documented as that made by Quibell because they were discovered at the beginning of the nineteenth century, when Egyptian archaeology was still in its infancy. Egypt first opened its borders to foreigners only after the expedition by Napoleon (1798–1801). Due to this campaign, Egyptian antiquities suddenly became fashionable in Europe, where people paid high prices to acquire them. As a result, it was the wrong kind of people who first started large-scale excavations: not devoted scholars, but treasure hunters and charlatans who did not keep a record of the exact conditions of a discovery or its location, and who often divided up their finds in order to sell them to the highest bidder.

One of these was the recently founded National Museum of Antiquities in Leiden. The Dutch museum posted a former army officer, Jean Emile Humbert, as its agent in the Italian harbor town of Leghorn, where shiploads of antiquities arrived from Alexandria and where whole collections were sold by the quayside. It was here that Humbert bought the collection of Maria Cimba in 1827 and the much larger collection of Giovanni d'Anastasi in 1828. D'Anastasi was consul general in Alexandria for Norway and Sweden, whereas the late husband of Maria Cimba had served as private physician to the British consul Henry Salt. Diplomats of similar rank were foremost among the persons who took advantage of their stay in Egypt to supplement their income with the lucrative antiquities trade. By the time they acquired the objects through a whole network of intermediaries, all records concerning the original archaeological context had already been lost.

Among the almost six thousand Egyptian objects from the Anastasi collection which poured into the Leiden Museum in 1829, there were numerous papyri with magical texts, five of which date to the New Kingdom. The first of these scrolls is about five meters long and inscribed on both sides with a total of fifty-three columns of hieratic. The first meter of this scroll was bought from d'Anastasi, the much decayed remainder from Maria Cimba—a sad example of the lack of care of the early antiquities dealers. This text is almost completely devoted to the treatment of two unclear diseases, or possibly a single disease described by two different names (*akhu* and *semen*). The latter word could be Asiatic in origin and refer to a new contagious disease contracted by the Egyptians during their conquests of Palestine and Syria. This might explain the invocation of numerous Asiatic deities such as Baal, Reshef, Anat, and Astarte by the magician who tries to stop the plague. It seems the physician was helpless in the face of these complaints, which could manifest themselves in any part of the body. All he could do was to shout that he acted on behalf of the gods, that the patient's limbs were protected by the gods, and that the ingredients of his unguents and other remedies had a supernatural origin.

The second scroll is 73 cm long and bears three columns of text for protection during the dreaded five intercalary days. The papyrus may originally have been longer and may have included a section on the other parts of the year, divided into lucky and unlucky days, as they are known from other papyri. In its present state of preservation, however, the papyrus starts with a copy of a Book of the Last Day of the Year that is not known from other sources, and with a charm against the twelve *murderers who stand in waiting upon Sekhmet, who have come forth from the Eye of Re, messengers present everywhere in the districts, who bring about slaughter, who create uproar, who hurry through the land, who shoot their arrows from their mouths, who see from afar.* Next follow five spells addressing Osiris, Horus the Elder, Seth, Isis, and Nephthys, who were born on the five epagomenal (or intercalary) days. The papyrus ends with the Book of the Five Epagomenal Days, a spell that identifies the speaker with the redoubtable Sekhmet in the hope that thereby he would not fall victim to her demons. At the bottom there is a vignette depicting twelve deities which must be copied

onto a linen bandage, to be worn around the neck for protection (fig. 61).

The third scroll is 242 cm long and has thirteen columns of magical texts. After an invocation to the gods Horus of Three-hundred Town and Horus of Athribis, the magician again identifies himself with a large number of supernatural powers. This spell concludes with the instruction that it must be recited over a linen bandage inscribed with seven jackals (fig. 62). The papyrus ends with the words: *Whoever reads this book, he will be favored every day. He will have neither hunger nor thirst. He will have no grief and his heart will not suffer. He will not end up in prison, he will not be sentenced. If nonetheless he is made prisoner, he will be released as a justified one. People will praise him as a god, his favor will not leave him, and slander will have no hold over him. He will not die from the plague of the year and bad luck will not hit him.*

The fourth scroll is 360 cm long and inscribed on both sides with a total of twenty-five columns. Unlike the other Leiden texts, this scroll displays at least five different handwritings. Most of the back is covered in model letters, the royal titles of Pharaoh Ramesses II (1290–1224 BC), and other writing exercises, whereas the front and the remainder of the back have been reserved for magical spells. It seems clear that several apprentice scribes had to share this precious scroll, and the gray hue of part of the surface suggests that they erased older texts to make the expensive writing material last longer. Fortunately the magic spells were not washed out. There are thirty-nine different charms, of which almost half deal with the treatment of headache, one quarter help against belly-ache, and the rest concern burns, phobias, and nightmares, and problems in childbirth. One spell is accompanied by an illustration (fig. 63).

Finally, the fifth scroll measures 61 cm and contains three columns with a total of eight spells to protect against scorpions. One of these charms refers to the myth of Horus-the-Child, who was attacked by scorpions in the

FIG. 61. The last column of the papyrus scroll for protection during the epagomenal days shows a model for the twelve divine figures that must be copied on a linen bandage. Photograph: RMO (acc.no. AMS 23a).

marshes when his mother Isis had left him for a moment: *Another spell against scorpions. Horus has been stung, Horus has been stung, the [orphan]. Horus has been stung, Horus has been stung in the evening, in the night. There is no wood, there is no fire, no charm has been brought for Horus, there is no saliva [for him] to spit out. May one go to Heliopolis of Re in order to fetch a charm for Horus. [Did he make] somebody come from Heliopolis, when Horus was stung? Sit up, Horus, save yourself! Your own words will be sufficient for you. May your mother Isis recite spells over you. All her words are effective!* On the back of this scroll too there are

writing exercises, in this case a model letter addressed to Pharaoh Ramesses II.

According to the list of the d'Anastasi sale, which includes all five papyri (except for the second half of the first), these manuscripts came from Memphis. But what does that mean? Surely not the ruins of Egypt's ancient capital, down in the Nile valley, humid from the annual floods and farmers' irrigation of surrounding fields, where such fragile manuscripts would never have survived. Probably the toponym refers rather to one of the more elevated terrains around the ancient city, such as the cemeteries in the western desert near the modern village of Saqqara, where all high officials of the New Kingdom were buried. It is well known that d'Anastasi occasionally

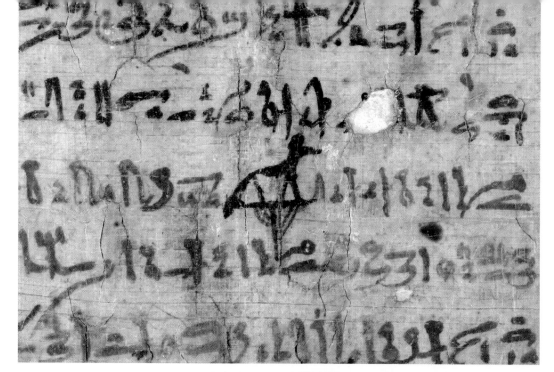

FIG. 62. The concluding remarks of the papyrus for Horus of Three-hundred Town are all written in red. However, the jackal sign and the name of Horus are in black. Photograph: RMO (acc.no. AMS 23b).

FIG. 63. The only illustration in the fourth papyrus from Leiden shows Osiris in a boat, flanked by Isis and Nephthys and with a god lifting a mummy on the left. When copied on a piece of linen, this vignette would protect against nightmares. Photograph: RMO (acc.no. AMS 26a).

FIG. 64. General view of the temple constructed by Khaemwas and recently discovered by a Japanese expedition on a high hill at Saqqara. Photograph: Egyptological Institute, Waseda University.

listed 'Memphis' as the origin of objects which have been proven to have come from Saqqara. Although he never says that the five magical papyri were in fact discovered together, this is possible in view of the Ramesseum find. The last two scrolls can be dated to the reign of Ramesses II, and the script of the first and third may also date to that period. Papyrus two is the only one which has to be dated to about 1425 BC and so would likely have been an heirloom. What was happening at Saqqara during the reign of Ramesses II?

In that period the cemetery was still in full use, and so the papyrus find may have come from the tomb of a contemporary magician. There are, however, other possibilities. Apart from a cemetery, there were also a number of sanctuaries situated at Saqqara, including the burial place of the sacred Apis bulls (later called the Serapeum). This complex was extended during the reign of Ramesses II, and the person responsible for that project was none other than the crown prince and high priest of Ptah, Khaemwas—whom we met above as one of the greatest sorcerers of pharaonic Egypt (figs. 22–24). Khaemwas also constructed a hilltop shrine that was probably sacred to

the goddess Sekhmet (fig. 64), who was a patron goddess of doctors and possibly some types of magicians as well. Everywhere in the desert he undertook the restoration of the ancient pyramids (already over a thousand years old in his time), identified their original owners, and commemorated this in newly carved inscriptions.

Presumably, all these activities must have entailed the foundation of an office center in the Saqqara desert. The Anastasi collection contained several administrative documents on papyrus, including the unique logs of a ship owned by the *sem*-priest of Ptah. Since the papyrus in question is dated to year 52 of Ramesses II, this priestly title can only refer to Khaemwas. The same collection comprised a number of Ramesside letters, one of which is addressed to Khaemwas in person (fig. 65). Thus it rather looks as if during their excavations in the desert d'Anastasi's workmen may have found the offices of the crown prince, and that indeed the Leiden magical papyri were found there. Two of them display a mixture of magical texts and writing exercises (the British Museum holds six other papyri from d'Anastasi's collections with similar exercises). It is a well-known fact that writing lessons were often given in government offices. If the office in question was so focused on magic, we may perhaps conclude that also the other three Leiden papyri were kept there in the archives. They display a markedly medical-magical character, and we might note here that medicine was an art protected by Sekhmet, a goddess considered to be the wife of Ptah. All the evidence seems to point to Khaemwas. It is possible that several other papyri from the Leiden collections belonged to his library, including literary and religious texts such as the Hymns to Amun (written on the reverse of the above-mentioned ship's logs), the Solar Hymns, and the Admonitions of Ipuwer (on the obverse and reverse of another Leiden papyrus). This would imply that the Memphite papyrus find was very similar to that of the Ramesseum!

Of course all of this is very speculative, and it cannot

be proved that Khaemwas ever touched these papyri personally, although he might well have owned them. On the other hand, it would perfectly corroborate the reputation he would gain in later generations. It is even possible to go a step further: the government office in question may have been located next to the later Serapeum. The Leiden collections contain more objects which demonstrate that d'Anastasi's workmen were active in that specific area. These include a large number of papyri dating to the Greek period and certainly having a close connection with the cult center of the Apis bulls, as well as numerous bronze votive statuettes of bulls and other deities. We can only hope that future excavations in this area will provide further clues. In the meantime, it is about time to leave Saqqara and return to Thebes in Upper Egypt.

AN END AND A NEW BEGINNING

More than fifteen hundred years passed, and Khaemwas became a mythical figure about whom the most fantastic stories were told. Pharaonic culture had reached its end, Greeks and Romans had assumed power in Egypt, but still there were Egyptian sorcerers who continued the ancient traditions. Around the beginning of the fourth century AD, one of them decided to hide his library in the ground. We will never know why he did so, or where he hid it, because once again this archive was excavated unscientifically at the beginning of the nineteenth century. The only thing we do know is that it must have been in Thebes, the religious capital of ancient Egypt. In view of the excellent state of preservation of the manuscripts concerned, we presume they were carefully stored inside a large pot, which was perhaps deposited in a tomb somewhere in the Theban hills on the west bank of the Nile.

D'Anastasi managed to acquire this find in its entirety. In 1828 he sold four papyri to the Leiden Museum, and the following year he donated the second half of one of

FIG. 65. This letter to Khaemwas was written by an overseer of cattle. It reports some problems involving royal messengers in central Egypt. Photograph: RMO (acc.no. AMS 25c).

these as an afterthought. Four years later he presented a fifth manuscript (plus one sheet of a sixth) to the Swedish Academy of Sciences. In 1839 the British Museum bought a seventh scroll at an auction of d'Anastasi's collections, and after his death in 1857 it acquired the other half of one of the Leiden papyri (although the match was only discovered in 1892). At the same auction, the Louvre bought a large magical papyrus undoubtedly belonging to the same Theban find, and possibly the same provenance can be attributed to six further manuscripts from this sale that wound up in London, Paris, and Berlin. If that is the case, the magical library in question would have been the largest preserved from antiquity. Even so, its importance does not lie only in its sheer bulk. It is of extreme interest that it contained not only rolled-up papyrus scrolls (the usual format for books during the pharaonic period), but also a number of bound books made of folded papyrus sheets. Such 'codices' were at the time quite a recent innovation. They would gradually take the place of the old-fashioned scrolls, especially as papyrus made way for parchment, and later paper.

Another characteristic of the Theban archive is that the manuscripts have been compiled in several languages and writing systems. During the Roman period people in Egypt employed a shorthand script for daily purposes known as demotic (literally 'popular'). This was ultimately derived from hieroglyphs and served for recording the colloquial language of the indigenous population. The country's ruling classes, however—first Greeks, and from 31 BC, Romans—spoke Greek, which meant that native Egyptians also had to use that language and script for their contacts with the government. In the manuscripts from the Theban archive, both scripts occur equally side-by-side. The obverse and reverse of a single scroll are occasionally in different languages, and sometimes the language shifts even within a single spell. Some words have been written in hieroglyphs or the obsolete hieratic script, presumably because it looked especially mysterious

and traditional. And some passages in the Egyptian vernacular have been annotated with Greek letters and demotic signs representing phonemes unknown to Greek, an experiment that would later evolve into the Coptic script of Egypt's first Christians. True, Egyptians did not approve of the translation of their sacred texts into Greek, and these Old Coptic notations are some kind of compromise. A Hermetic text states: *Leave the text untranslated, in order to prevent that such profound mysteries will be known unto the Greeks, and that the presumptuous, effete, and bombastic Greek language causes to disappear the loftiness, succinctness, and magic powers of our words. For Greeks employ empty words that are alleged to 'prove' things. Such is the wisdom of the Greeks: not philosophy but futility. We, on the other hand, do not use mere words but effective sounds which possess a magical potency* (Corpus Hermeticum XVI.2).

Foremost among the four manuscripts that came to the Leiden Museum is the famous Demotic Magical Papyrus, which it shares with the British Museum. Apparently d'Anastasi had cut the papyrus in two parts in order to get twice as much money for it! The total length of the scroll is almost five meters, but originally it must have been even longer because the beginning and end are now lost. With ninety-eight spells, this is the longest magical papyrus to have survived from ancient Egypt. The spells have been written in twenty-nine long columns on the obverse and thirty-three short ones on the reverse. The large columns are outlined in black framing lines. The demotic text is interspersed with three passages in Greek, annotations (so-called glosses) in Old Coptic, a spell in the Nubian language, and several notes written in cipher (fig. 67). The composer was mainly interested in techniques for predicting the future. He advises that a bright lamp be lit in a dark room and a young boy made to look into the flame until his blinded eyes see gods appear, while the magician creates the right atmosphere by reciting charms and burning stupefying herbs. The papyrus also contains spells to bring lovers together or separate them, to provoke dreams, or to ensure a successful career, and recipes for curing dog bites and eye complaints.

Equally famous is a second Leiden papyrus, the two halves of which were delivered by d'Anastasi with an interval of one year. This manuscript of 3.6 meters is especially renowned for the demotic animal fables on the obverse–a text which seems not, however, to have interested the magician, and which he partly covered by pasting on strips of papyrus to restore the scroll. The reverse carries the text of yet another magic handbook in thirteen columns of Greek and six of demotic. The demotic spells are written in the same hand as those of the Leiden–London papyrus, and again they are interspersed with Greek words, hieratic signs, and fancy letters. Moreover, the manuscript shows four illustrations included by way of models, for the benefit of those readers who wanted to administer a spell involving the manufacture of certain amulets (fig. 66). In total there are twenty-nine spells, varying from love charms, dreams, and predictions of the future to the instructions on the use of magic rings and the manufacture of a gold-colored solution. When the scroll arrived in Leiden, it clearly showed that it had been heavily used and well thumbed. Moreover, it could still be seen that it had been rolled up together with the Demotic Magical Papyrus.

The Leiden collection also holds two codices from the Theban papyrus cache. The first of these consists of six folded sheets plus a half-size sheet–twenty-five written pages altogether–with a blank sheet serving as its exterior cover. Each page is covered in closely spaced lines of neat Greek capitals. The title of the book is quoted in the first line as *A Sacred Book Called 'Unique,' or the Eighth Book of Moses Concerning the Holy Name* (fig. 68). This identifies it as a product of the Jewish influence on Hellenistic culture, which manifested itself particularly in the melting pot of Alexandria–the same metropolis that provided the cultural context for the codification of our Bible.

Contemporary scholars struggled with the question of which of the numerous available texts could be regarded as orthodox. In the end, they agreed that the five Mosaic books or Pentateuch would form the beginning of the Old Testament of our Bible. These texts show a Moses much resembling an oriental magician, who is able to change magic wands into snakes, strike water from a stone, and make a sea withdraw.

Numerous other, apocryphal books of Moses also existed, however, and soon the rumor spread that these had intentionally been rejected because the editors wanted to keep their wisdom and power for themselves. The Eighth Book is exactly such an occult compilation,

FIG. 66. In order to bring about the separation of a married couple, this figure of the god Seth had to be drawn on a potsherd which was then buried under their house. The concomitant spell has been written in a mixture of demotic and Greek. Photograph: RMO (acc.no. AMS 75).

From the demotic papyrus Leiden–London

The method of the scarab in the cup of wine in order to make a woman love a man: You should bring a scarab of Mars (which is this small scarab which has no horn), it having three shields on the front of its head—you find its face shrunken—or also the one which has two horns. You should bring it at the rising of the sun; you should bind yourself with a cloth on the upper part of your back; you should bind yourself at your face with a strip of palm fiber while the scarab is on the palm of your hand; and you should speak to it before the sun when it is about to rise, seven times. When you have finished, you should drown it in milk of a black cow. You should put ten pieces of olive wood to its head. You should leave it until evening in the milk. When evening comes, you should bring it up, you should spread under it with sand, and you should put a band of cloth under it upon the sand, for four days. You should put myrrh on a flame before it.

When the four days have passed, and it is dry, you should bring it before you, a cloth being spread under it. You should divide it in its middle with a copper knife. You should take its right half and nail parings of your right hand and foot, and you should cook them on a new potsherd with vine wood. You should pound them with nine apple seeds and your urine or your sweat (free from bath oil); you should make it into a ball; you should put it in the wine; you should speak over it seven times; you should make the woman drink it; you should take its other half, the left one, together with the nail parings of your left hand and foot also; you should bind them in a strip of byssus with myrrh and saffron; you should bind them to your left arm; and you should lie with the woman while they are bound to you. . . .

The invocation which you should recite to it before the sun at dawn: "You are the scarab of real lapis lazuli. Bring yourself out of the door of my temple! . . . I am sending you against A, daughter of B, to strike her from her heart to her belly, from her belly to her intestines, from her intestines to her womb, for she is the one who urinated before the sun at dawn, saying to the sun: 'Do not come forth!'; to the moon: 'Do not rise!'; to the water: 'Do not come to those of Egypt!'; to the field: 'Do not bloom!'; and to the great trees of those of Egypt: 'Do not grow green!' I am sending you against A, daughter of B, in order to beat her from her heart to her belly, from her belly to her intestines, from her intestines to her womb, so that she put herself on the road following after C, son of D, at all times.' . . .

I am sending you down to the heart of A, daughter of B; make a flame in her body, flame in her intestines. Put madness after her heart, fever after her flesh. Let her make the travels of the Shoulder constellation after the Hippopotamus constellation. Let her make the movements of the sunshine after the shadow while she is searching after C, son of D, at every place in which he is, she loving him, she being mad about him, she not knowing a place of the earth in which she is. Take away her sleep by night! Give her grief and anxiety by day! Do not let her eat! Do not let her drink! Do not let her lie down! Do not let her sit in the shadow of her house until she goes to him at every place in which he is, her heart forgetting, her eye flying, her glances turned upside down, she not knowing a place of the earth in which she is, until she sees him, her eye after his eye, her heart after his heart, her hand after his hand, she giving to him every favor. Let her put the tip of her feet after his heels in the street at all times, without a time changed. Quickly, quickly! Hurry, hurry!

(PAPYRUS LEIDEN–LONDON, RECTO 21.10–21.43)

FIG. 67. As this column of the great magical papyrus shows, the demotic is peppered with words in Greek, hieratic signs, and magical symbols. Photograph: RMO (acc.no. AMS 65).

combining the usual magical recipes with a creation myth occurring in two different versions in the Leiden manuscript. Otherwise it does not shun the use of 'abracadabra,' Hebrew and Aramaic magic words, and cipher, for instance: *Moses says in the treatise on the archangels: 'Aldazaô batham makhôr' or 'Ba adam makhôr rizxaê ôkeôn pned meôps psykh phrôkh pher phrô iaothkhô.'*

The other codex comprises ten sheets folded double, of which only sixteen pages have been inscribed. The handwriting is identical to that in the Eighth Book of Moses, but the contents are totally different. First it contains eighty-eight recipes for refining, annealing, alloying, and employing various metals, then proceeds with eleven prescriptions for dyeing cloth purple. It concludes with ten descriptions of metals derived from an older 'encyclopedia,' the *Materia medica* of Dioscurides (first half of the first century AD). Although it has the appearance of a strictly scientific treatise, in fact it is imbued with a strong link with the world of magic. The central interest of its author was notably the manufacture (or rather imitation) of silver and gold, suggesting that the border between illusion and reality had become utterly blurred (fig. 69). This manuscript is among the earliest alchemical treatises and so stands at the beginning of a long tradition. It should be noted that the codex which d'Anastasi donated to Stockholm formed a sequel to the book now in Leiden. The Swedish manuscript rather focuses on semi-precious stones and dyes.

Thus, on the one hand, the Theban sorcerer stood at the end of a long line of pharaonic magicians. As a highly educated priest he was still able to read texts in hieratic and demotic, and his books show him to have been a representative of ancient Egyptian culture. He appears not to have cared much for the animal fables, but otherwise he seems to have used his magical scrolls a great deal. Possibly they can be regarded as precious heirlooms, for the two demotic scrolls presumably date back to the second or third century AD. The sorcerer himself seems to have lived a little later, because his archives contained two modern codices which cannot be older than the fourth century.

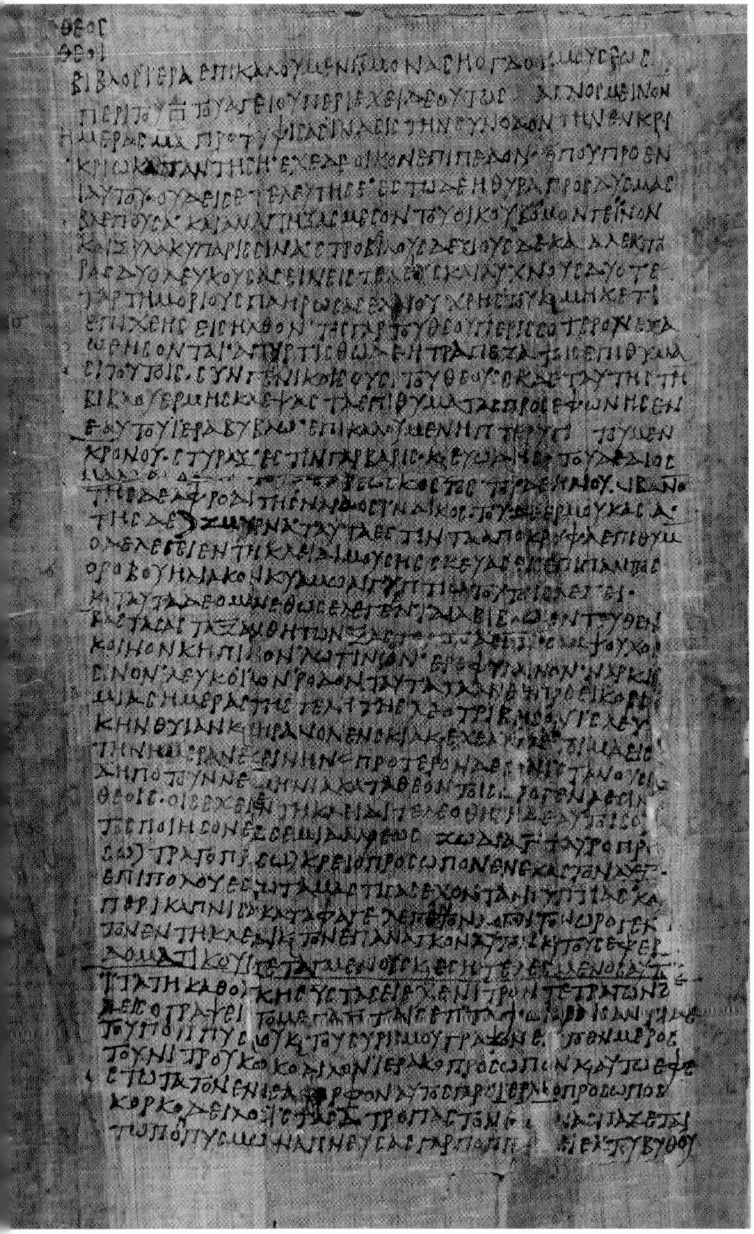

On the other hand, the magician in question was clearly a man who kept up with fashion, as demonstrated by his excellent mastery of Greek and the semi-scientific character of the alchemical treatise. Even the old-fashioned scrolls show a new period breaking through, which would be dominated by the Hellenistic culture of far-away, cosmopolitan Alexandria. The magical practices prescribed in the demotic papyrus hardly address dispelling evil forces and diseases (the traditional themes of Egyptian magic books), but rather focus on social and financial gain, status, love, and knowledge of the future. Frequent references are made to deities, authors, and prophets with Greek names, or to that strange magician from Jewish culture, Moses. People belonging to this international elite seem to have been aggressively interested in acquiring a better life, and they probably felt some disdain for the traditional Egyptian witch doctors. In spite of all this, ancient Egyptian magic was to have a long afterlife, as we shall see in the final chapter of the present book.

FIG. 68. The first page of the Eighth Book of Moses.

Photograph: RMO (acc.no. AMS 76).

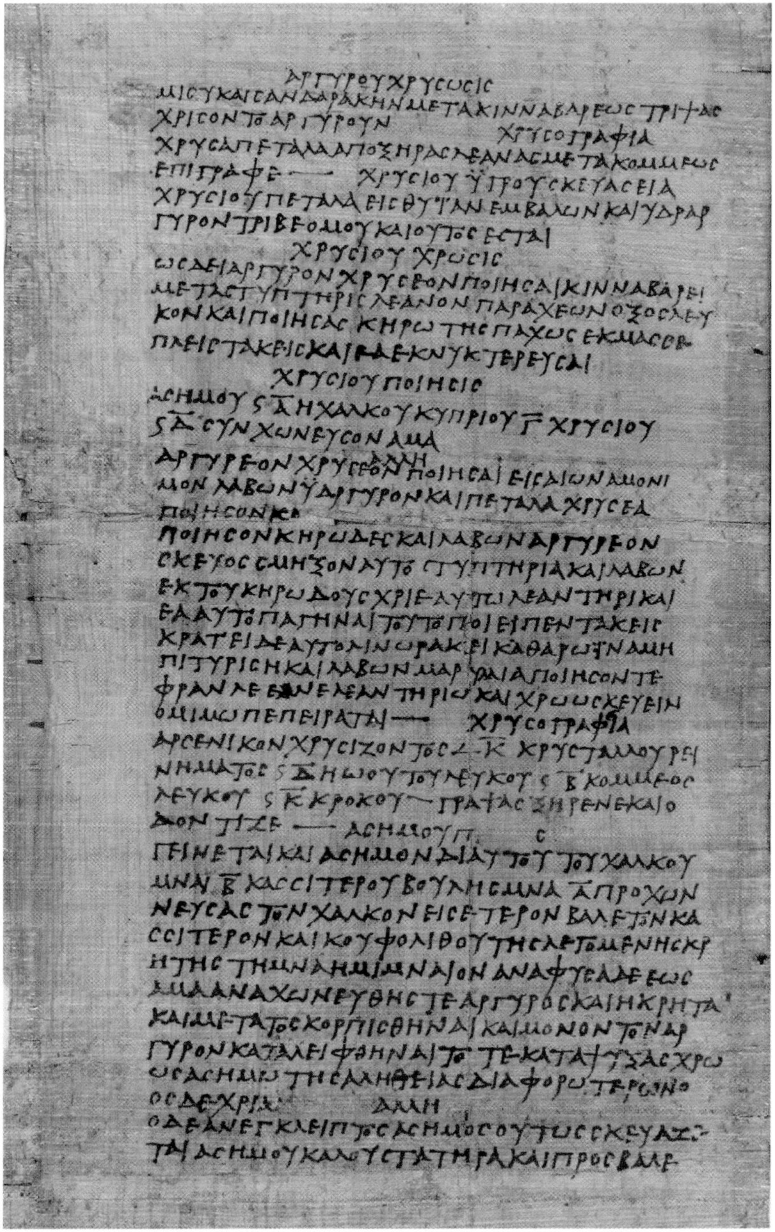

FIG. 69. Line 13 of this page from the alchemistic codex mentions a recipe for 'making gold': the dream of all alchemists. Photograph: RMO (acc.no. AMS 66).

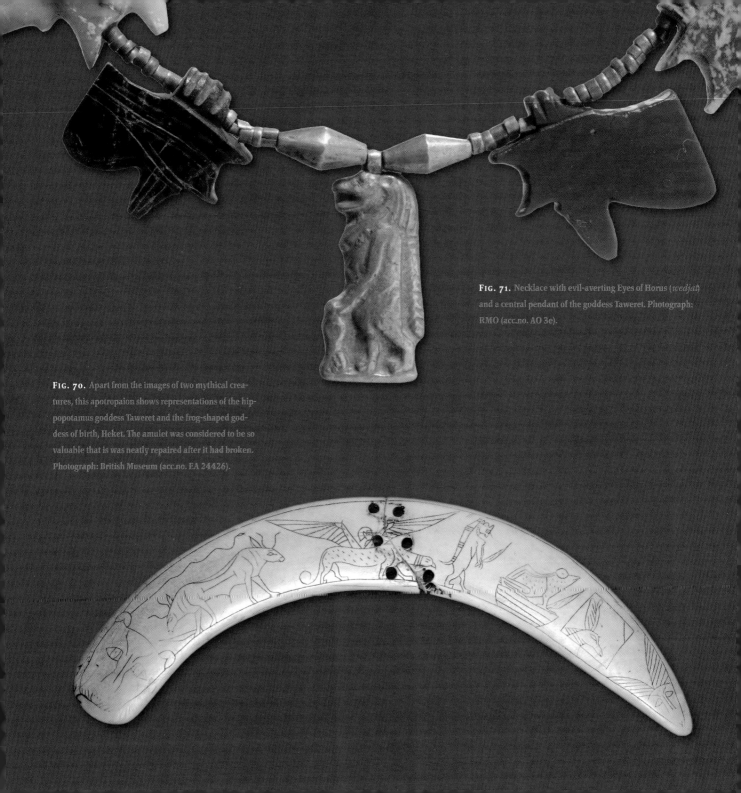

FIG. 71. Necklace with evil-averting Eyes of Horus (*wedjat*) and a central pendant of the goddess Taweret. Photograph: RMO (acc.no. AO 3e).

FIG. 70. Apart from the images of two mythical creatures, this apotropaion shows representations of the hippopotamus goddess Taweret and the frog-shaped goddess of birth, Heket. The amulet was considered to be so valuable that is was neatly repaired after it had broken. Photograph: British Museum (acc.no. EA 24426).

THE SOCIAL SECURITY SYSTEM

WOMEN AND CHILDREN FIRST

Many people today may regard magic as a detestable superstition of ill repute, mainly designed to scare or oppress others. That is because we tend to overlook a number of important issues. Superstition can be defined as a conviction which does not make sense in the context of a coherent world view. It is fair to say that magic has little place in the present-day world, since the universe is now generally understood through the prism of modern science. Yet, the preceding chapters have demonstrated that quite a different situation prevailed in ancient Egypt: there magic was an integral part of the world view, and one might even argue that it was its foundation. In that sense, magic did not result in fear, doubt, or remorse among those who were affected by it or made use of it themselves. On the contrary, magic served an important function in society and ensured a large degree of social cohesion. It was an indispensable means of protecting the weakest members of the community from dangers against which contemporary (medical) science stood powerless. In that way it offered reassurance similar to that of modern-day social security and medical or mental healthcare, and undoubtedly many people felt better because of it. Of course there is no denying the fact that magic was not only employed for defensive (evil-averting) purposes, and that occasionally it assumed the character of aggressive witchcraft. Still, one should not disregard the positive aspects simply because such malign excesses existed.

The important social function magic can exercise is well illustrated by the daily life of ancient Egyptians.

Backwards, enemy, fiend, male dead, female dead, and so on, who cause this suffering to X, son of Y! You have said that you would strike a blow in his head in order to force your entry into his forehead and to smash his temples! Retreat, recede for the striking power of his burning eye! It will ward off your attack, it will dispel your discharges, your seed, your harm, your feces, your oppressions, your wrongdoings, your torments, your inflammations, your afflictions, heat and fire, all the bad things of which you have said: 'He will suffer from them!' and which you have done accordingly!

(Papyrus Leiden AMS 26a, recto VI.4–8)

91

Nothing is more vulnerable than a newborn baby, and the degree to which a culture reflects humanitarian values can be measured by the care given to little children. Egyptian magic literature includes a separate category of spells designed for the protection of helpless infants. Several of these are contained in a papyrus now in Berlin: *A spell for a knot for a baby. Are you warm in the nest? Are you hot in the bushes? Is not your mother with you? Is not there a sister to give air? Is there no nurse to afford protection? Let one bring me some nuggets of gold and beads of garnet, and a seal with a crocodile and a hand, in order to defeat and ward off the 'beloved one,' to warm the limbs, and to vanquish the male or female enemy from the netherworld. Perish, this is a protection!—This spell has to be spoken over nuggets of gold, beads of garnet, and a seal with a crocodile and a hand. String them onto a strip of fine linen and make them into an amulet, to be fixed around the neck of an infant. Good!*

Indeed, ancient Egyptian children often wore necklaces consisting of beads and amulets, with the string knotted to 'tie up' the text of the charm inside it (fig. 50). Scarabs engraved with the figures of wild animals or evil-averting hands are also known. An alternative interpretation of the text above would be to regard the scarab, crocodile, and hand as three separate amulets. Obviously, these had to wield protection against jealous spirits who rose from the netherworld to take away the infant, spirits euphemistically named 'the beloved' to avoid unnecessary provocation.

If a mother in ancient Egypt had to leave her child for a moment, she would place a special amulet next to or on the baby to protect it in her absence (fig. 70). The amulet was carved from the canine (tusk) of a hippopotamus, the animal sacred to Taweret, patron goddess of mothers and children. The tooth was split lengthwise and the flat inner face incised with figures of lions and hippoptami, frogs and crocodiles, winged mythical animals and depictions of the dwarf god Aha ('the Fighter'). All of them carry

knives or hold coiling snakes in their hands or mouths. In Egyptian mythology, such deities counted as guardians to the young sun god, who was born as a defenseless infant every morning. In the present context their help was invoked for an ordinary baby, who was thereby equated to the solar child.

Such ivory amulets are called *apotropaia* (evil-averters) or magic knives; they date to the Middle Kingdom. Some scholars have speculated that the mother might use them to draw a 'magic circle' around her baby, a line that could not be crossed by demons. There is no evidence to support this hypothesis, however, because such circles are not mentioned in Egyptian texts and have only been recorded for later European witchcraft.

In spite of these precautions, ancient Egypt suffered extremely high infant mortality. Women in childbed and new mothers likewise were at high risk of death. Like their babies, they used to wear talismanic necklaces featuring figurines of Taweret and the dwarf Bes (fig. 71). There were also special magic spells to help women in childbirth, at the moment when the life of both mother and child was at risk: *Oh, benevolent dwarf, come for the sake of him that sent you, that is Re who is standing while Thoth is seated with his feet on the ground which Nun embraces and his hand on the roof beam. Come down, placenta, come down, placenta, come down! I am Horus who ensures that the condition of the woman in childbed gets better than at first, as if she has already been delivered. Oh, Support, the wife of Horus, Nekhbet the Nubian, the eastern goddess, and Wenut mistress of Wenut: come in order to do what you can! Look, Hathor will lay her hand on her with a charm for health! I am Horus who saves her!—To be recited four times over a dwarf of clay, laid on the forehead of a woman in childbed.*

In this spell the magician identifies himself with Horus and invokes the help of Bes and Hathor. The Creator Re himself sends assistance from heaven, while his deputy Thoth watches approvingly. Four goddesses will act as midwives, one for each direction of heaven, which will grant the delivery a cosmic dimension. Again, the power of the magic words is reinforced through the making of an amulet. This will help the woman in childbed to relax and thereby ensure the efficacy of the charm.

DOCTOR FOR INVISIBLE DISEASES

Apart from mothers and children, the weakest members of society of course included those suffering from disease. Today we know that many diseases are caused by bacteria and viruses: minute organisms that cannot be seen with the naked eye. Still, we believe our doctors who tell us that these invisible pathogens are everywhere around us. In antiquity, patients likewise put a blind trust in their physicians, except that they were told the invisible organisms in question were deities, demons, and the evil spirits of the dead (fig. 104). This did not make it any easier for doctors to fight their opponents, for as well as having knowledge of the human body and of medicines, they had to be experienced in magic.

We are perhaps inclined not to take the latter aspect of their work very seriously, but then we make a mistake. Because of the limited anatomical understanding and the rather ineffective drugs available in antiquity, the magical reassurance of the patient was probably the most efficacious part of the doctor's involvement! This psychological effect is often underestimated in modern medicine, even though experiments with placebos have demonstrated how essential the patient's own belief in recovery can be, if only because it significantly alleviates stress. This is where the invocations of the Egyptian witch doctors played a central part, and accordingly numerous

FIG. 72. Seated statue of Iuty, chief physician of the pharaoh. He is represented as a priest with shaven skull: because of his contacts with superior powers he had to observe the ritual obligations of purity. Photograph: RMO (acc.no. AST 10).

medical papyri conclude every recipe with the words: *A method which has been found effective many times!*

Much information about Egyptian medical knowledge has been preserved in these papyri. Most of them are hardly more than collections of recipes, often arranged according to complaints of a similar character or regarding a similar part of the body. Some of the recipes are purely magical and focus on the preparation of amulets or the recitation of charms, so it is more accurate to characterize these handbooks as magical-medical. Other papyri, however, offer clear proof that at least some doctors worked in a more scientific way. These physicians began by examining the patient, then they formulated a diagnosis, and finally they selected a recipe and made up the drug in question—for there were no pharmacists at that time. But even these doctors would recite a spell at the very moment when the patient swallowed the medicine, because that was believed to enhance its potency. Thus once again we recognize the fixed magical pattern of an action performed by means of specific materials and accompanied by a spoken charm. Only the most scientifically oriented papyri (especially Papyrus Edwin Smith) omit the spell and concentrate on the purely medical aspect of the treatment. The physicians who wrote these papyri sometimes had the honesty to admit: *A disease which cannot be cured.*

This class of doctors regularly trained as specialists. Egyptian texts mention the existence of oculists, dentists, and internists. The Greek tourist and historian Herodotus asserts that during his time (fifth century BC), all Egyptian doctors were specialists. According to him there were even doctors for the head or for 'invisible diseases,' which suggests that magicians (or whom we might term psychologists?) were among those specialists. The best doctors could become court physician to the pharaoh (fig. 72). The queen had her own doctor, and many papyri have a special section devoted to gynecological problems. Even a veterinary papyrus has been preserved.

The other extreme in the wide range of medical practitioners in ancient Egypt was represented by the village witch doctors, who also sold amulets and performed exorcisms for people possessed by demons. The treatment of snake bites and scorpion stings likewise belonged to the daily routine of such medicine men (fig. 17). They called themselves 'conjurers of Selkit' after the scorpion goddess, whose name can be translated as *She who gives breath*. Since one of the effects of the paralyzing venom of scorpions is that the patient feels short of breath, this is another example of the euphemistic terminology of the Egyptians, who liked to describe a negative quality in a positive way. Because the goddess could take away one's breath, she must also be able to restore it. Similarly, depictions of Selkit often show the innocuous water scorpion rather than its venomous cousin.

As stated above, one of the magical-medical papyri now in Leiden exclusively deals with the cure of scorpion stings. As a rule, the fate of the patient is equated with that of the young god Horus, who was stung by scorpions when, as a child, he had been hidden by his mother Isis in the marshes of the Delta. Thanks to Isis's sorcery and his own magical potency, the divine child survived. Dating from the later New Kingdom, this mythological tale gave rise to the development of so-called Horus stelae *(cippi)*: small tablets with a rounded top surmounted by the head of the apotropaic god Bes and a front dominated by a depiction of the naked Harpocrates (or Horus-the-Child, fig. 73). The god is standing on crocodiles and holds serpents, scorpions, lions, and gazelles in his hands. Thus the child wields protection not only against stinging and biting vermin but also against all wild animals living in the desert (the domain of the evil god Seth) or the river, and which were believed to endanger the well-ordered creation in the Nile valley.

The representation of Harpocrates is usually surrounded by roughly carved figures of various protective forces, whereas the sides and reverse of the

FIG. 73. The base of this Horus stela shows a scene of Isis feeding her child in the papyrus marshes of the Delta. Photograph: RMO (acc.no. H** 1).

stelae carry incised magical spells: *Hail to you, Horus, son of Osiris, born to the goddess Isis! I call your name, I recite your spells, I speak with your words of power. . . . Come to me quickly, like he who navigates the divine bark did for you, in order to protect me against the lions in the desert, the crocodiles in the river, and the snakes in their caverns. Make them for me as immobile as the pebbles in the desert and the potsherds in the alley. Remove for me the biting poison which has penetrated into the body of X, son of Y. Let him be saved from evil by the power of your words.*

Such Horus stelae, which were kept at home or deposited in tombs, are usually of small size. They were made in dark stone, with a preference for mottled or greenish rocks that imitate snakeskin. Larger specimens were erected in public places, such as the temple forecourts. Sometimes these assume the character of portrait statues of famous conjurers holding stelae or with magical texts and vignettes engraved over their entire surface (fig. 74). Both healing statues and Horus stelae proper are frequently quite eroded in places, their faces for instance, as a result of pilgrims and patients touching them. Many of the statues also have shallow basins carved out of their bases. People were meant to pour water over the statues or stelae to absorb the magical potency of the texts and vignettes; the water was believed thereby to become an effective medicine to be swallowed or rubbed on the wound.

Similar principles underlay the Egyptian practice of making amulets to protect against disease. They were made from specific materials believed to have a sympathetic bond with the disease or the part of the body affected. For instance, red stones would help against excessive bleeding during menstruation or childbirth (fig. 40). Of course the shape of the amulet could also play a part: a white cowrie shell could serve to ward off the evil eye because its shape is reminiscent of a human eyeball; it could also protect fertility because its slit-shaped opening rather resembles a vulva. Accordingly, cowrie shells were

FIG. 75. String of cowrie shells, probably used as a girdle for the burial of a young girl and recently excavated at Saqqara. Photograph: RMO.

FIG. 74. Priest carrying a Horus stela. His garment is completely covered with magical texts and images. Photograph: RMO (acc.no. F 1953/5.1).

often strung to form necklaces or girdles for women and girls (fig. 75). A spell had to be recited over these amulets before they could be sold, and a knot laid in the string would prolong their magical potency.

Ancient Egyptians also armed themselves with stone dust scratched from temple walls. This was believed to protect against all kinds of dangers, and all major temples of Egypt show the traces of this strange custom (fig. 76). Scratch marks can generally be found around the doorways to the sanctuary, for ordinary people were not allowed inside and only the priests had access to the interior of the god's mansion. In fact, the position of these scratch marks just outside the sanctuary suggests that at least some can be dated to the pharaonic period, although it is well known that the custom continued until quite recently. The walls flanking pylons and gateways are often covered with vertical grooves made by knives or other sharp implements. The powder ground from the stones would have been taken home and later carried around the neck in a pouch, or perhaps swallowed as a medicine. The supernatural power of the god would thereby spread inside the patient's body, for recall that the ancient Egyptians believed magic could

FIG. 76. The wall panel to the left of the entrance of the Egyptian temple from Taffeh (now in the RMO) clearly shows the slits carved out by worshippers who used the powdered stone as medicine. The numerous graffiti likewise indicate that the sacred building received many later visitors. Photograph: RMO (acc.no. F 1979/4.1).

be transferred through direct contact—from the god to the temple, and from the temple to the sufferer.

Other amulets consisted of a tightly rolled strip of papyrus inscribed with a magic spell or vignette (fig. 77). This might represent an Eye of Horus *(wedjat)*, one of the most popular amulets because it guaranteed the healing of wounds and protection against the evil eye. The texts of such amulets often have the character of a divine decree. Thus a papyrus amulet in the British Museum contains

a declaration of the god Khonsu on behalf of a little girl: *We shall protect her against Sekhmet and her son. We shall protect her against the collapse of walls and the impact of lightning. We shall protect her against leprosy, blindness, and against the evil eye during her whole life. We shall protect her against the seven stars of the Big Dipper and we shall protect her against the star which falls from the sky and strikes you down.* And so the papyrus continues, 140 tightly written lines long. Few present-day insurance

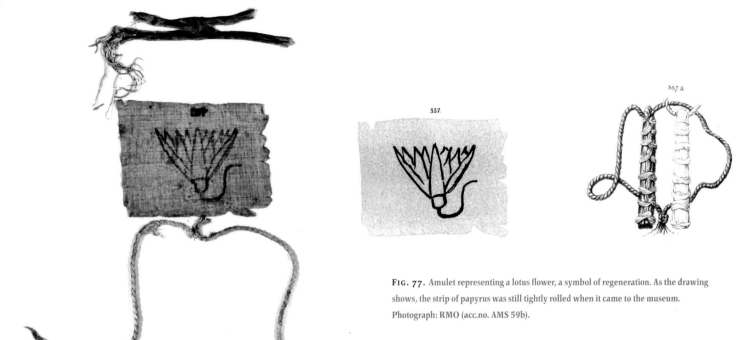

policies offer such all-encompassing coverage! People took care to store these contracts safely by carrying them around their neck in a wooden or metal cylinder (fig. 38).

HOME INSURANCE

Even the strong and healthy occasionally feel powerless against the dangers confronting them in daily life. In ancient Egypt, people thought demons could attack even the safety of one's own home, which they could enter through even the smallest aperture. To protect themselves from this threat, they applied lucky charms to their window grilles or the ventilation holes above their doors (fig. 78). They felt especially insecure while they slept, because in the dark of night the world is plunged back into primeval chaos. The life-giving solar god spent each night in the netherworld, fighting Apophis. Sleepers

were vulnerable, so apotropaic figures were depicted on the headrests they used as pillows. This ensured optimal protection for the fragile neck, where head and body are tied together. A wooden headrest now in the Louvre even displays large knots in the vertical supports of the curved neck part, so that no evil powers can rise from the ground to the sleeper's head. Other headrests show depictions of lions to either side of the vertical support, or of the deities Bes and Taweret (fig. 79). The gods are armed, catch serpents with their hands or mouths, or beat drums in order to chase away the forces of evil.

Similar representations appear on other types of furniture. Funeral beds were made in the shape of hippopotami, lions, and leopards. The latter two also symbolized the vault of heaven, and therefore the heads or legs of lions often graced thrones. The legs of folding chairs regularly terminate in duck's heads, emblems of the victory over untamed nature that threatens creation

Fig. 78. This window grille comes from the tomb of a high priest of the god Thoth in Hermopolis. Light fell through the slits next to the two symbols of durability *(djed)*, which are surmounted by apotropaic falcon's heads. Photograph: RMO (acc.no. F 1986/6.1).

and cosmic order *(ma'at)*. The dwarf god Bes is the favorite figure represented on all kinds of household articles, including cosmetic vessels and hairpins. His features also occasionally decorate the large vessels holding the household's water supply, a precaution against contagion by creatures like the serpents that haunted the moist floor around these vessels. A stand for a water vessel now in the collection of the Leiden Museum therefore shows a dwarf holding a serpent in each fist (fig. 80). During the Greco-

Roman period, however, there is evidence that people rather appreciated the presence of such a 'house serpent,' who was regarded as a supernatural guardian of the household. Several monuments to a serpent-shaped 'good spirit' *(Agathodaimon)* date to that period, and one cannot exclude the possibility that a similar concept was already known during pharaonic times.

FOR BETTER OR FOR WORSE

Sometimes the biggest impediment to good health is one's own state of mind. Like modern man, ancient

Egyptians occasionally suffered from irrational delusions, nightmares, or mental problems. They believed these were caused by evil spirits and demonic intruders, however, rather than internal factors. Lacking psychiatrists, they used to consult traditional healers, who might try to exorcise the demons attacking the mind using much the same tactics as they employed for bodily complaints. Some problems were attributed to spirits of the dead that continued to haunt the earth. In such cases one could instead write a letter to the dead, for instance on the drinking bowl where the spirit came to quench its thirst, or on a strip of papyrus which was then deposited in the tomb. One example is a letter, now in Leiden, written by a widower to his late wife (fig. 105). It seems as though she appeared in his dreams and accused him of adultery, an accusation he attempts to mitigate by describing in exhaustive detail how he always treated her well and threatening court action so the gods can judge the truth of his words. Presumably his conscience pricked him, but we will never know how clean it actually was.

Of course, unhappy love is a timeless phenomenon. Although today we may think there is no cure, ancient Egyptians would not agree. Magical papyri are full of spells to inspire love (or lust). Thus in the Demotic Papyrus Leiden–London we find: *Spell for bringing a woman to a man and for sending dreams, in other words to have dreams.* A line of occult symbols follows, and then the text continues: *Write this on a reed leaf and place it under your head when you go to sleep. It causes dreams and also sends off dreams. If you do this to send off dreams, place it on the mouth of a mummy. It can also bring the woman. You must write her name on the reed leaf with the blood of a . . . or of a hoopoe. And put a hair of the woman on the leaf and then place it on the mouth of a mummy. And you should write her name also on the ground, as follows: Bring A, daughter of B, to the house and into the bed of C, son of D.*

It is remarkable how often the dead were invoked in this regard. Those who were not professional magicians were a

FIG. 80. Pot stand in the form of a pregnant female dwarf holding two serpents.
Photograph: RMO (acc.no. F 1984/11.3).

bit reluctant to bother gods with their personal problems, and the spirits of the dead seemed more accessible, especially the spirits of those who had died prematurely or violently, which were believed to haunt the earth for some time. Thus charms for love or sex were frequently deposited in tombs or on mummies. The dead were also invoked through the use of lead as a writing material that would sink to the netherworld under its own weight. Especially during the Greco-Roman period, lead tablets *(lamellae)* were quite common for love charms (fig. 147). Some were accompanied by wax or clay figurines of the beloved that were occasionally pierced by needles (fig. 53). Some figurines contain human hair; also nails, blood, sweat, semen, and spittle could be added to a human likeness to gain power over someone, according to the magical texts.

If the desired contact occurred, other problems might yet materialize. Men in ancient Egypt donated phallic statuettes (fig. 81) to sanctuaries of Hathor, the goddess of love, or Bes, another patron of sex, where their modern counterparts might take Viagra. Excavations at Saqqara have uncovered the so-called Bes chambers, where life-size statues of the dwarf god were surrounded by hundreds of votive figurines left by hopeful pilgrims. Female figures of wood, stone, faience, or terracotta (fig. 82) have likewise been found in shrines, as well as houses and tombs. Often they display luxuriant hairstyles (which in Egypt were considered to be extremely sexy) and a prominent pubic triangle. Because some of these figurines have been represented feeding a baby, they are unlikely to have been meant as erotic, but rather votive figures to ensure fertility. This is supported by the fact that they have been found in female graves, so the traditional interpretation of these figures as 'concubines for the dead,' with its overtones of lust and sex, should be dismissed. Children were expected to take care of their elderly parents, and so were an essential investment toward a comfortable old age. A proper system of old age pensions was utterly unknown in antiquity.

FIG. 81. Of these two phallic figurines, the one on the right is all human but the other is baboon-headed. Photograph: RMO (inv.nrs. F 1936/10.6-7).

At the end of the calendar year, the whole of Egypt succumbed to a kind of national hysteria. In the astronomical year this event coincided with the height of summer, admittedly not the nicest season. The Nile was at its lowest level, the granaries were empty, and as a result of heat and hunger the people were particularly susceptible to contagious diseases. The 'plague of the year' was generally regarded as a manifestation of the goddess Sekhmet and her bow-carrying messengers (fig. 83). To make matters worse, people were afraid of a cosmic disaster. Twelve months of thirty days each add up to a year of only 360 days. The ancient Egyptian calendar therefore included five intercalary (or epagomenal) days. Since these were seen as outside the normal cycle of time *(neheh)*, they might result in a permanent halt of the cosmos *(djet)*. This would entail no end of calamity, for there would be no new inundation of the Nile and the balance between the well-ordered world *(ma'at)* and chaos would surely be upset.

Special protective formulas existed for these precarious five days, and as we have seen one of the Leiden papyri is devoted to them. One spell from this papyrus prescribes the preparation of a linen bandage depicting various deities, to be carried around the neck. A model showing twelve gods is added at the end of the papyrus (fig. 61). By unique coincidence, the Leiden Museum also possesses a set of the actual linen bandages used during

FIG. 82. Two concubine figures, the left one lying on a bed together with her child, the other of the more common type without a bed. Photograph: RMO (inv.nrs. A-1 en L.VII.12).

the epagomenal days (fig. 84). One displays twelve divine figures in almost the same order as those of the papyrus vignette; another shows a cortège of twelve different gods. Twelve, of course, corresponds to the number of months in the Egyptian calendar. The remaining bandages have separate depictions of Osiris, Isis, and Nephthys: three of the five gods who were born on the intercalary days. It rather looks as if the five bandages in question were tied together, perhaps with twelve knots (one for each month), as the ritual prescribes.

When the sun rose on the first day of the new year, everybody was relieved. This festive day was celebrated by the exchange of gifts, such as seals, scarabs, or lentil-shaped water flasks (fig. 85) symbolizing prosperity and fertility, all inscribed with the words 'Happy New Year.' Of course people wondered what the new year would have in store. This, however, was known only to the gods. Ancient Egyptians believed fate depended on the will of the gods (whereas the Greeks thought it was the other way round, and that even the gods were ruled by fate). The notion that it is possible to predict the future by observing certain omens was not clearly developed in pharaonic times. Astrology and the use of horoscopes were only introduced to Egypt as part of the Hellenistic culture, which had derived these traditions from Mesopotamia. Nor was consulting oracles very common in Egypt before the Greek period.

People did, however, put questions directly to the gods. The gods could answer during the annual processions with divine statues, for instance, when the god might cause the priests bearing his statue to take a sudden step forward or backward. Deities could also manifest their will in dreams, and the important pilgrimage sites in Egypt possessed special halls where visitors could spend the night in the hope of receiving such signs from heaven. During the Greco-Roman period these places assumed the character of sanatoria or health resorts, where visitors could also enjoy therapeutic baths.

FIG. 83. Sekhmet's serpent-headed messengers are often represented on the side-walls of the throne of their mistress. Photograph: RMO (acc.no. F 1982/12.4).

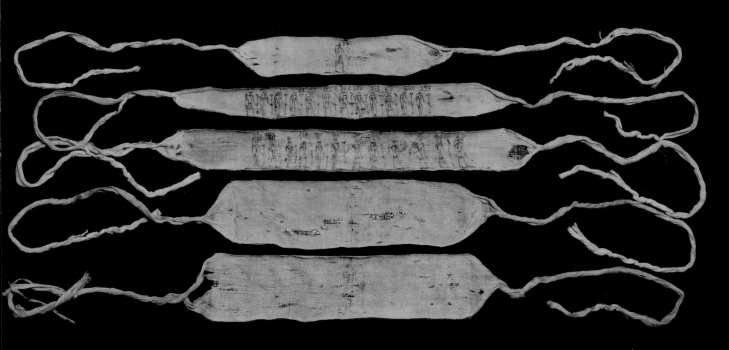

FIG. 84. This set of five linen bandages (two of them showing companies of twelve gods, the other three with single images of Osiris, Isis, and Nephthys) must have been used to invoke protection during the intercalary days. Photograph: RMO (acc.no. AU 30c).

Protection during the epagomenal days

Hail to you, gods there, murderers who stand in waiting upon Sekhmet, who have come forth from the Eye of Re, messengers everywhere present in the districts, who bring slaughtering about, who create uproar, who hurry through the land, who shoot their arrows from their mouths, who see from afar! Be on your way, be distant from me! Go on, you, I shall not go along with you! You shall have no power over me, you shall not give me to your authority! You shall not throw your net over

Careful observation of the events that followed these visions eventually seemed to reveal certain patterns, which Egyptians recorded in voluminous encyclopedias: *(If somebody sees himself in a dream) – while his hair grows: good! It means an increase of his property. – while he sees a large tomcat: good! It means he will obtain a large harvest. – shod with white sandals: bad! It means exile. – while he is bitten by a dog: bad! He is bewitched.* They also composed lists of lucky and unlucky calendar days (fig. 86). One example preserved on a papyrus now in Cairo states for the third and fourth day of the year: *Day 3: lucky (morning and afternoon). Feast of Sekhmet, instituted for her by Re when he had pacified her. Feast of Ptah the Great, the son of Re. Do not undertake anything during this whole day, do not eat fish, and do not start upon a journey, either by day or by night. – Day 4: unlucky. Feast of Hathor, mistress of Byblos. Feast of Nekhbet, the white goddess of Hierakonpolis. Feast of Nut. It is a great taboo to start work. Beware of making friends with another. As regards anybody with heart trouble, he will die.* Actually these customs do not really involve magic, except when people tried to determine their own fate. They are more akin to the much later almanacs, or with the horoscopes in present-day newspapers which still attract the attention of thousands of 'modern' readers.

FIG. 85. New Year's flasks are usually lentil-shaped. The neck is designed as a lotus bouquet flanked by two baboons, the sacred animals of the god Thoth, who records time. Photograph RMO (acc.no. AT 97).

FIG. 86. On this calendar the days of the year have been noted in vertical columns, each day followed by one to three signs signifying either 'lucky' (in black) or 'unlucky' (in red ink). Combinations of the two categories occur as well. Photograph: British Museum (acc.no. EA 10474).

FIG. 87. Gateway in the enclosure wall of the great sanctuary of Amun at Karnak, with behind it the pylon of the temple to the moon-god Khonsu. Photograph: P.J. Bomhof, RMO.

108

THE VIGILANT AUTHORITIES

You will be protected against a sudden death, you will be protected against fire, you will be protected against the sky (it will not fall down) and the earth (it will not capsize), and Re will not reduce the gods and goddesses to ashes.

(Papyrus Salt 825, XVII.8–13)

BATTLE AT THE TEMPLE GATES

The last chapter focused on private initiatives to protect oneself against all kinds of dangers. Ancient Egyptians had no need to worry, however, because the authorities also kept a watchful eye over the country and its inhabitants. The large temples effectively functioned as laboratories where priests worked day and night to preserve the balance of the cosmos. Some scholars have even compared the temples to our nuclear power plants because they generated energy using materials and techniques that might endanger the very life of the people who worked there, unless they subjected themselves to a strict routine of purification, social isolation, and fixed procedures. It was nonetheless a rewarding task, because tapping the magical energy that maintained the cosmos ensured the preservation not just of society, but of creation itself.

The Egyptians took it for granted that primeval chaos had not utterly disappeared from the cosmos. On the contrary, chaos and creation were believed to be codependent, for everything alive has been created from primeval water. The balance of the cosmos *(ma'at)* requires the interplay of opposing forces. Unfortunately this means that every day the sun must again fight Apophis and his confederates, every month the eye of the moon is torn from the face of the sky god, and periodically Seth releases sand storms or foreign armies on the Nile valley. In exchange for all the divine gifts that privileged humans over animals, the gods expected men to be loyal to their cause. One of these gifts was magic. It enabled priests to assist the gods in their battles and also, through daily ritual in the holy of holies, to demonstrate ongoing human allegiance. Every morning the priest woke the divine statue in its shrine and burned incense before it, washed, anointed, and dressed it, and finally presented it with food and drink. The energy contained in the food allowed the deity to replenish his or her life force *(ka)*. The offering ritual was thus not merely symbolic, but fulfilled a concrete and necessary purpose.

FIG. 88. Row of sphinxes in front of the temple of Amun at Karnak. The bodies of lions have here been combined with ram's heads, a reference to Amun's sacred animal. Photograph: P.J. Bomhof, RMO.

As the mansion of the god, the temple itself was vulnerable to the attack of evil forces. To repel them, an extensive decorative program was executed on the temple's exterior walls or at the gateways to the sacred compound. The temple enclosure was always surrounded by thick walls several meters high, constructed using millions of sun-dried bricks and pierced by only a few gateways (fig. 87). Like the fortifications surrounding Egyptian cities, such enclosure walls of course had a strategic function, but it is likely that the material aspect also played some part. In sorcery, unbaked clay is often used for modeling figurines (figs. 52, 95, and 98). The creator god Khnum made the first man on his potter's wheel, and clay was therefore regarded as a primeval life-giving substance. Sun-dried bricks were used in rituals to raise other magical objects above the unclean floor, or to guard the exterior walls of tombs against invaders (fig. 119). Thus the enclosure walls also formed a kind of sanitary cordon, separating the temple from the unclean exterior world. For the same reason, the sanctuary was constructed on top of a stratum of clean sand that was especially deposited during the foundation rites, similar to the pure sand used by magicians to delineate sacred space.

Fig. 89. Pylon of the Horus temple at Edfu. A scene to the left shows the pharaoh slaying his enemies as an offering to the god. Photograph: A. Groneman.

The gateways were the weakest parts of the temple enclosure. To prevent hostile forces from entering, rows of sphinxes were installed in front of them (fig. 88). These images of human-headed lions represented the aggressive aspect of the solar god or the pharaoh. The patron of magic, Tutu, was himself depicted as a sphinx (fig. 13), for instance in his role of guardian standing on the prow of the solar bark in which Re sails across the sky. Upon entering through the temple gates, visitors would see more sphinxes and statues of the warlike pharaoh before the entrance to the temple proper. This was designed as a pylon (fig. 89), a portal flanked by two towers that again stress the military and strategic character of such doorways. At the same time, this composition resembles the hieroglyph meaning 'horizon' *(akhet)*. The sun god fought his opponents each day on the eastern and western horizons. Evil forces that might try to slip through the temple gates could expect a similar battle.

Wall reliefs carved on the front of the pylon and on the temple's exterior walls depict the pharaoh defeating his foreign enemies on the battlefield or slaying dozens of bound prisoners to honor the chief god of the temple (fig. 89). Scenes of royals hunts are also depicted, because wild animals were seen to represent the primeval chaos that had to be controlled. Both types of representations are highly apotropaic. Alongside the local god, the cult of most temples included his divine consort and their son. The place where the goddess was delivered of her child was called the birth house *(mammisi)*, and its cornice was usually decorated with images of the protective god Bes (fig. 90). Because rains and thunderstorms were extremely rare in Egypt, they were much feared and were regarded as manifestations of the gods Apophis or Seth. To protect the sacred building against such terrifying phenomena, gargoyles ending in ferocious lion heads were installed to ensure that the water was immediately drained and thrown out far from the base of the walls. The temple floors might also become contaminated during offering ceremonies, for instance by the blood of the victims, or the oil and water of the libations. These liquids, too, were channeled to a place outside the building by an ingenious system of underground pipes. This was the only way to preserve the cultic purity that befitted the temple's status as a supernatural compound.

FIG. 90. Relief figure of the god Bes who dispels evil powers by sticking out his tongue. Presumably this image formed part of the decoration of the birth house of a temple. Photograph: RMO (acc.no. F 1979/8.1).

PLAYING FOR HIGH STAKES

To what extent the daily ritual in the temples can be regarded as an act of magic is a matter for debate. Many other religions involve offerings to the gods, for instance, which have become purely symbolic rites. Some of the rituals performed in Egyptian temples, however, can be interpreted as pure magic. Objects used in such rituals have frequently been found in or around the sacred enclosures. Several papyri which were once kept in the temples' Houses of Life have been preserved and are an important source of information. The rituals were also depicted on the temple walls, together with the accompanying texts.

Usually the pharaoh plays the chief part in these texts and representations, since he was the nominal high priest of all the country's shrines. In practice, he delegated his offices to the local high priests, and only made a personal appearance at the most important festivals. Generally such annual festivals were celebrated with a solemn procession: for a single day the divine statue was taken out of its shrine and carried around the temple walls on the priests' shoulders. Yet even then the statue could not be seen by ordinary people, because it was placed inside another shrine and carried aboard a model boat.

The magical rituals referred to above occasionally coincided with these annual feasts. In some cases they seem to have had the character of dramatic performances, which imply the presence of an audience. At the Horus temple at Edfu, there was an annual play on the sacred lake to celebrate the victory of Horus over Seth. The dramatic text has been carved on the inside of the temple's inner enclosure walls and is illustrated with a number of reliefs. Seth is portrayed as a ferocious hippopotamus, while Horus balances on an unstable skiff trying to harpoon the animal (fig. 91). Other gods assist him, while a choir on the banks of the lake encourages him and comments on the various episodes of the fight. Although Seth changes shape a number of times, he is finally defeated and his body cut to pieces. Had the part been played by a real hippopotamus this would have created a bloody mess indeed, but it is clear from the stage directions (also recorded as part of the dramatic texts on the Edfu wall) that only a model made of bread or cake was used, and other scenes may have relied on clay figurines.

The use of materials that, as we have seen, are generally connected with magic suggests that this was no innocent play, but rather an act of sorcery accompanied by magical texts. Instructions written on other papyri or temple walls suggest that similarly destructive rituals were also enacted elsewhere. Another text in Edfu explicitly refers to the destruction of a hippopotamus made of

FIG. 91. Relief on the enclosure wall of the Edfu temple: Horus, assisted by Isis and the pharaoh, harpoons a hippopotamus. Reproduction after *Edfou XIII,* pl. dviii.

red wax. During the annual procession in honor of the god Osiris at his sacred enclosure of Abydos, a red wax statuette of Seth (perhaps a human figure with the head of a donkey-like animal) was burned, fettered with a black string, and then harpooned.

Destructive rituals were also performed on a daily basis: two papyri have preserved the text of a Book for Slaying Seth, likewise derived from the Abydos rituals, which had to be recited over an image of a prisoner, made of red beeswax or wood and inscribed with the victim's name on the chest. During the recitation the following acts had to be carried out: *fetter it with the sinew of a red cow, spit on it four times, trample it with your left foot, pierce it with a lance, cut it with a flint knife, throw it in the fire, and spit on it again many times while it is in the fire!*

A daily ritual known to the priests of the temple of Amun at Karnak was intended to destroy Apophis. It has been preserved on the Papyrus Bremner-Rhind, now in the British Museum, and involves a ritual that had to be repeated several times a day. Apophis himself was presumably depicted as a serpent and was accompanied by wax figures of prisoners representing his confederates, bound with black string and locked in cages. A vignette drawn in red ink and representing such boxes or cages occurs in the famous Papyrus Salt 825, likewise in the British Museum (fig. 92). Each cage contains two figures tied back to back, one of an Asiatic prisoner and the other of Seth with the head of his mythical animal. Another cage holds the head of a large hippopotamus, and the lids of the cages are guarded by flames, cobras, lion heads, and baboons. The concomitant text is that of a Ritual for Preserving Life.

Few physical objects remain that can be connected with these terrifying rituals, probably because the priests took their job seriously and ensured that the enemy figures were utterly destroyed. Even so, a number of figurines depicting bound prisoners have come to light, as they were buried in massive numbers at the end of the rituals. In some cases this happened at the very spot

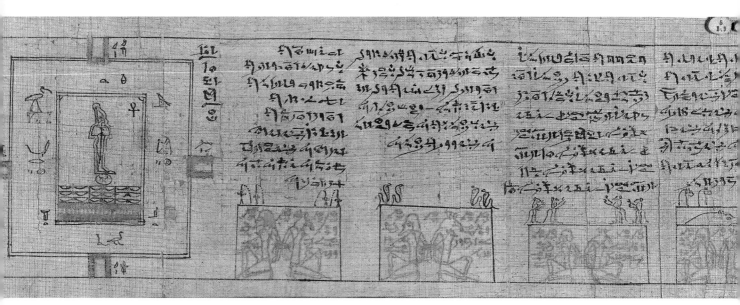

FIG. 92. Vignette from the Papyrus Salt 825, representing four cages holding prisoners and Seth figures. Photograph: British Museum (acc.no. EA 10051).

where the ritual was performed, as at the Middle Kingdom fortress at Mirgissa, which we have already mentioned. This fortress is situated on the Nubian border, and the magical deposit illustrates how the Egyptians tried to conjure their African opponents by means of rituals of destruction. Numerous clay figures from the deposit in question show severed heads or feet, headless and fettered bodies, blinded eyes, broken ships, and so on. A little distance away, there were also three limestone prisoner statues and the detached head of a fourth. Since the head has been cleanly severed, we can presume that the statues were used in a ritual for the destruction of enemies from all four directions of the sky. The actual bound body of a Nubian man was also found with the deposit.

Prisoner figurines have also been retrieved along Egypt's eastern borders in the Nile Delta. Others were deposited in the royal cemeteries, such as those around the pyramids of Giza and Saqqara. The earliest find of this nature dates to the end of the Old Kingdom, and such figures seem to have been especially popular during the Middle Kingdom. They were generally made of unbaked clay and buried inside ceramic vessels.

Part of a ritual deposit from Saqqara, comprising about 125 figurines, is now in Leiden (fig. 52). The statuettes depict bound prisoners and have intentionally been broken, decapitated, and pierced. Long execration formulas inscribed in red ink on their chests are directed against *every rebel of this country, all people, all patricians and all commoners, all men, all eunuchs, all women, every chief, every Nubian, every leader, every messenger, every confederate in any country who will be rebellious . . . or will conspire by speaking subversively or by slandering Upper Egypt or Lower Egypt forever.* Other texts are specifically aimed at certain Asiatic cities, or at domestic enemies of the king identified by name.

The materials preserved from these rituals also include several stone molds for making figurines of bound prisoners, presumably from beeswax. A limestone mold in the Leiden Museum shows a shallow recess in the shape of two prisoners, kneeling back to back with their arms bound

FIG. 93. Limestone mold for casting a wax figure depicting two bound captives. Photograph: RMO (acc.no. F 1992/7.1).

FIG. 94. This alabaster base for a statue of Pharaoh Nectanebo II is carved with the royal cartouches, bound captives, and the traditional nine bows. Photograph: © 2003 Musée du Louvre/ Christian Décamps (acc. no. E.11220).

together (fig. 93). A second stone for the other half would have created a mold from which the wax figures could be made, which were then destroyed in the temple's daily ritual. A specific type of bronze harpoon decorated with the falcon head of the god Horus must also have played some part in such rituals. Many royal statues show prisoners being trampled under the pharaoh's feet, alternating with the nine bows that symbolize Egypt's foreign enemies (fig. 94). Similar motifs occur on thrones and footstools, and Tutankhamun even possessed a set of walking sticks decorated at the lower ends with such figures of foreigners.

An interesting group of objects from the collection of Giovanni d'Anastasi is now divided between the Leiden Museum and the British Museum in London. This concerns seventy-eight magical figurines of unbaked clay that represent not the enemies of the gods, but evil-averting powers that might assist in battle (fig. 95). They include a statuette of a standing falcon-headed deity and three falcon-headed crocodiles, presumably images of Horus of Three-hundred Town, a well-known guardian against evil. There are also four uraeus serpents, which bring to mind the four cobras on the lid of one of the cages with prisoners depicted in the Papyrus Salt 825 (fig. 92). The cobra was regarded as a manifestation of the Eye of the Sun, spitting poison against the enemies of Re, and was also identified as the patron goddess of Lower Egypt—while the vulture was guardian of Upper Egypt. The cache contained no fewer than thirty clay vultures, obviously modeled by hand and not from a mold because they vary slightly in their dimensions and detail. It is probably no coincidence that the word 'protection' can be written in hieroglyphs using the sign of a vulture. The other figurines from the

FIG. 95. Some of the clay figures of the magical cache from Abydos. Photograph: RMO (inv.nrs. AT 101-106).

cache all represent ram's heads, a hieroglyph that expresses 'awe' and 'majesty'. Thus the cache as a whole appears to have been a collection of protective devices for a temple. The predominance of vultures and the few cobras might indicate a southern (Upper Egyptian) provenance. Indeed, similar figurines were found about fifty years ago next to the large Osiris temple at Abydos. It rather looks as if d'Anastasi's workmen made their discovery at that very spot, about two centuries ago.

There are no textual records, however, to inform us about the ritual in which such clay figures are presumed to have been used. The only indication that may be relevant is provided by the vignette of cobras in the Papyrus Salt 825. That this manuscript also concerns rituals performed at Abydos is probably no coincidence. The roof of one of the other cages depicted in the same vignette bears four lion heads. Sets of four clay heads of lions (or rather lionesses) have been recovered from shallow pits in the desert, where they formed a protective cordon around mummiform images of the god Osiris. In that context, they are generally identified as the four goddesses Sekhmet, Wadjet, Bastet, and Seshemtet, and of course they are connected with the four directions of the sky. Their heads likewise occur on a stone stand for an Osiris emblem now in the Louvre (fig. 96). Such parallels again seem to suggest a connection with the Osiris cult at Abydos. There, but also in other temples, priests used to throw four clay balls inscribed with the names of the lionesses to the four directions of the sky, as a symbolic defense against the god Seth. A related ritual consisted in hitting a ball with a wooden bat: not an innocent game, but a punishment of Seth's evil eye!

FIG. 96. This diorite base once supported a wooden standard surmounted by the emblem of Abydos. The heads of lionesses wielded protection against dangers from the four directions of the sky. Photograph: © 2003 Musée du Louvre/ Georges Poncet (acc. no. E.11072).

LIFE OUT OF DEATH

The end of the fascinating Papyrus Salt 825 is occupied by an instruction for making a so-called *Khenty-amentyu* figure. Literally this means 'First of the Westerners,' a designation of the king of the netherworld who at Abydos was originally held to be an independent god, but was later equated with Osiris. The figure in question had to be modeled from a mixture of clay, sand, fragrant resin, and wine. The semi-liquid substance was poured in a mold shaped like the mummiform Osiris, bearing his characteristic miter-formed crown and scepters. After it had dried, the figure was taken out of the mold, varnished with a mixture of resin and beeswax, and wrapped in linen. It was then placed inside a mummiform wooden coffin, covered with a sheepskin, and finally packed in a gold vase itself placed in a cedar wood box. To prevent any misunderstandings, the papyrus includes a vignette showing the figure with its various envelopes (fig. 97), for the ritual in question was of immense importance. The magical figure was briefly designated as 'Life' itself and was said to guarantee the preservation of the universe. The text adds that whoever unveils this grand mystery to the uninitiated will be killed.

How should we interpret this bizarre ritual for the preservation of heaven and earth? And did it only occur at Abydos? This appears in fact to have been one of the most common magical rituals in ancient Egypt, performed in every major temple in the country. Nonetheless, there were considerable local variations in the way it was executed. A long text inscribed in a roof chapel of the Dendera temple distinguishes no fewer than sixteen Egyptian towns where the ritual was known: mainly those where the inhabitants were the proud possessors of one of the relics of Osiris's body, which had been cut to pieces by the evil Seth. Assembling a clay figure from numerous ingredients must have symbolized the reconstruction of the corpse of Osiris from its various relics. Although this might sound abstract, one ingredient added to the clay made the resurrection much more concrete: grain. Most local recipes prescribed the use of barley. This was mixed with earth, poured in a mold shaped in the image of the mummified Osiris, and irrigated for a number of days. The result was that the whole mummiform figure was eventually furred in the fresh green stalks of sprouting vegetation, which, of course, is a universal symbol of life from death.

The origins of the god Osiris are most unclear, and it is usually accepted that his cult developed from the merging of various older deities. One seems to have been a grain god (or a general god of vegetation) who may have been worshiped by the earliest farmers during prehistoric times. It is suggested that this is why Osiris is often depicted with green skin (fig. 98). The custom of depositing germinated grain inside the tomb dates back at least to the Middle Kingdom. The burial chambers of royal tombs from the New Kingdom contained flat wooden boxes or seedbeds shaped like the body of Osiris and filled with earth and tiny seedlings of cereal (usually called 'Osiris beds').

A contemporary text refers to an annual ceremony for preparing such grain-mummies for non-royal persons as well. This might be corroborated by a slightly later burial custom, wherein a side-chamber in the tomb remained accessible after the burial so that people could place a fresh grain-mummy there every year and take away the old one. The dates mentioned for this ceremony–days 18 to 25 of the fourth month of Inundation (known as *Khoiak* in late antiquity)–would have coincided perfectly with the season specified in the Dendera text. These were the last few days preceding the season of Emergence, when the farmers could resume their work in the fields. It is certainly no coincidence that at this time of year everybody's mind was fixed on the origin of new life.

Archaeological finds of grain-mummies prove that such rituals were performed across Egypt. They have generally been found in shallow pits along the desert edge, not far from the local temple. So far the most important

FIG. 97. Osiris figure depicted in the Papyrus Salt 825. Reproduction after Derchain, *Papyrus Salt*, Fig. xx.

finds have been made in the so-called Valley of the Monkey Tombs in the Theban hills (fig. 98), and in Central Egypt at Tihna al-Gebel, al-Sheikh Fadl, and Bahnasa. All these sites comprise cemeteries with hundreds of grain-mummies in small, individual graves, suggesting that indeed these were part of an annual ritual. The figures are fully rounded and range in length from 35 to 55 cm, whereas the texts prescribe a standard length of one cubit (52 cm). Ancient Egyptians considered the cubit to be the basic measure of the whole universe, and for that reason they also used it as the standard size for the gold images of their gods that were kept in the inner sanctum of the temples. The body of each grain-mummy is made of mixed earth and barley (either germinated or ungerminated) and finished with layers of resin and linen. Often the mummies

From the ritual of Khoiak in Dendera

As regards what is being done in Busiris, it is performed there on the fourth month of Inundation, day 12, in the presence of Shentit [the Widow = Isis] who resides in Busiris, with 1 hin [= 0.45 liter] of barley and 4 hin of sand. Put it likewise in a basin. Pour divine water over it every day, ¾ hin, from a pitcher of gold and in the presence of Shentit, while you recite the spells over it regarding the 'Pouring of Water over the Bodily Remains'. The guardians of the basin will protect it until the advent of the fourth month of Inundation, day 21.

Take it out of the basin and give it the form of a mummy with the White Crown by means of 1 deben [= 91 grams] of incense. Tie it with four lengths of papyrus rope, and the basin of the divine remains likewise. Allow it to dry by exposing it to the sun for a full day.

Make a water procession with it on the fourth month of Inundation, day 22, on the eighth hour of day. Let there be many torches around it, together with their guardian gods, viz. Horus, Thoth, Anubis, Isis, Nephthys, the Sons of Horus, and 19 gods. They stand in 34 barques. Dress these gods in four fabrics of the Northern and Southern Mansions. Lay them to rest in the grave, wrapped in the linen of the Khenty-amentyu of the previous year and of the basin of the divine remains likewise. Lay it in a coffin of sycamore wood, with an inscription for Khenty-amentyu in ocher. Bury them on the nebeh-hill under the sacred persea trees on the last day of the fourth month of Inundation.

(DENDERA, INSCRIPTION OF THE KHOIAK FESTIVAL, 18–23)

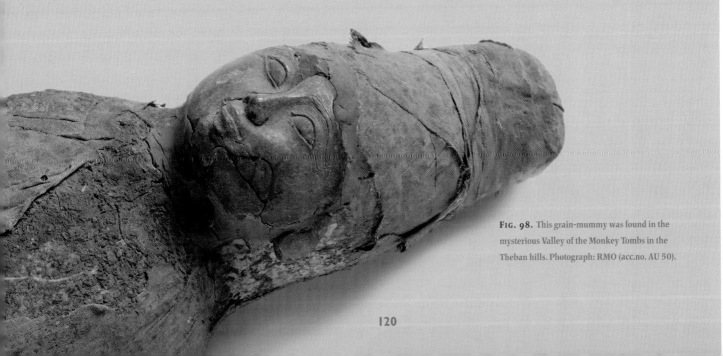

FIG. 98. This grain-mummy was found in the mysterious Valley of the Monkey Tombs in the Theban hills. Photograph: RMO (acc.no. AU 50).

have various special attributes, such as a garland around the head, a crown and mask made of beeswax or metal, four miniature mummies symbolizing the four Sons of Horus (which likewise were used to protect ordinary human mummies), or four clay balls or lioness heads to guard the god against evil powers.

Grain mummies have never been found in the many envelopes prescribed by the Papyrus Salt, or in gold vessels. Often they were buried in simple wooden coffins, usually black-varnished mummiform ones with falcon-headed lids. As a result, they have often been mistaken for the burials of sacred falcons. The falcon head here represents the funerary deity Sokar, who was closely linked to Osiris. The Dendera text refers to the making of two different figures: a *Khenty-amentyu* and a Sokar figure. It seems to have been the custom in some towns to make two distinct images during the annual festival, whereas others only prepared a Sokar figure, without grains of barley but still presumably expressing the same magical intention.

Examples of such Sokar figures have been recovered from a corner of the vast precinct of the Karnak temple of Amun, where the ground between a number of Osiris chapels is occupied by numerous dome-shaped brick tombs, as well as by an underground gallery comprising dozens of niches, all of them containing small statuettes made of stucco or plaster. According to the local priests this was the location of the primeval hill, the first dry land to emerge from the waters, where life first manifested itself during creation. A similar gallery must have been present at some distance to the south of the Giza pyramids, where according to an Egyptian tradition the access to the underground realm of Sokar is situated. Numerous Osirian figures, modeled in terracotta and overlaid in black varnish and linen (fig. 99), were recently found at this site. The images in question occasionally still lie inside wooden boxes inscribed with the names of several Greek pharaohs of the second century BC. Although one cannot call them real grain-mummies, they can be regarded as

variations on one of the basic themes of Egyptian religion. Everywhere in Egypt, at the precarious moment at the end of the Nile inundation, priests sought to ensure the continued existence of the cosmos by generating life from dead matter. The fresh, green grain-mummy was brought to the temple to replace the dried-out specimen of the previous year, which was removed and interred in the local cemetery.

SEX AND VIOLENCE

The ritual involving grain mummies seems clearly to have derived from the magical habits of Egypt's first farmers. The texts from the Dendera temple or the Papyrus Salt, however, reflect the evolution of this agricultural ritual. At stake was not just the fertility of the fields, but the start of a whole new cycle of life, both on earth and in the hereafter. Similar annual rituals involving puppets made of greenery and flowers and intended to increase the fertility of the new crop are performed by agricultural communities across the world. In Europe, such rituals died out only recently, and in some places they even live on in rudimentary form under the guise of the 'maypole.' Similarly, numerous cultures recognize a connection between harvest rituals and the fertility of humans or animals. This was a common link in ancient Greece, for instance, where the cult of the god Dionysus involved a great deal of licentiousness. Still, the Greek tourist and historian Herodotus could not believe his eyes when he witnessed an Egyptian procession in the fifth century BC: *In most aspects there is hardly any difference with the Greek cult of Dionysus, although choral dances are unknown in Egypt. Neither do they carry phalluses around. They have found another solution: puppets of about half a meter in height. The women carry these from one village to the other, while moving the penis—which is almost as long as the rest of the body—up and down by means of a string. An oboe player*

FIG. 99. This statuette from Giza is an example of a
so-called Sokar figure. Photograph: RMO (acc.no. F 1996/1.2).

*walks ahead, while women follow behind singing a hymn
to honor the god. Some pious legend connected with this
custom explains why the genital is so out of proportion, and
also why it is the only movable part.*

Unfortunately Herodotus does not tell us which legend
this is, or perhaps he did not quite understand what was
going on. We do not need him to make an educated guess
ourselves. An erect phallus was a common characteristic
of grain-mummies and Sokar figures (figs. 98–99). It is of
course a general symbol of fertility, but in the framework
of the Osiris myth such an erection played a special part.
When Isis restored the corpse of her murdered husband
by rejoining the severed limbs, she was so successful in
her endeavors to revivify him that she was impregnated
at that very moment. The child would be born as Horus,
the avenger of his father. In this mythical context the
phallus symbolizes the return of life after death, although
the processions described by Herodotus seem rather to be
about agricultural rituals.

Initially, however, the account by Herodotus appeared
problematic: no depictions of such phallic processions
had ever been found on Egyptian temple walls, which
raised some doubts about the veracity of the story. In
1971, however, proof was found in a temple precinct at
Saqqara. Here a whole group of phallic figurines rose from
the desert sand, including a terracotta model representing
exactly the kind of procession that Herodotus described
(fig. 100). Two persons with long garments (either priests
or women) and two dwarfs with the leonine mask of the
god Bes carry an enormous phallus. The god Harpocrates
seems to squat at the end, or perhaps the phallus is his.
The god is naked and wears the common lock of youth on
one side of his head. He beats the time on a tambourine,
while a monkey (the usual companion of the god Bes)
sits on his shoulder. We can guess that such processions
took place at a particular time of year and that they were
intended to increase the fertility of crops, cattle, and
people. Once again this appears to be a periodical festival,
organized by the priests on behalf of the community as a
whole. Unfortunately, Herodotus does not specify in which
season these processions took place.

The exact date of other rituals is better known. I have
already mentioned the anxieties accompanying the start
of the New Year, when ancient Egyptians feared attack

by the goddess Sekhmet. They never forgot how, soon after the creation of the world, she nearly eradicated humankind—and would have but for Re's intervention. Ordinary citizens could not possibly cope with such a powerful and violent opponent; they required the protection of the state. This constituted a heavy burden for Egypt's priests, who worked the entire year to keep the lioness calm, their exertions reaching a peak during the intercalary days. They performed endless rituals in the temples, which involved the singing of hymns and the performance of dances. The singers were accompanied by the rhythmic jingle of sistra (a kind of rattle consisting of a loop of bronze, pierced by transverse bars from which hung small sheets of metal) and *menat*s (necklaces with numerous strings of beads, provided with a counterweight at the back of the neck). The resulting sound must have had a hypnotizing effect reminiscent of the rustle of papyrus plants in the marshes, the abode of the cow goddess Hathor and the place where Isis brought up her child Horus. The priests hoped the sound would send Sekhmet to sleep, or at least pacify her enough that she would manifest as one of the benevolent goddesses. Thus the fierce lioness or the dangerous cobra goddess Wadjet who was connected with Sekhmet might also transform into the lovely cat goddess Bastet, the patron of song and dance. Both sistrum and *menat* are often decorated with depictions of this cat, or of the cow-eared head of Hathor (fig. 101). The collar-shaped attributes known as *aegis* with which the dancers accentuated their movements (fig. 102) also often show a cat's head, instead of that of a lioness.

At Karnak we can still see for ourselves how seriously these pacifying rituals were taken. Here the goddess Mut, the consort of Amun, possessed her own temple precinct. Because Mut's identity was as fluid as that

FIG. 100. A unique terracotta model proves that processions as described by Herodotus actually happened. Photograph: RMO (inv. F 1975/11.2).

of all other goddesses, she could also manifest herself in the guise of Sekhmet. Therefore her temple is still surrounded by a sacred lake in the shape of a horseshoe, to isolate the dangerous compound from the surrounding area. At the same time this layout possibly refers again to the papyrus marshes of the Delta. Even nowadays there still are many seated or standing statues of the goddess Sekhmet around the precinct (fig. 103). Most of them were erected by order of Pharaoh Amenhotep III (1391–1353 BC) and carry inscriptions invoking the goddess under various names. More Sekhmet statues were put up in

FIG. 101. The handle of this sistrum is formed by an evil-averting Bes figure, surmounted by a Hathor head. The loop above frames a figurine of a cat, the animal sacred to the goddess Bastet, whereas on top of it three cats seem to be attacking a rooster (a scene whose significance is unclear). Photograph: RMO (acc.no. F 1953/10.1).

FIG. 102. Gold objects such as this one are scale models of the *aegis* (the head of a goddess wearing a large collar), which dancers held in their hands. Sekhmet's head of a lioness has remarkably pointed ears, like a cat's: a sign that the goddess allows herself to be pacified? Photograph: RMO (acc.no. F 1940/8.8).

this pharaoh's mortuary temple on the Theban west bank, and their total number probably surpassed seven hundred. This set of statues seems to represent some kind of eternal calendar, with one statue for each day and another for each night of the year. Attempts to pacify the goddess should not relent for a single moment, or she might launch a new assault on humanity, as she did in primeval times.

FIG. 103. One of the numerous Sekhmet statues which can still be found in the ruins of the Mut temple at Karnak. Photograph: W.D. van Wijngaarden.

A MAGICAL FUNERAL INSURANCE

Furnish your station in the valley,
The grave that shall conceal your corpse.
Set it before you as your concern,
A thing that matters in your eyes.
Emulate the great departed,
Who are at rest within their tombs.
No blame accrues to him who does it,
It is well that you be ready too.

(THE INSTRUCTION OF ANY, IV.14–17)

THE TROUBLESOME DEAD

It has already been noted that magic was performed especially to protect the weakest members of society. These included mothers and children, people with diseases or mental problems, and also . . . the dead. In Egypt, the dead continued to be counted as members of the community, and every family treasured the memory of their departed relatives. The eldest son was responsible for looking after his parents' tomb and supplying it with food and drink at regular intervals. When the spirits of the dead came to the tomb chapel to enjoy their meal from the offering table, this created an opportunity to consult them about family matters or problems. As long as this was done prudently, it prevented the spirits from haunting the earth, intimidating the living or making them ill. Just like the gods, the dead had a dual nature: they could be loved or dreaded, for if they were not befriended they could make one's life miserable.

The spells of the medical papyri stress time and again that many complaints were caused by 'any male or female deceased.' In particular, those who had died prematurely or as a result of violence could seek to avenge themselves. Thus the effort relatives made to ensure a proper funeral was not just an expression of piety, but also a means to protect the living against unwanted contact. Threats and aggressive magic could be resorted to as necessary. Those spirits which caused trouble were sometimes depicted as fettered prisoners (fig. 105). Even the official stamp of the necropolis, which on the day of the funeral was pressed

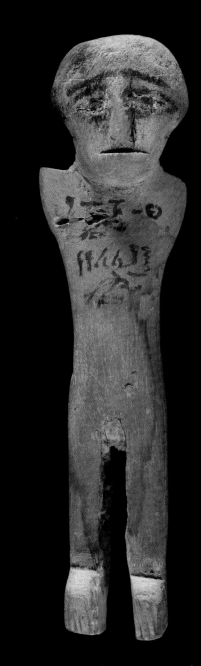

in the wet clay of the sealed doors to the most important tombs, depicts the jackal god Anubis standing guard over a group of bound persons. For the peace of mind of the living, the dead had better keep quietly to their graves!

Despite all precautions, things could occasionally get out of hand. Bad luck experienced shortly after the burial, gloominess, remorse, or nightmares were attributed to interference by the dead. Sometimes the Egyptians wrote letters to the dead in attempts to put an end to such harassment, or to invoke the assistance of the late head of the family. Of course such messages had to be posted at the tomb, and an effective way of doing so was to write the summons on a drinking bowl. This ensured that the *ba* of the deceased would find the letter when it came to refresh itself. As the Instruction for King Merikare clearly states: *The* ba *comes to the place it knows. It does not miss its former path. No kind of magic holds it back. It comes to those who give it water.*

Some of these bowls bearing letters to the dead have survived. In a bowl inscription now in Berlin, a widower addresses his late wife: *You have been brought here to this city of eternity without bearing a grudge against me. If these complaints have been caused with your knowledge, then look how the house with your children has been plunged into fresh misery. If they have been caused without your knowledge, then your father in the realm of the dead is great! If you bear a grudge against me, forget it for your children's sake. Be merciful, be merciful, and the gods of Abydos will have mercy on you!*

A long letter to the dead now kept in Leiden was written on a sheet of papyrus which was then rolled up and tied to a female statuette made of wood (fig. 106). Apparently the woman it represents is the same Ankhiry to whom the letter is addressed, which came from her widower, a high-level army officer. In this case the widower's complaints concerned mental troubles, and it rather looks as if Ankhiry pestered her husband with reproaches in his dreams. After having endured this situation for three years, the poor man had had enough

Letter to the dead

To the excellent spirit of Ankhiry. What have I done wrong, that I have ended up in this awful situation in which I am? What have I done to you, that you did this: laying your hand on me though I have not done anything to you? From the time that I was your husband till this day, what have I done to you that I should hide? What is it which urges me to lodge this complaint? What have I done to you? I shall dispute with you in court with my own words, in the presence of the Ennead of the West, and one will administer justice over you and me on the basis of this letter, which contains a complaint against you, that about which it reports.

I made you unto my wife when I was still a young man. I stayed with you when I performed all kinds of offices. I stayed with you, I did not repudiate you and did not make your heart unhappy. I acted likewise when as a young man I performed all kinds of important offices for the Pharaoh (may he live, be prosperous and healthy!). I did not repudiate you, for I said: "She has always been with me," so I said. And everybody who came to me in your presence, I did not receive them for your sake, saying: "I shall do as you wish." But behold, you do not consider my desires! I shall take you to court and one will tell falsehood from truth!

Mind you, when I trained officers for the army of the Pharaoh (may he live, be prosperous and healthy!) and for his cavalry, I made them come to prostrate themselves before you with presents, all kinds of nice things to put them down before you. I never had reason to hide anything from you, as long as you lived. I never hurt you by bossing you around in any respect. You never had to notice that I cheated you, as a crook who enters the house of somebody else. I never gave another man cause to rebuke me for my conduct toward you.

When I was given the position which I still have, and I could no longer travel as I used to do, I did what everybody does who stays home like me. Your ointments, your food, and your clothes, they were all brought to you. I never had them delivered anywhere else, but I said: "The mistress lives there," so I said, for I did not cheat you. But behold: you do not realize how well I treated you. That is why I send you this letter, in order to let you know what you did to me.

When you came to suffer from this disease which you had, I summoned a specialist who treated you. He did everything of which you said: "Do it!" And when I had to leave in the following of the Pharaoh (may he live, be prosperous and healthy!) in order to go south, and you got in that condition, I spent a period of eight months without eating or drinking as would suit a man. And as soon as I had come back to Memphis, I asked leave of the Pharaoh (may he live, be prosperous and healthy!) and went to the place where you were, and I wept profusely with my people in the presence of the whole neighborhood. I gave sheets of linen in order to wrap you and had many clothes made. And I did not omit anything good by not doing it for you. Behold, I spent three years on my own, without entering a single house, though it is not just that somebody like me has to act like this. But look, I did it for your benefit! Mind you, you do not make the distinction between good and bad! Let one administer justice between you and me! For behold: the girls in the house, I have not entered at a single one of them!

(PAPYRUS LEIDEN AMS 64)

FIG. 106. Together with the letter once tied to it, the statuette of Ankhiry is an effective means to contact the deceased. Photograph: RMO (inv.nrs. AH 115 en AMS 64).

and so wrote a confused epistle full of misspellings, additions, and repetitions. He omitted the usual greeting formulas with which a letter ought to start, while at the end he found himself short of space and his writing got smaller and smaller. The widower immediately threatens to summon his wife to appear in a divine court of justice. He lists all the charities he conferred on his wife during her lifetime, and it is not until the very end that he seems to come to the point. Here we find a passing reference to girls in a brothel. It is possible that the widower was possessed by feelings of guilt about frequenting them. Thus the dead and the living in Egypt held each other firmly in their grasp.

GOING OUT BY DAY

Letters to the dead represent only one aspect of the manifold magical concepts related to the hereafter. They clearly demonstrate ancient Egyptians' firm belief that life could continue after death, even within one's family circle, provided that the proper funeral arrangements had been made.

Every Egyptian with some money to spare began at a relatively young age to collect the necessary burial equipment: coffins, a funerary mask, jars for the embalmed intestines, funerary figurines (*shabti*s), and a whole array of magical objects for warding off the various dangers in the realm of the dead. In fact, almost all the objects deposited in the tomb possessed magical significance, because they were intended to wield a positive influence on the fate of the deceased. They were therefore inscribed with magical spells, or spells were recited over them while they were being made or deposited in the tomb. They were made of materials with supernatural potency or coated in paints and varnishes that had a magically effective color scheme. Often they were decorated with symbolic vignettes or functioned as scale models of an ideal situation. An intact

tomb thus has the appearance of a kind of magic toolbox, and perfectly illustrates the religious convictions of the deceased. Unfortunately most tombs were plundered in antiquity, and all that remains today are isolated objects in museums and private collections. It is impossible to discuss them all here; instead we will concentrate on the chief objectives of Egyptian sorcery connected with death and the afterlife.

The Egyptian notions of life after death were codified in elaborate texts that continually evolved and shifted their emphasis over thousands of years. The oldest version is known as the Pyramid Texts, since they were carved on the walls of the burial chambers inside the pyramids of the Old Kingdom (fig. 104). The first pharaoh who had this done for himself was Unas (2356–2323 BC), and his example was followed by all his successors and soon in the pyramids of the royal consorts as well. The texts themselves are probably a good deal older than that: they were undoubtedly passed down in oral form for generations before Unas or recorded on papyrus scrolls in the House of Life (these have not survived).

The Pyramid Texts are a heterogeneous mix of ritual instructions for use during the royal burial and ensuing offerings; they include hymns to the gods, invocations, and outright magical spells. Originally they were used by the mortuary priests charged with prolonging the pharaoh's life in the centuries after his interment; they were responsible for performing the daily offerings of food and drink in the enormous mortuary temple at the foot of the pyramid. For some reason, however, Unas did not trust this system. He felt safer having all the spells at his personal disposal inside the burial chamber. If the priests neglected their duties, he would still be able to help himself by reciting the required spells, for the power of words could take the place of actual offerings.

A central concept in the Pyramid Texts is the idea that after death the pharaoh will ascend to heaven, there to join the solar god Re or to shine as a star in the

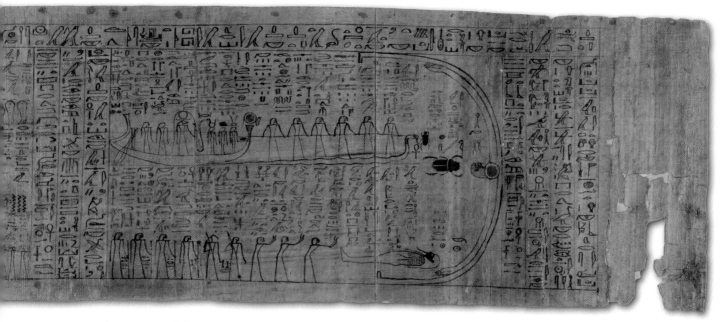

FIG. 107. Depiction of sunrise in a so-called *Amduat* papyrus. The god Re rises from the eastern horizon as a disk pushed by a scarab. Meanwhile the corpse of Osiris, from which he has risen, stays behind in the netherworld. Photograph: RMO (acc.no. AMS 46).

firmament. However, toward the end of the Old Kingdom another divine figure began to manifest himself: Osiris. The Egyptians preferred not to talk too much about the god's earthly existence and miserable death. The story of his early days as king on earth was not recorded until the Greek period, when a coherent account of the Osiris myth was finally written down by European tourists. The Egyptian texts restrict themselves to passing references to this part of the tale, and rather stress Osiris's glorious resurrection, when he conquered death thanks to the good care of his widow Isis and assumed the position of king of the netherworld. This is what attracted the dead pharaoh, and the king's association with Re is combined in the texts with his complete identification with Osiris.

Modern readers might say that the concepts are mutually exclusive, but Egyptian theologians cleverly managed to intertwine them by stating that every evening Re in his celestial bark enters the netherworld through the western horizon. There the sun god unites with Osiris, to be reborn in the east at dawn (fig. 107). However, these kinds of reflections were not committed to paper until a thousand years after Unas.

In the beginning, ordinary men and women did not expect to have access to such an afterlife. Toward the end of the Old Kingdom, however, the notion that they too could become 'an Osiris' became predominant. In funerary texts inscribed on tomb items the deceased's name is therefore preceded by the epithet 'the Osiris,' and distinguished Egyptians even appropriated the royal mortuary texts for their own use. This led to the development of the Coffin Texts of the Middle Kingdom, which were written on the interior walls of the wooden coffins of the wealthy (fig. 108). The upper parts of the

FIG. 108. The inner walls of the coffin of Asetweret have been inscribed with Coffin Texts along the bottom. These are surmounted by a frieze representing vessels, mirrors, jewelry, and weapons which the deceased would need in the hereafter. Photograph: RMO (acc.no. F 1966/2.1).

walls were decorated with painted friezes of attributes the dead might need in the hereafter. That these include crowns and scepters is a clear sign of the royal origins of this funerary ritual. One should not, however, interpret the phenomenon as proof of democratization; the custom was restricted to the members of a clearly defined elite. Most were men, although a few women were also interred with such luxuries. Referring to the deceased as 'he,' as we will do hereinafter, is thus apt in this context.

A thorough revision of the funerary texts took place during the early New Kingdom. They were now often inscribed on the linen shrouds of the mummy, or on scrolls of

papyrus inserted between the bandages or laid on top of the corpse (fig. 117). We generally refer to these texts as the Egyptian Book of the Dead, although they still consist of a heterogeneous compilation of magic spells. The Egyptians themselves called it *The Book of Going Out by Day*, since these spells allowed the soul to leave the tomb at will and return to the safe haven of the mummified body by night. However, the Book of the Dead also deals with numerous other themes, such as solar hymns, transformations, the identification with specific deities, justification in the divine court of justice, and so on. It also provided the passwords needed to enter through the various gateways that led to Osiris and contained selective charms for warding off hostile demons, wild animals, and other dangers, and for procuring certain commodities. Thereby the Book of the Dead served as a travel guide for the hereafter, and at the same time functioned as both a passport and a credit card for the deceased.

Every manuscript represents a fresh selection from the known corpus of about two hundred spells, copied in an individual order. Thus we should not refer to the Book of the Dead as a 'book' in our sense of the word. It was not until the Late Period that the order of the texts was more or less fixed, and our modern numbering of the individual spells is based on a manuscript dating to that period. Another peculiarity of the Book of the Dead is that the various spells are generally illustrated. Thus the magical potency of the vignettes reinforced that of the words.

THE BODY AS MICROCOSMOS

These books of magic for the dead inform us about all kinds of rituals and magical acts which existed to smooth the transition from life to afterlife. This is also true of other texts, such as those regarding the Opening of the Mouth or the Ritual of Embalming. Finally, we can study the actual objects buried in the tombs which prove that such rituals were really performed. These items include the mummies themselves.

Modern scientific research has taught us a great deal about the process of mummification. It is clear that sensible technical practices were carried out alongside rituals of purely magical significance (and lacking all practical efficacy), a situation that resembled the way in which medical care for the living was organized. The application of the various substances meant to preserve the body, and of the linen bandages, was accompanied by the recitation of charms. Several of the materials used in this process are well known from the magical domain, such as beeswax or fragrant resin. Even commonplace materials such as sand, clay, natron, and linen were generally associated with mythological tales or cosmic events. While these substances were in fact effective for drying out the mummy or isolating it from external influences, the texts rather focus on their supernatural origin and mythical-magical efficacy. One good example is natron, a mixture of ordinary salt and soda which helped to dehydrate the corpse but was also used as soap in daily life. Our word 'natron' and the international symbol for sodium (natrium, Na) are derived from the ancient Egyptian adjective *netjery*, which means 'divine.' For the Egyptians, the treatment of the body with natron was not primarily to dehydrate but rather to purify it, resulting in divine status. In our analysis of the various funerary rituals we should be aware of such differences in perspective.

Symbolically, the mummy had to be reassembled from its constituent parts, just as Isis rejoined the dismembered body of her late husband Osiris (fig. 109). Therefore the mortuary priests addressed the deceased as follows: *I am Horus. I have come to cleanse you and purify you, to resuscitate you and collect your bones for you, to reassemble your intestines and rejoin your dispersed limbs, for I am Horus who protects his father. I killed the one who killed you.* Thus the embalming was symbolically elevated to

FIG. 109. Headless representation of the god Osiris, a reference to the mythological event when Seth cut his opponent's body to pieces. Photograph: RMO (acc.no. F 1955/10.3).

represent the victory of Osiris over Seth, of the ordered world *(ma'at)* over chaos. The body's integrity was protected by four gods known as the Sons of Horus. Their fourfold company is an unmistakable reference to the four directions of the sky, and indeed the Sons of Horus were associated with the four supports of the celestial vault. This indicates that a sympathetic equation was felt to exist between the preservation of the corpse and the continued existence of the cosmos. If the body suffered decay, then the whole universe would also perish; surely the gods would never allow such a catastrophe!

Certain rituals imply that during the embalming process the body was laid in a north–south direction, and in the burial chamber the mummy was likewise deposited with the head toward the north in most periods. This suggests that the fate of the deceased was intimately connected with the basic structure of the ordered world. As soon as he lifted his head, he would see the creator god Re in the sun's zenith, the highest point of its course through the southern sky.

The four Sons of Horus were also regarded as guardians of the internal organs of the deceased. These were usually removed from the body and conserved separately. The embalming priests stored them inside four so-called canopic jars (fig. 110), which usually had stoppers provided with the heads of the Sons of Horus: a human head for Imset, a baboon's for Hapy, a jackal's for Duamutef, and a falcon's for Qebehsenuef. As a rule these jars were meant to contain the liver, lungs, stomach, and bowels, in that order, although scientific analysis of the dried-out contents has shown that in practice many mistakes were made. It rather looks as if the embalmers just took a symbolic sample from each of the four directions of the abdominal and thoracic cavities. Indeed, considering that they took these samples by inserting their left hand through a narrow incision in the corpse's abdomen, mistakes are hardly surprising. It was primarily the magical intention that was important. While

FIG. 110. The canopic jars of a man, Horwedja, are provided with stoppers showing the heads of the four Sons of Horus. Photograph: RMO (acc.no. AAL 2a-d).

the quick removal of the moist organs was essential for preventing the total decay of the corpse, the symbolism rather stressed the opposite notion: that they remained an integral part of the body, and that their importance for its preservation was as fundamental as that of the four supports of the sky. Occasionally the four packages of dehydrated intestines were wrapped as miniature mummies or interred in small coffins. In the same way, the canopic box holding the four jars usually matches the mummy's sarcophagus in color scheme and decoration. One item closely followed the other in the funeral cortège, and they stood side by side in the burial chamber.

Canopic jars were not used in all periods. From about 1150 BC onward, the Egyptians restored the packages with the embalmed organs to the abdominal cavity after they had finished with them. To accentuate their relationship with the Sons of Horus, figurines of the four deities were attached to the packages. The use of these figurines, always made of beeswax, was restricted to the eleventh and tenth centuries BC (fig. 111). Thus once again we observe the use of this material that played such an important part in the magical practices of the ancient Egyptians. For a brief period in the early Middle Kingdom, it was the custom to place a miniature wax figure of the naked corpse in the burial chamber: a spare body in case the mummy itself was lost (fig. 112).

Apart from its usual symbolic associations, the Egyptians must have discovered that the use of beeswax in mummification was particularly effective because it perfectly sealed off the skin and various orifices from fungi and bacteria. The side-plate that covered the embalming incision in the left side of the abdomen was likewise often made of beeswax, provided with an additional depiction of the apotropaic Eye of Horus *(wedjat)* to increase its

FIG. 111. This set of four wax Sons of Horus was once tied to the packages containing embalmed internal organs. Photograph: RMO (acc.no. AC 7a-d).

magical power. Several other attributes of the mummy were made in wax as well. For instance, mummies dating to the Greco-Roman period sometimes possess nipples or navels of (gilt) beeswax, and in the Third Intermediate Period miniature images of the phoenix (the bird of resurrection) were added. These lay on the chest alongside amulets in other magical materials: hearts or scarabs made of a mixture of wax and resin (fig. 47) or protective falcons made of lead (fig. 45). The side plate was sometimes made of lead, whereas the funerary mask (fig. 44) and the sheaths around the fingers and toes were generally gold or at least gilded. Such supernatural substances were of course very suitable for preserving the body, while gold was a clear sign of the divine status that the deceased had obtained by conquering death.

THE DAILY BREAD

The Egyptians preferred to have no witnesses during the actual embalming process. The body was first transferred to a workshop at the desert edge. The embalmers were not just specialist craftsmen, but also priests, and so bound to secrecy about the exact mummification procedures. Moreover, it was not only human witnesses who were kept out of the way, but also the soul of the deceased. It

FIG. 112. The custom of manufacturing *shabtis* lasted several millennia. It originated in early Middle Kingdom wax figures meant exclusively to act as spare bodies for their owners. Photograph: RMO (acc.no. F 1980/6.1).

had left the body at the moment of death in the shape of a human-headed bird (fig. 28), so the corpse was just a lifeless object that could be manipulated. According to the Egyptian traditions, the soul's absence lasted seventy days, exactly the time needed for the body's dehydration by means of natron, the anointing, and the final wrapping with linen bandages. Seventy days is also the length of time during which stars around the equator disappear from the nocturnal sky: they rise above the horizon by day only and therefore remain invisible. One of the beliefs about the hereafter was that the soul would become a star in the firmament. Thus the god Osiris was connected with Orion, and when the constellation reappeared on the eastern horizon after an absence of seventy days, this symbolized the god's resurrection. In the same way, the *ba* of the deceased was believed to return to the body after mummification was complete, causing it to live again.

Yet this did not happen automatically; a special ritual was required to transform a dead body into a living person again. This was the Ritual of Opening the Mouth, which has already been mentioned several times. It was performed on the day of the funeral in the open court of the tomb. The mummy was set on a layer of sand to isolate it from the unclean environment (fig. 32). It stood upright on its feet, facing south, aligned with the basic directions of the universe. Then the *sem* priest touched its mouth, nose, eyes, and hands with an array of ritual implements (figs. 56–58), so that the mummy would be able to resume breathing, eating, and drinking—all those faculties which distinguish the living from the dead. This was followed by the presentation of a first offering of food and drink. After this transition ritual the mummy would be able to live on forever and form a suitable abode for the *ba*. A well-known vignette from the Book of the Dead shows the soul bird flying down the vertical shaft which leads to the burial chamber, while upstairs the priest is still conducting the funeral rites in front of the tomb chapel (fig. 113).

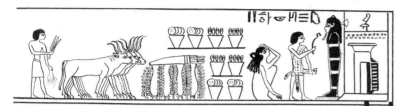

Thanks to the Ritual of Opening of the Mouth the deceased could be served food and drink. Such offerings were not made every day but only at certain festivals. For instance, in Thebes we see the development of the Feast of the Valley, a festival celebrated from the Middle Kingdom onward during which bark processions of Amun, Mut, and Khonsu crossed the Nile from Karnak and visited the most important mortuary temples of the pharaohs in the necropolis. Wealthy Egyptians selected burial plots along the route followed by the procession, believing that the annual passage of the gods would give them a boost of vitality. During the Feast of the Valley, all Theban families used to visit the tombs of their ancestors, where they had a communal meal with the dead. Small lights burned the whole night long across the hills as a symbol of new life brought to the dark netherworld.

On ordinary days the cemeteries were practically deserted, apart from the occasional visitors who had some business in the chapels of their relatives. The eldest son bore the primary responsibility for the care of his deceased parents, but to carry it out he was permitted to hire the services of a professional mortuary priest: one of the priests of low rank attached to a local shrine, who would sign several such 'maintenance contracts' to earn extra income. Of course Egyptians could see with their own eyes that the offerings of food and drink remained untouched. They were nonetheless convinced that the inherent vitality would benefit the *ka* of the deceased, which was believed to live inside the chapel and especially

in the statue depicting the tomb owner. During the Old Kingdom, the statue was generally locked in a small chamber *(serdab)* which communicated with the offering room via a slit-shaped aperture.

In spite of all this, the Egyptians were not entirely confident that their relatives would in fact observe these pious obligations. They could see for themselves that such practices rarely endured beyond a single generation. That is why actual food and drink was entombed along with the mummy. One alternative was to provide empty storage vessels, which could be filled through magical means so long as the deceased had knowledge of the proper magic spells. Another was to provide only miniature versions of the usual offering vessels, a solution which was already common by the Old Kingdom

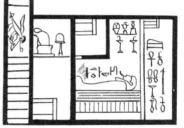

FIG. 113. While above the *sem* priest performs the Ritual of Opening the Mouth on the mummy, which is standing in front of the tomb chapel, below the soul bird speeds down the shaft on its way to the mummy in the burial chamber. From the Book of the Dead of Nebked in the Louvre, chapter 1. Reproduction after Naville, *Todtenbuch* I, pl. iv.

(fig. 114). Other miniature models have also been found in tombs, for instance those depicting silo-shaped granaries. Offering tables and the walls of tomb chapels include relief representations of food and drink and hieroglyphs listing the various victuals: thus the magic of word and image would ensure a well-provisioned dining table forever.

FIG. 114. Miniature vessels such as these come from Old Kingdom mortuary temples, where they served as a magical replacement for actual food offerings. Photograph: RMO (acc.no. F 1953/9.101–108 and F 1957/10.13–14).

But what was to be done with the qualified kitchen personnel who had to prepare all this choice food? The barbaric custom of killing one's domestic servants so they could accompany their master in the afterlife was abolished very early; it was only practiced for the burials of the first few pharaohs. Instead the royal mortuary temples introduced extensive wall reliefs, which would soon be copied for private tomb chapels too: lively scenes showing farmers, hunters and fishermen (figs. 15 and 54), butchers and cooks, bakers and brewers, who would continue to serve the deceased after death. We could regard these scenes as 'art,' amusing wall decorations full of information about daily life and abounding in

funny anecdotes. This is utterly wrong, however, for such illustrations did not serve to amuse the living but to provide for the dead. They depict a magical ideal, and certainly not the reality of life on earth.

Alongside these two-dimensional images the Old Kingdom tombs also contained three-dimensional representations of milling servants (fig. 115), bakers, brewers, and other specialists. These were placed in the *serdab*, next to the tomb-statue of the deceased himself. They too had been given life during the funeral rites and were supposed to perform their work magically in the hereafter. During the Middle Kingdom the dead preferred to keep these statuettes to themselves inside the underground burial chamber, mainly for safety reasons. This meant they no longer needed to be made of stone, and wooden model workshops now became popular, producing bakeries, breweries, granaries, weaving shops, and so on. Also common were the model boats used by the deceased for transport in the hereafter (fig. 116). This enabled them to go on pilgrimage to Abydos, the place where Osiris lay buried and which all Egyptians hoped to visit, if not during their lifetime then at least after death. A sailing ship was often provided for the trip south so the pilgrim could sail against the current by making use of the prevailing northerly wind. All that was necessary for the return journey was a model rowboat with its crew, consisting of oarsmen, a pilot in the prow to assess the depth of the water, and a helmsman in the stern; the deceased himself—or his coffin—sat amid ships under an awning.

FIG. 115. This woman performs the heavy labor at the millstone that the deceased does not fancy doing himself. Photograph: RMO (acc.no. F 1934/12.1).

The ancient Egyptians fretted constantly about the problem of obtaining food in the hereafter. Some feared it might be necessary to earn one's living by carrying out heavy labor on the fields. In the vignettes of spell 110 from the Book of the Dead the deceased is depicted plowing, reaping, and threshing (fig. 117)—a rather unattractive prospect for wealthy people who were not used to toiling in the hot sun. For this reason the Egyptians invented the *shabti*, a term whose original meaning was soon lost, but which probably signified 'he who answers.' The word is explained in spell 6 from the Book of the Dead: *Oh, you* shabtis*, if the Osiris X is called and summoned to do all the work which is wont to be done in the hereafter—to plow the fields, irrigate the riparian lands, and transport by boat the sand of the east to the west (or vice versa)—and a task is given him as a man under his obligations; if one calls him at any time, you will say: 'I shall do it, here I am.'* Shabti*s are small figurines of the deceased as a mummy or in the shape of a living person, inscribed with his name and sometimes with the complete spell from the Book of the Dead (fig. 118). Often they are depicted with agricultural tools: holding two hoes for tilling the soil, carrying a bag to contain sand or seed corn on their back, and occasionally bearing a yoke with pots for irrigating the fields. Separate miniature tools have also been found. During the Middle Kingdom no individual possessed more than a single *shabti*, but this increased to about ten figurines during the New Kingdom. Later it became the custom for each person to be buried with about four hundred statuettes: one for each day of the year, and an overseer with a whip for each group of ten.

Yet still the Egyptians worried whether the figurines would really reply on their behalf when they were summoned for forced labor in the hereafter. Two contracts were therefore displayed in the burial chamber of Nesikhonsu, wife to the high priest Pinudjem II. In these texts, the god Amun-Re explicitly confirms that Nesikhonsu acquired the *shabti*s from the faience-

FIG. 116. This model ship comprises nine rowers, a helmsman, and a pilot, with a figurine of the deceased shipowner inside the cabin. Photograph: RMO (acc.no. F 1939/1.3).

FIG. 117. A vignette from the Book of the Dead of a woman, Taiuheryt, shows the work in the fields of the hereafter: plowing, sowing, reaping, and pulling flax, followed by offerings to the gods. It is remarkable that the lady is assisted here by male laborers. Photograph: RMO (acc.no. AMS 40).

FIG. 118 Group of *shabtis* of various owners dating to the New Kingdom. The two figures on the left are mummiform and hold hoes for tilling the fields, whereas the two on the right wear the clothes of the living. Photograph: RMO (inv.nrs. AF 131, CI 249, L.VII.15b en L.VII.17a).

makers honestly, and that the price paid for them should also be regarded as the wages for the figurines themselves to compensate them for their field labor! These contracts can be compared to the divine decrees that the living used to wear as amulets around the neck. The magical concept involved is quite touching; it demonstrates the importance with which ancient Egyptians regarded concluding a fair deal to the full satisfaction of all parties concerned.

Fig. 119. The top of this magic brick is incised with a protective formula for the deceased. Photograph: RMO (acc.no. ad 52-a).

ETERNAL LIFE

O, you who lead the perfected spirits to the house of Osiris, lead my spirit with you to the house of Osiris! May it hear as you hear and see as you see! May it stand as you stand and sit as you sit! O, you who give the perfected spirits bread and beer in the house of Osiris, give my soul bread and beer with you at the proper times! O, you who open the roads and open up the paths for the perfected spirits in the house of Osiris, open the roads and open up the paths for my spirit with you!

(BOOK OF THE DEAD, SPELL 1)

DEFYING DEATH

A proper burial gave the deceased an excellent start in the afterlife. Even so, after the mummification, the funeral, and the Ritual of Opening the Mouth were done, he had to face the darkness of the sealed burial chamber alone. Fortunately he was provided with his Book of the Dead to lead the way and help to overcome the various dangers that might threaten him on his journey. Hostile demons might overwhelm him even before he could leave the burial chamber. After all, he was now an Osiris and so exposed to the revenge of the jealous Seth. To avert this danger, a shallow niche was built into each of the four walls of the burial chamber—one for each direction of the sky—and a brick (fig. 119) placed within each niche inscribed with a protective formula and surmounted by an amulet: a faience *djed*-pillar (symbol of durability, connected with Osiris) in the west wall, a clay jackal representing the god Anubis in the east, a torch in the south, and a wooden mummiform figure in the north. The spell on the northern brick reads as follows: *You who*

come in order to capture, I will not allow you to capture! You who come in order to make a prisoner, I will not allow you to make a prisoner! I will capture you, I will make you a prisoner! I am the guardian of the Osiris X.

Inside the burial chamber, the mummy or its coffin was occasionally laid on a funerary bier, similar to the ones used during mummification. This item wielded extra protection, for it often had leonine legs, two lion's heads at one short side, and two tails at the other. Thus the deceased was reclining on the body of a lion that not only dispelled evil but also symbolized heaven. The tomb of Tutankhamun was found to contain no fewer than three such biers, with the bodies of, respectively, a leopard, the cow of the goddess Hathor, and the hippopotamus of Taweret—all of them referring to the King's ascension and rebirth. Private individuals were sometimes given biers with legs in the shape of the god Bes, again combining apotropaic qualities with care for the newborn.

A whole cordon of protective demons was put up around the bier of royal tombs (fig. 120). They were known as the guardians of Osiris, keeping watch over

the dead god day and night. In their hands they carried frightful knives, and they were known by ghastly names such as 'dung-eater,' 'the fiery one,' 'the vigilant one,' or 'he who throws into the flames.' Their most frightening feature was their head, which might belong to a falcon, bull, or crocodile, or have the features of Bes with his leonine mane and his tongue sticking out, or even be shaped like a whole tortoise! But all this was for the good, because the opponents were the demons who tried to attack Osiris, and defeating them was the only way to avoid instant death. These statues were usually made of wood and coated with a layer of shiny black varnish, the color associated with night and the netherworld.

As soon as the deceased left the safe haven of the burial chamber, he had to face the hostile forces in a more direct way. For that purpose, the images of two bound prisoners (one usually an Asiatic and the other a Nubian, fig. 121) decorated the soles of his feet, or rather those of his sandals or of the cartonnage foot cover that came into fashion in the Greco-Roman period. The traditional representation of nine bows also appears on these items: a symbolic image of the foreign tribes recruited by the Egyptians to serve as mercenary archers in their armies. Thus the deceased would crush his opponents with every footstep. Other enemies manifesting themselves in the guise of large carnivores or poisonous animals could only be defeated with the help of the protective spells 31–37 and 39–40 from the Book of the Dead. The concomitant vignettes illustrate how the deceased wields a harpoon to fight crocodiles, serpents, or an enormous beetle (fig. 122). The crocodiles were believed to rob the dead of their

FIG. 120. This guardian from the tomb of Ramesses IX has turned his head in order to look at us: a spooky effect in Egyptian art, which is used to depictions in profile. He has the lion's mane of the god Bes and holds his beard with both hands. There is a cavity in the back for holding a papyrus scroll or amulet. Photograph: British Museum (acc.no. EA 61283).

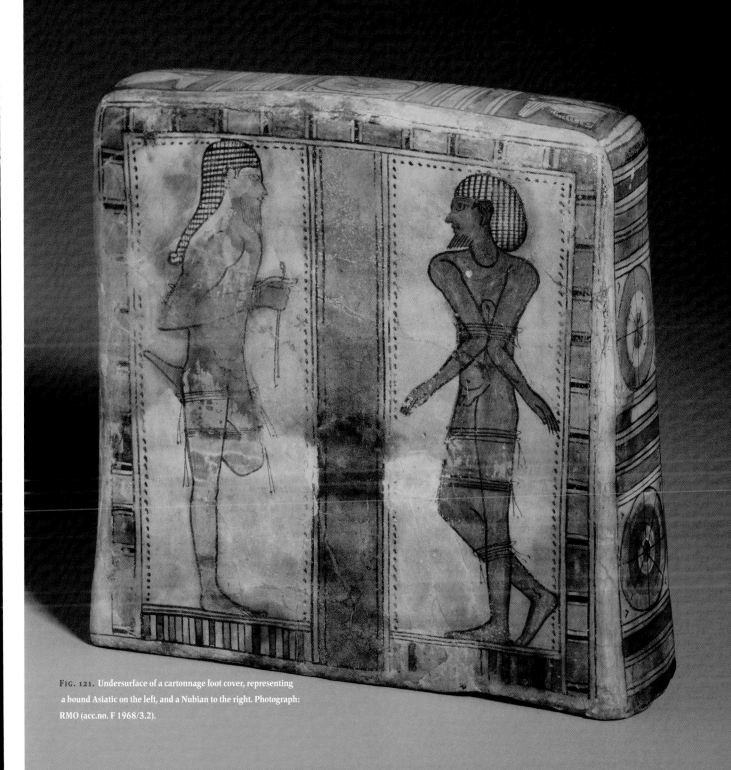

Fig. 121. Undersurface of a cartonnage foot cover, representing a bound Asiatic on the left, and a Nubian to the right. Photograph: RMO (acc.no. F 1968/3.2).

magical faculties, while the serpents were regarded as manifestations of Apophis.

Like the living, the dead also wore amulets to protect themselves from all kinds of danger. Some were identical to those worn in life, such as figurines of the divine guardians Bes and Taweret, or the Eye of Horus (fig. 71). Others had the specific aim of ensuring resurrection or reinforcing the vital functions, and therefore differed from the amulets of daily life. Many were inserted between the mummy wrappings, while others were strung onto necklaces, wristlets, or finger-rings worn by the mummy, or laid atop the outer shroud (figs. 40–41). Among the latter are the bead nets consisting of blue-glazed cylinder beads that undoubtedly refer to celestial regions. Ancient Egyptians associated the lozenge-shaped cells formed by these beads with feather patterns, and so they were reminiscent of the wings of the sky goddess, which

she wraps around the deceased for protection. Usually figurines of the four Sons of Horus or of winged scarabs were included in such nets. These dung beetles were a common symbol of life after death. The Egyptians did not know that the insect lays its eggs in the pellets of dung it buries in the ground. Great was their surprise, therefore, when this inert material suddenly produced living creatures. Moreover, they observed a similarity between these pellets of dung and the sun disk that is rolled across the sky, so they depicted the god of dawn, Khepri, as a scarab which propels the reborn sun into the sky (fig. 107).

Most amulets had to be placed in a specific position on the mummy in order to wield their influence on that spot. Thus a miniature headrest was generally put under the neck (fig. 43), to assist the deceased in raising his head and to emphasize that death is nothing but a temporary sleep. Heart amulets or heart scarabs (figs. 47 and 128) lay on

FIG. 122. The deceased fights crocodiles (Book of the Dead chapters 31–32), an empty base (chapter 36?), and a donkey (chapter 40). From the papyrus of Nesnakht. Photograph: RMO (acc.no. CI 11a).

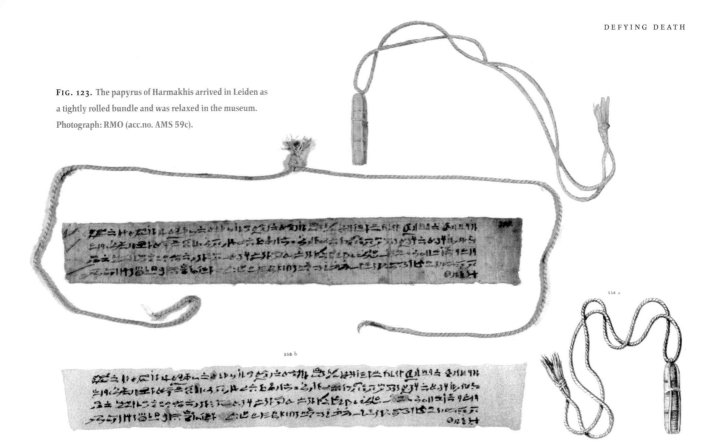

FIG. 123. The papyrus of Harmakhis arrived in Leiden as a tightly rolled bundle and was relaxed in the museum. Photograph: RMO (acc.no. AMS 59c).

the chest, often forming the centerpiece of a breastplate or pectoral. The incision in the left side, opened to remove the internal organs, was often covered with an amulet of black stone in the shape of two outstretched fingers, presumably in imitation of a protective gesture to ward off evil forces trying to enter. At the end of the Book of the Dead, spells 155–60 contain magic formulas meant to charge certain mummy amulets with extra power: a gold *djed* pillar, a *tyet* knot of red jasper sacred to the goddess Isis, a gold vulture with outstretched wings (likewise connected with Isis), a gold collar amulet, and two charms in the shape of a papyrus column (*wadj*, a sign of prosperity).

Talismans written on papyrus form a separate category. In the same way that the living armed themselves with divine decrees and other charms, the dead also wore tightly rolled papyrus scrolls around their neck. Among such papyri is an amulet made for the high priest of Amun, Harmakhis, which is now in the Leiden collection (fig. 123). It hangs from a knotted cord and reads as follows: *O, you who throw his lasso, you shall not throw a lasso around the high priest of Amun and royal son, Harmakhis! O, injurer, you shall not injure him! O, robber, you shall not rob him! O, you who tear out hearts, you shall not tear out his heart! O, powerful one, you shall have no power over his limbs! He is the corpse without head, the mummy without face. He is the bull which changes its color, the general who commands eternal silence, the god who circulates every day, the great creature of morning. Do not approach him, have no power over his limbs! Nothing bad or evil can be done against him, he will not feel it. He is the fibers of Geb, wrapped in*

149

a dog skin which is in the Mansion of the River at Coptos. Amun-Re, uniter of the Two Lands who is in Karnak, is the protection of his body. He is the Heliopolitan.

Thus the protection against dangerous demons follows the traditional pattern: the deceased is again equated with superior powers, such as Osiris (the headless mummy, fig. 109, the fetish of a stuffed dog skin), Amun-Re (the supreme god who decides over life and death), the sacred Bukhis bull, or the solar god (who circulates every day, the Heliopolitan). Thereby the text ensures that demons will think twice before they set out to attack him!

TRAVEL NERVES

It was generally believed that the deceased had to undertake a journey toward the throne of Osiris. Like the setting sun, he had entered the netherworld from the western horizon, and his final destination was near the eastern exit from which the disk rose again at dawn. There was a long road ahead of him, leading through unknown regions. Fortunately, in the Book of the Dead he possessed an excellent travel guide giving full descriptions of anything he might encounter. Moreover, it included magical formulas and passwords required to negotiate all the obstacles he would face. The realm of the dead was subdivided into a number of sections, separated by strong gateways. Each was guarded by a formidable gatekeeper whose appearance was as hostile as that of the demons protecting the pharaoh's funerary bier (fig. 124). The various texts do not agree about the exact number of these gateways.

The Book of That Which is in the Netherworld (*Amduat* in ancient Egyptian) divides the realm crossed by the solar bark during its nocturnal journey into twelve hours (figs. 51 and 107). All kinds of terrifying creatures populated the banks of the river of the netherworld, where sinners and the enemies of the gods received their due punishment by the application of terrible tortures. Of course the

deceased tried to remain seated in the comparative safety of the bark, but even so he could expect to meet Apophis somewhere in the dark, the opponent who, every night, endeavored to overwhelm the tired sun god.

According to spells 144 and 147 from the Book of the Dead, meanwhile, there were only seven gates, whereas spells 145 and 146 mention no fewer than twenty-one (three times the sacred number seven). The dead person had to report at each of them, shouting complicated formulas transcribed in his guidebook: *Hail to thee, twelfth gate of the Weary of Heart* [Osiris]*! Make way for me! I know you, I know your name, and I know the name of your occupant: she who summons the Two Lands and slaughters those who arrive at dawn, the bright one, mistress of spirits who hears the voice of her master every day–that is your name, and you are under control of the realm of the dead.* If there were no complications, a voice would then be heard to reply from inside the gatekeeper's lodge: *Go ahead! You are pure!* Once again we can observe how knowing the name gave a person command over a demon's actions. The disadvantage was that the deceased had to carry around a complete encyclopedia, for nobody could possibly remember all the different passwords (a problem we also face today, in this world dominated by computers).

Apart from the gateways, the deceased also encountered other obstacles. Like Egypt itself, the netherworld was crisscrossed with waterways and irrigation canals. To cross it without a boat of one's own required a ferry: it should be noted that in the texts from the Book of the Dead the deceased is not the constant passenger of the sun god's bark, as in the book *Amduat*, and therefore he might face transport problems. Spells 98 and 99 from the Book of the Dead describe a confrontation with an unwilling ferryman. He is called 'He who looks behind himself,' a fitting name for a person who rows a small skiff and must look over his shoulder every now and then to see where he is going. The ferryman starts firing questions at the deceased and complains that his boat is not fit for the crossing and lacks all kinds of essential parts. An endless series of questions and answers follows, which forces the dead person to demonstrate his familiarity with a wide range of mythological tales and to confess his final destination. When finally the ferryman seems to be convinced of his passenger's trustworthiness, each of the boat's components begins to question him in turn to discover whether he knows its true name: *Tell me my name,' says the mooring post. 'Your name is: the Lady of the Two Lands in the shrine.' 'Tell me my name,' says the mallet. 'Your name is: the leg of the Apis bull.' 'Tell me my name,' says the forward rope. 'Your name is: the knot tied by Anubis during the embalming.'* Etcetera, etcetera, enough to drive a person mad! But the deceased keeps his composure, consults his notes, and thanks to the magic words eventually reaches the opposite bank. This spell also stresses the importance of knowing and guarding the name.

To prevent this kind of trouble, it was far preferable to bring a boat of one's own to the netherworld. Wooden ship models could fulfill this function and had the extra advantage of being fully equipped with an expert crew (fig. 116). Such boats mainly date to the Middle Kingdom, although older specimens are known. An exceedingly old model ship can be dated to Egyptian prehistory, around 3500 BC. It is a little skiff made of baked clay. The prow and stern are occupied by the front and rear part of a frog, respectively (fig. 125). In the ancient Egyptian religious tradition, this animal was sacred to the goddess of birth,

FIG. 124. The deceased confronted with the fearsome gatekeepers of the hereafter: chapter 145 from the Book of the Dead of Nesnakht. Photograph: RMO (acc.no. CI 11a).

FIG. 125. This terracotta model is one of the earliest depictions of a funerary boat. Photograph: RMO (acc.no. F 1962/12.1).

Heket, so presumably the boat model helped to ensure the rebirth of the deceased. He is represented in a fetal position (perhaps asleep?), lying in the boat's oval central section which resembles a womb. Thus he sails to the other world, hoping to be reborn in a new life. It is rather striking that concepts of the afterlife had developed at such an early age in Egyptian history, and that people already used magical models to realize the imagined.

As an alternative, one could request to sail with the sun god Re in his own boat, which crossed the netherworld from west to east every night. Spells 100 to 102 provided the deceased with the necessary boarding passes. It was recommended that these invaluable documents be carried in a visible way, preferably around the neck or on the chest—rather like people about to enter a classified zone in a modern office building. The Leiden Museum possesses such a sheet of papyrus inscribed with the vignette of spell 100 from the Book of the Dead (fig. 126). Spells 133 and 134 have a rather similar purpose. They prescribe drawing a divine bark in white ink on a pottery bowl, with Re and the deceased on board (spell 133), or even the complete Ennead (the nine primeval gods, spell 134). The vignettes accompanying the spells demonstrate that the Egyptians themselves had some trouble in correctly interpreting the complicated directions. Thus some of the representations show a boat transporting a large round bowl on which the nine gods have been drawn—not really what was intended!

Some people got it right, however, and quite a number of bowls have survived which bear the correct depictions. One of these has indeed been found inside a tomb,

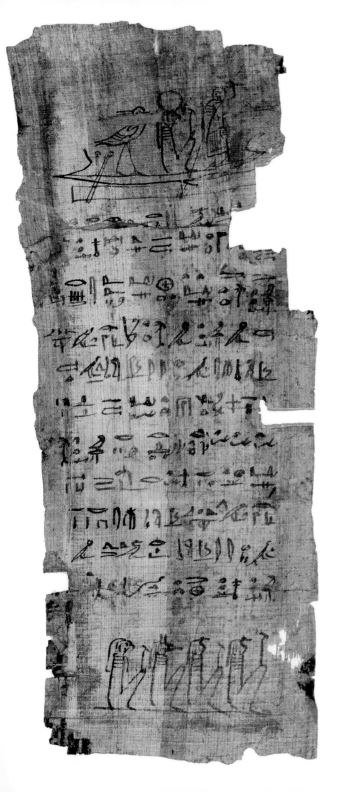

where it had been deposited in front of the sarcophagus, together with a number of boat models in clay and wood. Most magic bowls came from the temple precinct at Abydos and were apparently produced there in large numbers by the local priests. Again, this was a discovery made by the treasure hunters working for Giovanni d'Anastasi, who divided the finds between the Leiden Museum (thirty-two pieces) and the British Museum (eight pieces). Fragments of even more bowls were found in the same spot during American excavations in the 1960s. Whereas some of the Abydos bowls illustrate the prescribed divine barks (fig. 35), others just show companies of primeval deities, or even images of isolated gods. Most popular is the local god Osiris, but the rare deity Werheka ('Great of Magic') is also present. It rather looks as if the kilns of the Osiris temple produced so many bowls that the priests found it impossible to sell them all. They seem therefore to have employed the magic bowls themselves in the unguent workshop where fragrant perfumes were prepared. All the bowls bear black ink dockets mentioning the numerous ingredients of a mixture for censing, thereby relegating these valuable instruments of magic to the rank of plain storage vessels!

AT THE WEIGHT WATCHERS'

Provided that the deceased managed to pass all the gatekeepers and ferrymen, he would finally come to a large building. Its cornice showed alternating cobras and ostrich feathers. The feathers were the emblem of the goddess of justice, Ma'at, because according to the Egyptians the truth was as light as a feather. In this Hall of the Double Justice (as the courthouse was called) the gods would weigh the deceased's conscience, but it was not easy to get inside.

FIG. 126 Boarding pass for the hereafter: a papyrus inscribed with the text and vignette of chapter 100 from the Book of the Dead. Photograph: RMO (acc.no. CI 3-a).

153

First, the defendant had to pronounce the correct name of the gateway, its lintel, and its threshold as a last check of his identity. Fortunately, the correct answers could be found in the text of spell 125 from the Book of the Dead, which also helped the individual clear all the procedures in court. Upon arrival, the god Anubis took his hand and led him to a large pair of scales (fig. 127). Forty-two judges representing all provinces of Egypt were seated along the walls, but the deceased would probably be distracted by the terrifying monster sitting on a pedestal next to the scales: the notorious Swallower of the Dead whose body was part lion and part hippopotamus, and whose head was that of a crocodile.

Now the precarious moment had come when the heart of the deceased was taken from his chest and laid on the scales. During embalming, when all other internal organs were removed, the heart was generally left in the thoracic cavity especially for this occasion. According to the ancient Egyptians, the heart was the seat of conscience and the organ for thinking and feeling. All sins committed during life would therefore increase the heart's weight, which was now compared to that of the feather of Ma'at to determine whether the deceased was worthy to be admitted to the presence of Osiris. If he was not, he would fall prey to the Swallower of the Dead!

Egyptians were very much afraid of this final test; they were only human and naturally most would have committed at least some small transgression during their lifetime. Again the Book of the Dead provided assistance. Spell 125 gave directions for the 'declaration of innocence' to be read in court, an enumeration of all the misdeeds *not* committed by the deceased which begins: *I have not done wrong to anybody. I have not maltreated anybody. I have not committed any sins in the Place of Justice. I have not sought to know what should not be known. I have not done evil.* The list goes on for some time, and then the deceased addresses each of the forty-two judges in turn, calling them by their correct name and again denying that he has done any harm.

The Egyptians put a blind trust in the efficacy of magic words, and therefore the final words of spell 125 were almost redundant: *This has proved to be effective a million times.* But even so there were some qualms about the outcome of the weighing. Would the evidence presented by the poor heart on the scales support the words of its owner? To make sure it did, a particular magic charm had been placed in the tomb of the deceased: a heart scarab (fig. 128). This was generally a large stone image of a dung beetle, placed on the mummy's chest or hung from a necklace. Sometimes instead of a beetle there was a heart-shaped amulet of stone, resin, or beeswax. Both types of objects are inscribed on the reverse with a copy of spell 30B from the Book of the Dead, in which the deceased instructs his own heart not to yield the whole truth to the tribunal: *Oh, heart of my mother, heart of my mother, cardiac muscle of my various ages! Do not rise against me as a witness, do not oppose me in court, do not be hostile to me in the presence of him who wields the scales! You are my Ka* [vitality] *that is in my body, the* [creator god] *Khnum who keeps my limbs healthy. Go for the good things that are being prepared for us there! Do not give my name an evil smell with the judges that assign people their places! That is good for us and good for him who listens, and it pleases the judge. Do not make up any lies about me in the presence of the great god* [Osiris], *for behold: your behavior decides whether we shall be justified!*

Ancient Egyptians may not have considered that this might amount to unjust manipulation of a witness. We might say today that what began as a fair trial of ethics was being corrupted by this intervention. In magic, however, all tricks were permitted. And the postscript of spell 30B clearly states that this charm was discovered by none other than Prince Hordedef under the feet of an image of Thoth–the same god who served as clerk to the court by writing down the outcome of the weighing and thereby deciding the fate of the deceased (fig. 9). Clearly, this meant that the celestial powers approved the spell.

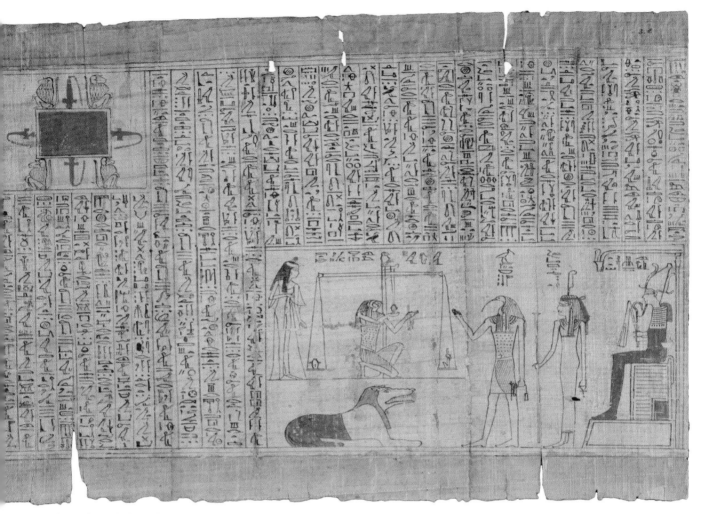

FIG. 127. The weighing of the heart is here performed by Horus. He is being observed on the left by Thoth, Ma'at, and Osiris. Below, the Swallower of the Dead impatiently awaits the outcome. From the Book of the Dead of Taiuheryt. Photograph: RMO (acc.no. AMS 40).

Once he had passed this test, the deceased finally acquired the status of one 'true of voice' and was allowed to become a follower of Osiris. As a token of his vindication he was crowned with a wreath of flowers, as specified in spells 19 and 20 from the Book of the Dead: *Your father Atum ties this beautiful garland of justification around your forehead. As the beloved of the gods lives, so you shall live forever. Osiris, the first of the westerners, declares your victory over your enemies, and your father Geb hands you his inheritance.* That both Atum and Geb are said to be the father of the dead man is proof that he has become an Osiris and is ready to begin his eternal existence.

Of course, depositing a copy of these two texts inside the tomb was yet another magical trick meant to ensure

a positive decision by the tribunal. Indeed, ancient Egyptians were so certain of a favorable result that, even before the trial had been held, they added the predicate 'true of voice' to the name of the deceased in all funerary inscriptions. In the same way, they liked to tie a floral wreath around his head, or a replica in stucco or gold leaf. Such naturalistic garlands made of gold leaf were most popular during the Greco-Roman period, perhaps because they were confused with the trophies given to victorious sportsmen or generals by the Greeks and Romans. That same period saw the rise of yet another type of funerary text, the Book of Breathing, which usually included the Spell of the Garland. A papyrus scroll bearing this spell was found next to the mummy of the Romano-Egyptian girl Sensaos, which shows that the belief in a 'last judgment' (and in the possibility of affecting its outcome) still existed as late as AD 109, when she was buried.

THE QUEST FOR ENLIGHTENMENT

So far, we have learned how eternal life could be acquired. But what did it look like? What did one do all day, and where did one stay? The Egyptian texts are rather vague about these questions, but one thing is clear: because of the great mobility of the *ba* (soul), which flies around as a bird, the deceased could be in several places at once. Moreover, apart from the soul the Egyptians distinguished several other immortal aspects of a human being, such as the vitality or identity (*ka*, fig. 29), the blessed spirit *(akh)*, the shadow, the name, the fate *(shay)*, the corpse *(khat)* or the mummy *(sah)*. During life all these were linked together, but after death they parted company and each went its own way. This explains how all concepts regarding the afterlife could be true simultaneously: the deceased lies in the burial chamber, receives offerings in the tomb chapel, resides in the subterranean realm of Osiris, and at the same time

FIG. 128. This luxurious heart scarab of green stone is mounted in gold and suspended from a gold chain. The undersurface is inscribed with the text of chapter 30B from the Book of the Dead. Photograph: RMO (acc.no. AO 1).

he is sitting in the bark of the solar god. Like the god Osiris he is alive and dead; like the god Re his existence consists of continual transformations. The book known as The Litany of the Sun distinguishes no fewer than seventy-four forms of Re. The dead do not change shape that often, but they still do so frequently.

Some spells from the Book of the Dead describe these transformations in detail. Thus spell 76 helps one *to assume all the appearances which one likes to assume.* Spell 77 serves for transforming oneself into a golden falcon, and spell 78 for appearing as a divine falcon. The next few spells enable one to become the president of the divine tribunal (79), a god who fills darkness with light (80), a lotus flower (81, fig. 77), the god Ptah (82), a phoenix (83), a heron (84), a living *ba* (85), a swallow (86), a serpent (87), or a crocodile (88). The common denominator in this heterogeneous company is the element of mobility, because unlike humans these creatures can speed through the air or dive to the mysterious depths of water or earth. The concomitant illustrations help the deceased to fulfill his requests, as do the amulets that were occasionally laid on the mummies: gold falcons, soul birds, or a gold Ptah around the neck, or a small beeswax image of the phoenix in the region of the heart.

The phoenix *(benu)* is a rather mysterious creature in Egyptian mythology. The Greek traveler Herodotus asserts that it manifested itself once every five hundred years, while other classical authors write that the bird was resurrected from its own ashes. These stories differ from the real pharaonic traditions, however, and the Egyptians themselves rather stressed the connection of the bird with Atum, Osiris, and Re, with eternity and resurrection, and with the heart and the soul. It was generally represented as a heron, for instance in the common limestone molds found in Late Period tombs (fig. 31). These consist of two stone tiles with a bird-shaped recess in the center, which fit together. Remains of beeswax demonstrate that these molds served for modeling wax figures, doubtless in order

to help the deceased magically transform into a phoenix and thereby to obtain resurrection.

For that was the final aim of these transformations: to live forever. Various magical objects placed in the burial chamber helped the deceased to realize this goal. Among them are the so-called concubine figures (fig. 82), statuettes depicting naked women, often lying on a bed. In fact their common designation is utterly wrong, because it suggests that such figurines were only given to men to provide for their sexual needs. However, these statuettes in ceramic or stone are also found in female tombs, which implies they must have had a quite different function. Often the women are depicted together with children, sometimes breast-feeding them. This rather implies that the statuettes represented general fertility for both men and women, resulting in the magical ability to produce offspring even after death. As mentioned previously, similar figurines were presented to the shrines of the goddess Hathor by the living. This patron deity of love and sex was also considered to be a guardian for the dead, and so the presence in tombs of votive offerings to Hathor is not surprising. Presumably, yet another aspect connected with these 'concubines' is that humans were thought to live on in their children. Having numerous offspring was therefore almost synonymous with living forever.

Another symbol of new life consisted of small bowls made of bright blue faience, also deposited in the burial chambers (fig. 129). The decoration in black lines on their exterior and interior is generally dominated by lotus patterns. Often the flower petals on the exterior walls are represented in such a way that the bowl itself looks like an open lotus umbel. On the inner walls the lotus and papyrus motifs are grouped around a central rectangular element which can be identified as a pond. Other elements occurring here are masks of the goddess Hathor, fish, and sometimes birds. The blue color of the glaze may refer to the blue lotus (although the flowers represented occasionally show the rounded petals of the white lotus),

FIG. 129. This bright blue bowl symbolizes the primeval water. This explains the pond motif in the center, from which grow a lotus and a Hathor head. Two tilapia fish are also represented. Photograph: RMO (acc.no. F 1981/5.2).

of life that the Egyptians compared to that of the scarab. Therefore the tilapia was a symbol of new life, not only on these bowls but on other objects as well. Scholars used to assume that the 'Nun bowls' were originally filled with water. However, the white encrustation and cheesy smell of several specimens rather points to the use of milk, a liquid that often appears in lists of funerary offerings. After all, the reborn individual was like a newborn baby, and milk would give him the strength he needed (see fig. 48).

In temple ritual we have already encountered yet another efficient means to ensure resurrection: the grain-mummy (fig. 98). The royal tombs of the New Kingdom contained wooden seed beds in the guise of the body of Osiris, sown with germinating barley. Texts dating to the same period imply the presence of grain-mummies in private tombs as well, although none have ever been found. It is not before the Late Period that some monumental Theban tombs seem to include a special underground chamber in which a grain-mummy could be placed (and periodically renewed). The same period saw the development of an alternative form of grain-mummy, so unobtrusive that it has only recently been recognized as such. These are small figurines made of clay and barley and wrapped in linen. Sometimes they were inserted between the mummy wrappings of the deceased, but in most cases they were hidden inside a cavity in the body or in the base of a wooden Osiris statue set next to the coffin of the deceased (fig. 130). Osiris is here identified with the god of resurrection, Ptah-Sokar, and wears an unusual headdress of ram's horns, a solar disk, and ostrich feathers. Both the texts inscribed on these statues and the other decorations (in which the blue color of the primeval water recurs) stress the notion of new life after death. The grain-mummies enhance the magical assurance of rebirth in the same way as they do in the annual temple rituals. This custom survived until well into the Ptolemaic period.

With the combined effect of all these magical objects, the deceased could be certain to acquire a divine status

but it is also reminiscent of the primeval water *(Nun)*, the source of all life. This accords well with the pond motif, while Hathor adds a specific funerary aspect. In this respect the fish are also interesting, because they are always depicted as tilapia, a species that carries its own eggs in its mouth until they hatch. At that moment, the adult suddenly spits out its infants, a mysterious origin

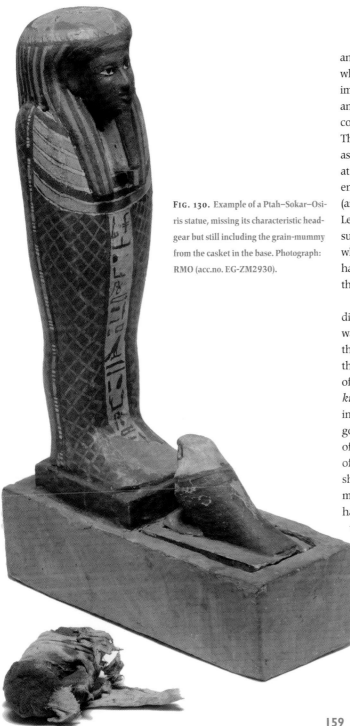

FIG. 130. Example of a Ptah–Sokar–Osiris statue, missing its characteristic headgear but still including the grain-mummy from the casket in the base. Photograph: RMO (acc.no. EG-ZM2930).

and the ensuing eternal life. Although it is not quite clear whether the Egyptians regarded their gods to be quite immortal, at least they believed in an eternal cycle of life and death. The deceased would now become part of this cosmic cycle and would thereby enter a new phase of life. The Egyptian texts express this by designating the deceased as an 'illuminated being' *(sehedj)* or an *akh*: a spirit having at his disposal all those faculties (including magic) that enable him to survive and even to affect the life of others (an *akh iker* or 'effective spirit,' as they are called in the Letters to the Dead). One of the manifestations of this supernatural status was the light spread by the deceased, which indicated his affinity with the solar god. His body had become gold-colored like that of the gods, as shown by the funerary masks of coffins (fig. 44).

This effusion of light was a direct effect of achieving divine status. According to Egyptian magic, however, there was no distinction between cause and effect. Might it not therefore be possible to deify the dead by first helping them to disperse light? To that effect, most manuscripts of the Book of the Dead end with spell 162, a *formula for kindling a flame under the head of a spirit*. It involves an invocation to the sun god, the son of the celestial cow goddess, begging him to provide the deceased with a bit of light. The spell had to be recited over a gold figurine of the celestial cow, which had also to be drawn on a sheet of papyrus to be placed under the head of the mummy. Indeed, such amulets of papyrus, linen, or metal have survived, generally in the shape of disks inscribed with magical pictures and texts (fig. 131) known as *hypocephali* (Greek, meaning 'under the skull'). They are a relatively late phenomenon in Egyptian tombs and are usually dated between the fourth and second centuries BC.

And with this last chapter of the Book of the Dead we leave the mysterious world of the hereafter, reassured by the conviction that the deceased has become a source of light *whose rising never ends* (as

spell 162 puts it). Indeed, one can observe a circular spot of light or nimbus behind the head of the deceased in late-pharaonic funerary portraits and shrouds (fig. 132). It is only a small step from there to early Christian art, where the halo became a fixed attribute of saints. As we shall see, numerous other magical concepts and practices would survive the transition from one religion to another.

FIG. 132. A shroud from the Greco-Roman period represents the deceased with a blue halo behind his head and the wreath of justification in his hands. Isis stands to the right; Anubis is just visible to the left, holding out the key to the netherworld. Photograph: RMO (acc.no. F 1968/2.1).

FIG. 131. Apart from the Cow of Heaven, this hypocephalus shows the barks of sun and moon and the god of the four cardinal points. Photograph: RMO (acc.no. AMS 62).

A CHANGING WORLD

As my teacher Hermes used to tell me in confidence . . . , to those who read my books my writing style may appear to be simple and clear, but on the contrary it is obscure, because the words have a deeper, occult significance. And this style will become even more obscure when the Greeks will later translate our Egyptian language into their own language. That will result in total distortion and corruption.

(Corpus Hermeticum, XVI.1)

FIG. 133. Marble colonette of the Greco-Roman period. The baboon and the ibis are the two animals sacred to the god Thoth. Photograph: Allard Pierson Museum, Amsterdam (acc.no. 07946).

ORIENTAL WISDOM

In 332 BC the Macedonian prince Alexander the Great conquered Egypt after a short-lived Persian occupation. He founded the harbor city of Alexandria as the country's new capital, visited the oracle in the oasis of Siwa, and then immediately continued the conquests that would eventually bring him as far as India. Upon his death ten years later, the rule of Egypt fell to his general Ptolemy (I), who founded a dynasty of Greek pharaohs. In 31 BC the last ruler of that royal line, Cleopatra VII, lost her country to the Romans.

The arrival of the Greeks, and later the Romans, changed the character of pharaonic culture. While Egypt had always been rather isolated from foreign influence, the cosmopolitan city of Alexandria now opened up the country to the rest of the world. As the Ptolemies embellished the city with public monuments and large temples and palaces, great throngs of foreign artists and scholars arrived with the intention of contributing to the development of a new culture: Hellenism. This amounted to an amalgamation of elements derived from Greek civilization with oriental traditions valued in the conquered regions. Material remains of the resulting culture can still be seen around the Mediterranean, but Alexandria formed one of its focal points. Even after the annexation of power by the Romans and the loss of Alexandria's status as a royal residence, the harbor city continued to be the absolute center of culture in the eastern Mediterranean.

The cosmopolitan climate was dominated by the Greeks, and Greek also became the language of the new elite. Cultural life was concentrated around the Mouseion, Alexandria's sanctuary of the Muses. This was connected to an extensive library unrivalled in all the world. Here poets and authors, historians and geographers, philosophers, astronomers, and natural scientists studied the thousands of scrolls in which all available knowledge of the era had been collected and recorded. These included translations and editions of indigenous sources. To the Greeks and Romans, Egyptian culture was already incredibly ancient and incomparably learned. In their opinion, a civilization which had managed to erect so many miraculous monuments at so early a period had to possess supernatural wisdom. Part of that occult knowledge had doubtless been recorded in the Egyptian texts, especially in the mysterious hieroglyphs. Since bilingual people could still be found at that time, the Egyptian texts might now reveal their secrets to the newcomers from Europe. The texts being studied included the Egyptian books of magic, which were treated with the same kind of awe nowadays reserved for the publications of top scientists. Like these, the ancient scrolls were believed to demonstrate how the universe functioned and how the gods had allowed humanity to glimpse that superior truth. This concept perfectly matched the Greek philosophical theories of authors like Plato and Pythagoras, who likewise asserted that what can be seen on earth by mortal eyes is only a poor reflection of the harmony of higher spheres.

The findings of the Greeks' remarkable quest for knowledge were codified in the so-called Hermetic treatises. Seventeen have been preserved, some of which date to the last centuries before the Christian era while others were composed during the Roman imperial period. These seventeen texts are very diverse, varying from discussions of theological issues such as the relationship between God, humanity, and the world, to astrological,

FIG. 134. This relief presents a good example of the merging religious traditions of the Hellenistic period. Isis and Osiris have been depicted as serpents, by association with the agathodaimon or guardian spirit of the house. Osiris sports the hair and beard of the new god Serapis. The serpents flank an image of the god Osiris Canopus, represented as a vessel with life-giving Nile water. Photograph: RMO (acc.no. F 1960/9.1).

medical, or alchemical texts, or even magical formulas comparable to those known from the Eighth Book of Moses (fig. 68) and related compositions. Again this suggests that no distinction was yet made between what we would regard as scientific knowledge on the one hand, and esoteric or occult wisdom on the other.

One common feature of the Hermetic treatises is that their authorship is attributed to none other than the Egyptian god of wisdom, Thoth, now often called Hermes Trismegistus ('the thrice great' Hermes, fig. 133). It is noteworthy that Hermes Trismegistus is regarded as a human prophet and teacher, rather than as a god. Finally the magic book of Thoth had been found, and in its Greek edition it became a best seller. The philosophical and Neoplatonic ideas about the good God and the evil world, about the material and spiritual aspects of human nature, and about enlightenment as a divine gift were further elaborated in the Gnostic teachings, which aimed to acquire superior wisdom by studying the widely divergent revelations of all kinds of religions. Rather more down to earth were the so-called Gnostic amulets, usually gemstones carved with images of various oriental divinities and provided with captions in Greek and a variety of magic signs and symbols (fig. 34).

While these new ideas were developing in European circles, the pharaonic traditions survived as before in the Egyptian hinterland. For several centuries more the priests continued to present offerings to the numerous gods and their sacred animals, while the local population kept to the age-old funerary customs. Egyptian officials still wrote their documents in the demotic script and the villagers

kept the ancient Egyptian language alive. Contacts with the Greek government were restricted to the registration of important administrative acts and tax declarations. In fact, the important political changes which characterized these declining years of Egyptian civilization rather increased people's trust in magic. People sought comfort from the gods and the sorcerers as a reaction to the vicissitudes of anarchy and foreign occupation. There is no other period which has produced so many magical texts, partly because the priests realized that the traditional way of life was under threat. To preserve the precious texts, which had hitherto been handed down only in the fragile papyrus scrolls kept in the Houses of Life, they carved them onto the stone walls of the major temples being erected everywhere by order of the Ptolemies (fig. 91). As a result of this fortunate decision we can still find copies of the purely pharaonic esoteric treatises, so different from contemporaneous Alexandrian sources.

Gradually, the two distinct worlds started to merge. The local people made increasing use of imported articles from Alexandria or neighboring Mediterranean countries. Well-educated Egyptians began to learn Greek, dressed according to the latest fashion, and furnished their homes in a new way. They also derived new ideas from the cosmopolitan foreigners, including religious views—as we have seen from our discussion of the fourth-century Theban papyrus archive. All kinds of oriental cults began to form, both in Alexandria (where whole districts were inhabited by Jews, Persians, and other immigrants) and in the countryside. These cults included downright mysteries such as those connected with Demeter, Cybele, or Mithras, mysteries which promised their initiates a better life and an existence after death. Such ideas were easily accepted by the Egyptian population, long used to similar concepts from their own religion, especially those connected with the god Osiris (fig. 134). In the urban centers, the new ideas amalgamated to some extent with notions derived from Hermetism or Gnosticism. The authorities generally tolerated these exotic religions, as long as their followers did not upset order, behaved as loyal citizens, and took part in the obligatory cult of the ruler.

It was this last requirement which generated conflict with yet another new creed: Christianity, which expected its adherents to acknowledge the existence of only one god. This led to the well-known persecution of the earliest Christians. In Egypt some of them fled to the deserts, where they could also escape from the increasing burden of taxation and other obligations imposed by the central government. Here the first monastic communities of Christianity were formed, institutions which did not spread over the rest of the Empire until much later. In AD 312 the Emperor Constantine converted to Christianity, and eighty years later Theodosius proclaimed it the official religion of the Roman Empire. Now it was the turn of the traditional polytheistic cults to be persecuted, while schisms and councils made an effort to strip the new religion of unorthodox notions derived from Hermetism, Gnosticism, and other sources.

In Egypt the Christians decided to go their own way, because they refused to distinguish between the divine and the human natures of Christ (one of the most hotly debated issues of the early Church). The Egyptian Monophysite Church therefore split from the Orthodox Church after the Council of Chalcedon in AD 451. This led to the gradual disappearance of Greek influence, as represented by the learned theologians and philosophers of Alexandria, and the increase of indigenous and popular elements. The Egyptian Christians preferred to recite the liturgy in their native language—which was none other than the last phase of the ancient Egyptian colloquial language that had been spoken for thousands of years. They banned the use of the traditional writing systems, however, to prevent any association with paganism. The Coptic language was therefore written with Greek letters, with the addition of a number of demotic signs for rendering phonemes unknown to Greek (figs. 137–40).

A CHRISTIAN VARNISH

Magic had always been an essential aspect of ancient Egyptian religion, which in its turn formed the foundation of pharaonic culture. The advent of Christianity resulted in a radical change. The temples were closed, divine statues and wall reliefs were smashed, and the meanings of the hieroglyphs were forgotten. In spite of all this, several ancient traditions survived under a Christian varnish, and these included concepts about magic. We may rightly call them superstitious, because officially they clashed with the ideas of the new religion. Tradition, however, was stronger than orthodoxy, so that finally even priests and bishops surreptitiously permitted all kinds of practices that were not at all Christian. These included the vandalism unleashed against the pharaonic monuments, which was based as much on the superstitious fear of the intrinsic life of the pagan images as on the fanaticism of the recently converted. This explains why eyes, in particular, were cut out, from both human and divine figures, because people continued to fear the evil eye. There were persistent stories about the appearance of ghosts in certain deserted areas, where some of the ancient deities and demons were said to manifest themselves.

An unpleasant encounter with one such figure is described in the hagiography of Apa (Saint) Moses, a saint who lived at Abydos during the second half of the sixth century. After having destroyed the local shrine of Apollo (Horus) through the force of his prayer, Apa Moses met with much more violent opposition in the age-old temple of Osiris, a little to the north of the monastery he had founded. This place was haunted by a demon called Bes, after the former dwarf god and protector of the domestic sphere who used to possess an oracle here (figs. 12 and 90). The present apparition was much more malignant, though, and liked to harass innocent passersby, many of whom emerged from their encounter partially blind, lame, or unable to speak. Moses decided to put an end

to this threat and spent a night praying in the temple, accompanied by seven monks. Exactly at midnight the demon showed himself in an orgy of thunder and lightning, the temple was in danger of collapse, and a host of apparitions overwhelmed the poor brethren. Of course, victory belonged to the true religion. The defeated representative of the ancient cult retreated and was never seen again.

This is only one of the manifold miracles worked by the adherents of the new creed. Although the Copts were careful to attribute such miracles to the power of God, in everyday practice the distinction between the Christian priest and the pagan sorcerer was negligible. Both claimed to be able to heal patients, dispel demons, domesticate wild animals, speak with the dead, and find treasure. Examples of such works of wonder can be found in the *Apophthegmata patrum aegyptorum*, a well-known book containing instructions by the fathers of the Coptic Church: *Once upon a time one of our fathers sent one of his disciples to fetch water. The pit was very far from the monk's cell, and he had forgotten to bring a length of string. Arriving at the pit, he discovered that he had not got the string with him. Therefore he prayed as follows: 'O pit! My father says: "Fill my jar with water!"' And immediately the water rose up, the brother filled his jar, and the water receded to its former level.* Such exploits are strongly reminiscent of those performed by Djadjaemankh at the court of Snefru three thousand years before, when he folded back the water to retrieve a piece of jewelry from the bottom of a pond.

Like their pagan counterparts, the Coptic priests also sold amulets to those believers who called upon their help. Instead of the figurines of deities, sacred animals, or hieroglyphic signs, the Christian Egyptians now wore crosses around their necks, or medallions and bracelets inscribed with protective formulas and the figures of saints (fig. 135). Especially popular were equestrian saints such as St. George, commemorating the fate of the numerous

FIG. 135. Coptic bracelet of iron and copper. The rectangular elements are inscribed with a protective formula; the rounded medallions show mounted saints and other decorative motifs. Photograph: RMO (acc.no. F 1943/3.2).

Roman army officers tortured to death for their adherence to Christianity, but at the same time bearing a rather suspicious resemblance to the armed and occasionally mounted evil-averting divinities of the Egyptian pantheon (such as the popular statuettes depicting Horus on horseback). A bronze plaque in the Louvre shows a male figure carrying a palm branch and dominating a serpent, a dog, and a crocodile: wild animals with no Christian connotations at all, but which reflect rather the well-known images on Horus stelae (fig. 136).

The belief in the power of the written word was another traditional notion. Thus the Copts, too, liked to arm themselves with inscribed strips of papyrus that functioned as amulets. A portion from the confession of faith, followed by downright abracadabra, could protect against fevers; complete books could also be used as talismans. An example of the latter is a leather-bound codex in the Leiden Museum (fig. 137). The thirty-two pages of papyrus contain a number of prayers by St. Gregory, an exorcism of the devil, a list of martyrs, and the opening words of the four Gospels. The book derives its main significance, however, from the nine pages containing copies of the correspondence between Jesus and Abgar. The latter was king of Edessa, in southern Turkey, and an inveterate pagan. In this book, he has been confused with another Abgar, a successor who lived centuries later and converted to Christianity. The correspondence is thus a blatant forgery, although this did not prevent the third-century author Eusebius from including these apocryphal texts in his ecclesiastical history. Translations into numerous other languages soon added the story that the presence of these letters in Edessa

FIG. 136. This bronze tablet is inscribed with several unclear texts in Greek and Arabic. The representations include a human figure carrying a palm branch and triumphing over a serpent, a lion, and a crocodile. Photograph: © 2004 Musée du Louvre/ Georges Poncet (acc. no. AF 11704).

169

Letter of Jesus to Abgar

(PAPYRUS CODEX LEIDEN AMS 9, PAGE 24)

The letter of Jesus Christ, our Lord, to Aukaros. Amen.

The copy of the letter of Jesus Christ, the Son of the living God, which he wrote to Aukaros, King of Etessa.

"Greetings! Blessings to you and good things will happen to you and blessed is your town, of which the name is Etessa. Because you have not seen and yet you have believed, you will be rewarded in accordance with your faith and in accordance with your good intention. Your complaints will be healed, and even if as a man you have committed many sins, these will be forgiven you. And Etessa will be blessed until eternity. The majesty of God will increase among its population, and faith and love will shine in its streets.

I, Jesus, it is I who commands and it is I who speaks. Because you have greatly loved, I shall make your name to be an eternal memory and a reverence and a blessing among the generations which will come after you in your whole fatherland, and it will be heard till the end of the world.

I, Jesus, it is I who wrote this letter with my own hand. The place where one will publicly affix this manuscript, no force of the devil and no impure spirit will be able to approach or to touch this place until eternity.

Fare you well in peace! Amen."

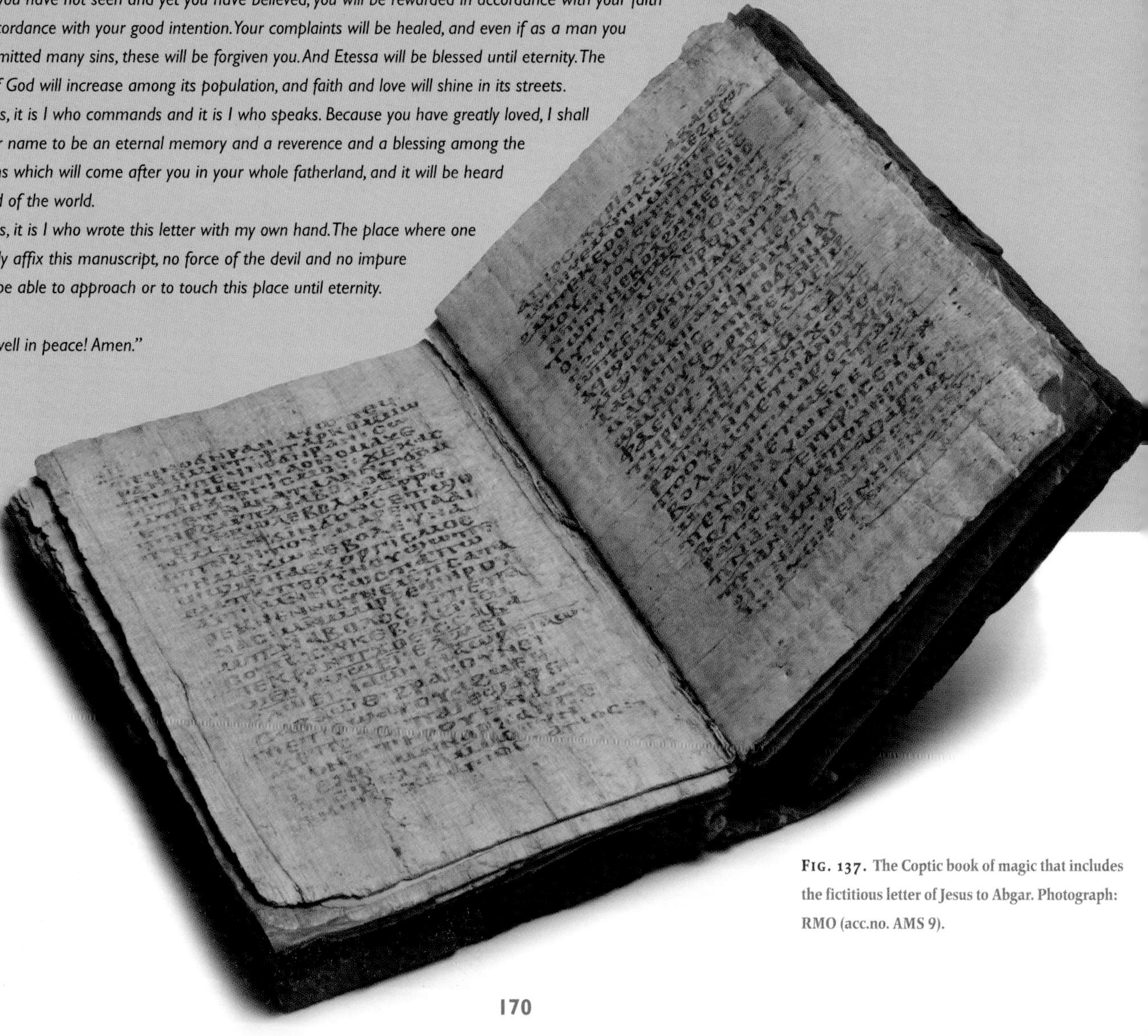

FIG. 137. The Coptic book of magic that includes the fictitious letter of Jesus to Abgar. Photograph: RMO (acc.no. AMS 9).

had prevented the town from being conquered on several occasions, especially when they were nailed to the wall above the city gates. The inclusion of a Coptic version of the correspondence in the codex thus made it effective in protecting against the devil and his henchmen! A similar protective function can be attributed to a large limestone ostracon inscribed with the text of Exodus 15:1–19 (fig. 138). This is the hymn sung by Moses after he had safely crossed the Red Sea, a song which glorifies God's power over the enemies of Israel.

The examples above might suggest that Coptic sorcerers obediently practiced only permitted forms of magic: as long as they invoked God to save his flock in its distress, all was well. The pages of contemporary books of magic, however, show that 'black' magic was practiced as well. One sheet, now in Leiden (fig. 139), shows a vignette of a human figure whose head is pierced by an arrow and who is flanked by two winged demons. At the bottom of the page a magic circle has been drawn by tracing the inner and outer contours of a finger-ring, a common prescription known from the Greek magical papyri. Both illustrations are surrounded by weird letters with strokes ending in roundels, so-called *charaktères* which became popular in the second century AD. This cipher script was considered especially suitable for communicating with superior powers.

The text on the rest of this page concerns a spell for obtaining control over a woman. A copy of the spell in question had to be buried near the door to her house during a full-moon night, and this ritual had to be accompanied by a burnt offering. The reverse of the page is inscribed with the abstracts of several spells for manipulating other people: enchanting them, separating or matching couples, causing ruin or death. In short, these can hardly be regarded as good Christian actions. To make matters worse, the sorcerer invokes a number of supernatural beings that are quite unrelated

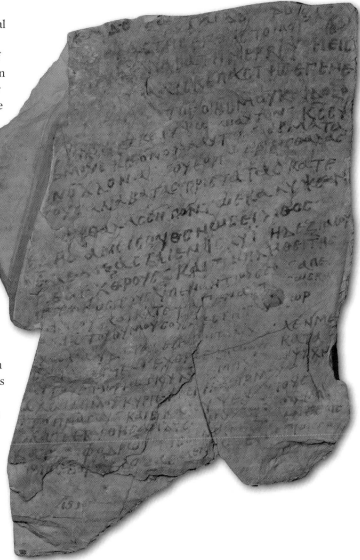

FIG. 138. Perhaps this large slab of limestone was put up to keep evil demons away from a house or shrine. It carries a protective spell from the Old Testament, written in Coptic script. Photograph: RMO (acc.no. AAL 161).

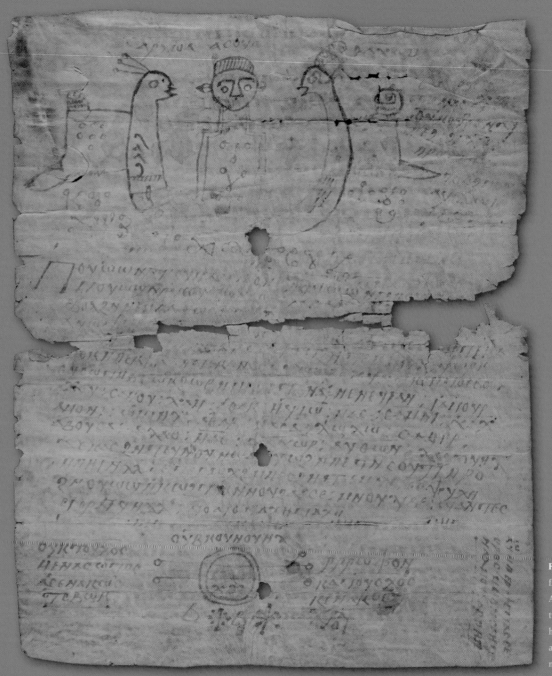

FIG. 139. Sheet of parchment from a Coptic book of magic. Above, there is a vignette depicting two winged demons flanking a human head which is pierced by an arrow. Photograph: RMO (acc. no. F 1964/4.14).

to the Biblical God. They belong to the company of the twenty-one 'decans' (three times seven, a well-known magical number)—the direct successors of the ancient Egyptian personifications of the ten-day 'weeks' and the henchmen of Sekhmet who attack humanity at the end of the year. The names carried by these avenging angels have an exotic ring. Some are reminiscent of their pharaonic precursors, others are derived from Hermetic or Gnostic sources. And yet this text can be dated to the eleventh century, long after the Coptic Church had officially severed its links with paganism.

Even more striking is a text that has been preserved on a camel rib now in Leiden (fig. 140). The writing material itself is already rather macabre and thereby betrays the magical intention with which it was selected. The red ink in which the text is written also suggests magic, for red was the color of evil and was associated with blood. The obverse and reverse bear the same text, and a third copy was inscribed on another rib. Threefold repetition was an approved method in Egyptian magic. The text, which is full of misspellings and other errors, reads as follows: *Kouchos, Trochos, Aphonos, Pesphokops and Plemos and Ouliat: these are the six powers of death, these which bring every soul out of every body. They are those that will go to Aaron, the son of Tkouikira. I adjure you, O dead one, by the way you were taken and the manner in which you went and the fearful places and the raging river of fire which you saw and all your sufferings: may you bring all your suffering on Aaron, the son of Tkouikira. Yes, quickly! I adjure you, O dead one, by the way you were taken and the fearful places to which you were taken and the fearful places which you saw and the raging river of fire, that you may bring all your suffering; that, as soon as I place this bone beneath you, you*

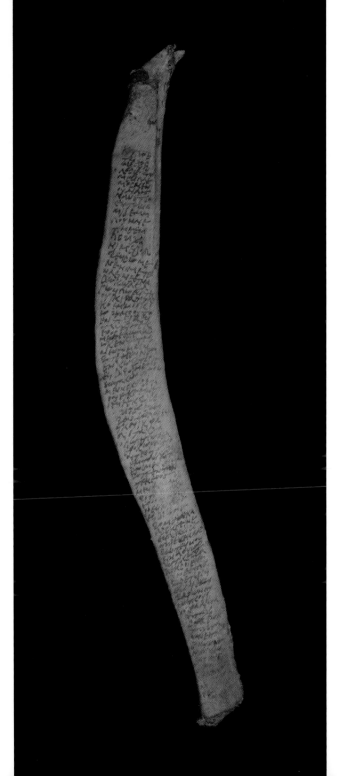

FIG. 140. Camel rib inscribed with a Coptic curse in red ink. Photograph: RMO (acc.no. F 1965/8.5).

bring all your suffering over Aaron, the son of Tkouikira.
Yes, quickly, quickly! Come, come! Quickly, quickly!

This tenth-century document is a product of pure black magic, not only because the sorcerer threatens to plunge someone into distress, but also because to that end celestial powers are invoked which bear no relation to the Christian God. Admittedly, the six genii of death occur elsewhere in Coptic apocryphal literature, but that does not mean they were acknowledged by the official religious doctrine. The practice of taking vengeance on someone by calling for the assistance of a recently departed soul originates rather in ancient Egypt, where letters to the dead (fig. 105) and the invocation of the spirits of those who had died young or violently were common. As a rule, the Christian Church taught that this was not just witchcraft but also heresy, and that such practices therefore called for capital punishment. These doctrines were more characteristic of Europe, however, where the persecution of witchcraft was not restricted to the 'dark' Middle Ages but claimed the lives of thousands of innocent men and women during the so-called centuries of Enlightenment. In the Middle East people were perhaps less barbaric, because they managed to reserve a special position for this kind of anomalous behavior. This concerned not just the Christians, but also all those who converted to the new religion of Islam.

JINN AND BURIED PEARLS

In the year AD 639 a small army of Arabs commanded by Amr ibn al-'As conquered Egypt, a country which by then had become thoroughly Christian under the rule of the Eastern Roman (or Byzantine) emperors. The Copts rather liked this conquest, which put an end to the detested burden of taxation, the conscription for military service, and the religious repression by the Byzantines (who had always regarded Monophysitism as a form of heresy).

Their rule was now replaced by the relatively tolerant government of the caliphs, who resided in Damascus or Baghdad, and their local governors in Cairo. This new capital of Egypt grew from the army camps of the Arab invaders and soon assumed the position of cultural center for the Near East that had formerly been occupied by Alexandria. The new rulers permitted the indigenous population to stick to their traditional convictions, but financial and social incentives nevertheless stimulated large numbers of Copts to convert to the religion of the newcomers. Gradually they even gave up their own language in favor of Arabic, a vernacular that allowed them to seek their fortune as migrant workers, merchants, or mercenaries anywhere in the Islamic world. Even so, the majority of the Egyptians continued to live in their own country, and some of them kept the faith of their fathers alive. Today, Coptic Christians still make up about 10 percent of the Egyptian population.

Conversely, Islam in Egypt became subject to the influence of the age-old culture that still lingered at the time of Amr's conquest. Thus all kinds of traditions were adopted which were unrelated to the official religious doctrines, including well-defined magical convictions. Officially Islam rejects sorcery, unless it is practiced in the name of God and makes use of Qur'anic texts. Indeed the Qur'an contains some evidence for the existence of pre-Islamic magical traditions on the Arabian peninsula. For instance, Sura 113 ensures protection against black magic and refers to the use of knotted cords, which was already known from Middle Kingdom Egypt: *Say: I seek refuge with the Lord of daybreak from the evil of what He has created, from the evil of a dark night when He appears, and from the evil of those who blow on knots, and from the evil of an envious person in his envy.* The last clause is a clear reference to the widely held belief in the evil eye, a conviction which is often rejected by the more orthodox clerics even though Muhammad himself is said to have accepted it.

A frequently professed Islamic conviction is that all magical knowledge ultimately derives from King Solomon. He is alleged to have composed a series of books summarizing all occult wisdom—a new edition of the magic book of Thoth perhaps? Although Solomon himself is said to have owed his knowledge to revelations from jinn or Satan, his strong personality would have enabled him to turn this into something positive. This explains why Islamic treatises on magic often attribute all kinds of ideas to Solomon as the ultimate authority. It had the further advantage that those who merely followed his example could never be accused of heresy, since Solomon was regarded as a pious Muslim. Thus sorcery became an inherent part of everyday practice in Islamic countries.

Of course, it is nonsense to claim that this is due to the exclusive influence of ancient Egypt. Long before Islam was codified as a religious doctrine, the Near East went through an era characterized by the free circulation of numerous other cultural traditions, in which Greco-Roman civilization and the ideas of Hermetism left important traces. The earliest translations into Arabic of the Hermetic treatises probably date back to the third century and so predate the rise of Islam. These texts exerted a strong influence on Persian astrology, and the astrologers in their turn disseminated them at the court of the eighth-century caliphs. In Arabic tradition, Hermes Trismegistus acquired the reputation of having been a prophet, legislator, and the founding father of philosophy and natural science. Such scientific traditions were designated in Arabic as 'Egyptian' (*kimiya'*), a word derived from *Kemet* (literally 'the black land'), which was the name the ancient Egyptians used for their own country. Our words chemistry and alchemy are derived from this term.

Alongside the court culture dominated by scholars and their Hermetic background, all regions conquered by the Arabs had their own particular folklore. Naturally, this differed from one country to another, and evidently the ideas derived from pharaonic tradition played a more

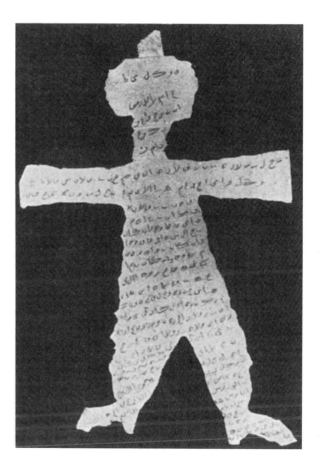

FIG. 141. Figure torn from a sheet of paper and inscribed with an Arabic spell. Reproduction after Blackman, *The Fellahīn of Upper Egypt,* fig. 117.

FIG. 142. Example of a modern 'hand of Fatima' or *khamsa* from Morocco.
Photograph: RMO (private collection).

important part in Egypt than in other regions of the Islamic world. The early twentieth-century anthropologist Winifred Blackman describes how, in those days, every Egyptian village still had its local sorcerer. He or she specialized in exorcising evil spirits and healing simple complaints, gave advice in case of fertility problems, and sold amulets.

It appears these sorcerers also practiced black magic, tossing wax images in the fire or piercing them with needles, or dissolving clay figurines in water to torture or kill an opponent. To force a victim to come to their home, Egyptians of this period were advised to hang above a bowl of incense a figure torn from a sheet of paper and inscribed with an enchantment (fig. 141). The text in question reads: *O King Tarish, King Kasura, and King Zoba who has four heads! Go, you three great kings of the netherworld, and order your servants to bring X, the son of Y. If he is seated, make him stand up, and snatch him up, mount him on a horse, and fly with him through the air till you arrive at my house!* Equally well known was the use of magic squares containing combinations of letters or numbers. Some rituals required killing a black chicken, or hiding a hen's egg in a tomb to engage the spirit of the deceased.

All of these magical practices already occur in the demotic and Greek papyri of the Ptolemaic and Roman periods! In modern Egypt, such customs are rapidly disappearing, although in the rural areas in particular some traditions live on, such as the Egyptian habit of organizing a picnic on the graves of their ancestors at the occasion of the Bairam festival: a communal meal taken with the spirits of the deceased, which has a direct relationship with pharaonic customs such as the Feast of the Valley, and is thus distinctly un-Islamic.

The belief in amulets is still a common phenomenon in contemporary Egypt. Much use is made of texts from the Qur'an (for instance the Islamic profession of faith, the text of Sura 1, or the 'Throne Verse' of Sura 2). These talismans

FIG. 143. String of glass eye-beads from present-day Egypt.
Photograph: RMO (private collection).

are engraved on sheets of copper, to be worn around the neck or hung on the mirror of a car, or they are inscribed on strips of paper which are kept rolled up inside a small tube *(higab)*. Another common type are the hand-shaped amulets, often known as 'hands of Fatima' or, alternatively, as *khamsa* (five) because the fingers symbolize the five pillars of Islam and the five daily prayers (fig. 142). In spite of this Islamic interpretation, it is easy to recognize the ancient apotropaic gesture of the raised hand, which in Egypt occurred as early as the Middle Kingdom in the spells for mother and child.

Certain metal breastplates or pectorals *(luha)* inscribed with hands alongside daggers or serpents are also common. The belief in the evil eye is omnipresent, and as a precaution against it people wear finger-rings set with a rounded glass bezel, or necklaces consisting of eye-beads in blue glass with details in black and white (fig. 143). This is comparable to the similar use of the Eye of Horus *(wedjat)* in ancient Egypt, where eye-beads were also already known. Color symbolism is still a determining factor in the choice of jewelry: red is the color of blood, the heart, and love; blue symbolizes water and heaven;

FIG. 144. Modern silver *zar* amulets from Egypt.
Photograph: RMO (private collection).

green refers to plants and prosperity; yellow is connected with the sun. Amber is still widely used. The exact number of beads or pendants of a necklace is not randomly chosen but reflects a deeper significance.

The pharaonic remains themselves play a major part in the belief in the efficacy of amulets. Until well into the twentieth century, women who were unable to conceive would walk three times around the ruins of Egyptian temples. Authentic pharaonic figurines or amulets and their modern imitations were much in demand, and so were fragments of ancient mummies. Women with fertility problems were advised to step over them, seven times forward and backward, and were assured that this would lead to pregnancy. In 1850 the French archaeologist Auguste Mariette complained that he continually had to chase away the local women of Saqqara village, who came over to his excavations of the Serapeum to ride a newly found statue of the Apis bull! Another popular custom inherited from ancient Egypt (fig. 76) is the use of powdered stone scraped from the walls of temples and tombs and made into amulets or medicines. Even nowadays the superstition has not died out that evil spirits (jinn or *afarit*) haunt ancient ruins and that one should not go there after dark.

In modern Egypt, people (mostly women) who despite all precautions become possessed by such a spirit have to undergo an exorcising ritual *(zar)*. To this end a number of musicians armed with drums and tambourines visit the patient at home, to sing special songs and to dance. All participants wear strings of beads and silver pendants engraved with the depiction of the specific spirit concerned: Islamic saints, mermaids, or even ancient Egyptian sphinxes (fig. 144). Squares with numbers, the five- or six-pointed star of Solomon, and Qur'anic texts appear as well. If the ritual is successful and the spirit reveals his or her desires, a ritual of conciliation follows one week later, after which the patient is declared to have recovered. Evidently, such rituals fulfill an important social

role, forming an acceptable means for these patients to vent certain legitimate feelings of frustration.

An equivalent outlet (especially for men) is to take part in the religious processions performed on the occasion of the birthdays of Muslim saints. This can easily involve the gathering of thousands of neighborhood people at the local mosque, which becomes the center of an enormous fairground. Here magicians or holy men (*faqirs*) display their mastery over knives, fire, serpents, and scorpions. Doubtless, this is at least partly inspired by the age-old tradition of the 'conjurers of Selkit.' Ordinary people rather dread vermin and seek to drive scorpions from their homes by hanging protective bowls made of pottery or bronze (fig. 145). These depict evil-averting eyes, hands, scorpions, magic squares, or Qur'anic verses. Water from such bowls can be used as medicine for the treatment of scorpion stings, because it assumes magical power from the texts and representations on the bowl itself. A bizarre superstition perhaps connected with the fear of untamed desert animals is illustrated in a recent photograph taken of a window in Edfu, in which the dead bodies of a gazelle and a large lizard are suspended to ward off evil desert spirits (fig. 146).

In the *Thousand and One Nights*, constant reference is made to the discovery of hidden treasures. In Egypt such stories could acquire additional popularity from the fact that treasure troves are by no means rare. Thus, in the year 2000 an expedition of the Leiden Museum found a hoard of 246 silver coins at Saqqara, where it had been hidden in the ground by its owner during the turbulent events immediately preceding the accession of Queen Cleopatra. Other treasures consist of the considerable riches of gold and semi-precious stones deposited in the ancient tombs of some of the wealthiest Egyptians, or of the partly gilt and inlaid votive figurines of gods hidden under temple floors or in cavities in the walls whenever the priests decided to clear away the abundant gifts, left by pious pilgrims, which were obstructing the chapels of

FIG. 145. This modern ceramic bowl from Morocco protects the house against the evil eye. The decorations include an evil-averting hand, two scorpions, and two eyes. Photograph: © 2010 Wereldmuseum, Rotterdam (acc.no. 48330).

the sanctuary. During the Islamic period, most people would have heard of such finds in the ancient ruins, but very few had the courage to confront the dangerous jinn guarding the treasures.

This, however, proved to be a field where magicians could display their mastery. None other than the fourteenth-century historian 'Abd al-Rahman ibn Khaldun wrote a book about magic and amulets that contains a number of sections devoted to finding treasure. He prescribes killing a rooster on the spot suspected to hold treasure, and then smearing its blood onto a copper plate inscribed with magical texts and vignettes. Next, he advises that incense be burned and the plate covered with a piece of silk, tied with threads of wool. The text, which is directly inspired by the magic books of the Greco-Roman period, was regarded by countless generations to be an efficient charm and was even copied on to the copper plates in question. These also bear incised depictions of demons and other symbols, as well as fantastic writing allegedly derived from the long-forgotten scripts of ancient Egypt.

Another handbook for finding treasure is the fifteenth-century *Book of Buried Pearls*, which was so popular that it can be held responsible for much of the serious damage done to Egyptian antiquities by treasure

hunters. In an effort to put an end to this vandalism, the archaeologists Gaston Maspero and Ahmad Kamal published cheap Arabic and French editions of the book in 1907, hoping these would convince everybody that the book's instructions were utterly ridiculous. Their efforts, however, were in vain, for years later Winifred Blackman still described the practices of a village conjurer looking for treasure by means of a divining rod: a palm branch suspended from a construction of four sticks of olive wood, pomegranate, apricot, and tamarisk, planted in the

FIG. 146. Dead gazelle and lizard, hung from the window grille of a house in Edfu, Egypt. Photograph: Rob Demarée.

ground and tied together at the top. The rod was inscribed with magical signs referring to the four directions of the sky and was supposed to indicate which way to go. Even today nocturnal fortune hunters, now using bulldozers, still occasionally destroy the walls and floors of archaeological monuments in Egypt, so that the country's real treasures are lost forever in the quest for purely fictitious ones.

'ENLIGHTENED' EUROPE

Ten measures of magic came into the world. Egypt received nine of them, the rest of the world only one measure.

(TALMUD, B.QID. 49B)

BETWEEN WITCHCRAFT AND EGYPTOMANIA

As we have seen, the ancient Greeks and Romans took Egyptian magic very seriously. They were convinced that only the supernatural wisdom possessed by the Egyptians could explain the extraordinary things realized by this mysterious civilization. This conclusion was aptly summed up in the motto *Ex oriente lux* (all enlightenment comes from the east). Accordingly, the scholars of the Mouseion at Alexandria tried to record as much of the ancient occult knowledge as possible before it was lost forever. Thus a whole array of previously unknown magical practices became part of Greco-Roman folklore.

Gradually these concepts also spread outside Egypt, at first to the countries around the Mediterranean, and then also to Northern Europe, where the expansion of the Roman Empire resulted in a thorough Romanization of culture. A lead tablet inscribed with what seems to be a curse has even been found in the soil of Leiden in the Netherlands, where the Roman army camp of Matilo was once located (fig. 147). Soldiers of the Roman legions often originated from other provinces of the empire, and this caused the rapid dissemination of all kinds of exotic traditions throughout the known world. In fact, the Matilo tablet shows that the soldier who put it in the ground was well informed about the most recent innovations in the field of magic, since its inscription already comprises a few signs ending in roundels, just like the Greco-Egyptian *charaktères*.

FIG. 147. Lead tablet from a Roman army camp, inscribed with a curse. The letters OBA possibly refer to the Hebrew God Jahwe (Jehova). Photograph: RMO (acc.no. h 2008/12.1).

ISIS so auch Iuno genant wird ein Königin
der Egyptier hat das pflugen, baumpflanzen,
den saat aus den Weintrauben zu trucken, und die
Egyptijue Buchstaben gelehret A:Mundi. 1456.

p. o. n. m. l. l. k. i. h. g. f. e. d. c. c. b. a.

bi. ni. si. ka. sch. z. y. x. w. u. t. s. r. q.

It was not long, however, before the Roman Empire itself began to decline. In AD 476 a Germanic invasion put an end to Rome's position as capital of an empire, after numerous other provinces had already been lost. The eastern half of the empire, which was ruled by the emperors of Byzantium, withstood the pressure of the Germanic tribes, but here the Arabs soon arrived and conquered one country after the other. Thereby medieval Europe was effectively sealed off from the Orient. Only the most audacious travelers and pilgrims managed to enter Egypt and the Holy Land.

Yet there were several other channels by which the eastern civilizations continued to affect the west in an indirect way. First, the scriptoria of the monasteries, where the written records of antiquity (including many oriental traditions that are even older) were copied and provided with learned commentaries, at least insofar as these literary sources did not clash too seriously with Christian morality and doctrine. Second, there was a continuous exchange of information with the Moorish Kingdoms that existed in Spain and Portugal from the eighth to the fifteenth centuries, and where culture and science preserved many elements originally deriving from classical and ancient oriental sources. A third factor consisted of the Crusades (eleventh to thirteenth centuries), which enabled European noblemen and citizens to obtain firsthand experience of all kinds of oriental traditions. Finally, one should not forget the influence of the gypsies, who began to roam across Europe from the fifteenth century onward, causing a fresh influx of exotic practices not unlike those spread by the Jews at a much earlier stage.

FIG. 148. Isis teaching humanity 'plowing, planting trees, pressing wine, and the Egyptian script.' German eighteenth-century miniature, probably from an alchemical treatise, with 'Egyptian' signs below. Photograph: RMO (coll. Bibliotheca Philosophica Hermetica, Amsterdam).

All these events left their traces in the contemporary magical practices of the western world. Often these superstitions were restricted to popular belief, although other applications of the 'black arts' were readily adopted by the Church, or even regarded as the privilege of rulers and other figures of authority. The framework of the present book does not allow us to sketch an outline of all traditions prevailing in this bizarre field from the Middle Ages down to modern times. Instead, we will endeavor to determine to what extent the occult sciences of ancient Egypt affected the practice of magic in Europe and inspired the foundation of several cultural and religious movements. This is not an easy field of study because it is riddled by a veritable confusion of tongues and complicated by intentional mystifications. The issue may be summarized as follows: (1) people who assert that their occult principles stem directly from ancient Egyptian traditions are seldom right, and (2) European folklore indeed contains numerous anonymous concepts which ultimately derive from ancient Egyptian inspiration.

Since late antiquity the average witches' cauldron would contain a magic potion in which the various cultural ingredients—Egyptian, Jewish, Persian, Babylonian, Greek, and Roman—could hardly be distinguished from each other. Because Egyptian culture was considered to be much more ancient and distinguished than the others, magicians liked to assert that they followed pharaonic traditions only (fig. 148). The third-century Church father Clement of Alexandria wrote: *Egypt is the mother of all magicians.* Many eastern miracle workers and soothsayers therefore chose to emphasize their 'Egyptian' roots, which were usually purely fictitious, but which served as the best possible advertisement for their craft. A similar distortion of the facts explains the common designation 'gypsies' (Egyptians) for people who originally came from India.

In fact, the 'sympathetic' world view of late antiquity survived the Middle Ages, and witches, sorcerers, and naturalists continued to work according to the ancient

DAS
(WAHRE)
SCHATZ-HEBER
(SIEGEL)
(MOSIS)

AUF DEN BERG SINAY GEGEBEN MOSI BIB. ARCANORUM LIB. X CAP.

DAVIDS, WIE AUCH SALOMONIS (R)

GEOFFENBAHRET)
MIT WELCHEN MOSES
GROSE SCHÄTZE DER
DAVID ALLEIN SEINEN
DERT (TAUSEND)
MAHL TAUSEND
ZU DEN TEMPEL
VERLASSEN HAT, WIE
CHRONIC (XX) STEN
BLOS ALSO AN GOLD
ERN GERECHNET
TAUSEND, UND SECHS
UND AN SILBER SECHS
GOLDES REICHS THALER
LEN AUSMACHT EIN UND
GOLDES AN REICHS THALERN, DA
SIEGEL MOSES, DAVID, SALOMON SO GROSE SCHÄTZE GEHOBEN, HAT ALLHIR

MOSI AUF DEN BERG SINAY
DAVID, UND SALOMON SO
ERDE GEHOBEN, DAS NB
SOHN SALOMON HUN
GOLDS UND TAUSEND
CENTNER (SILBERS)
BAU NACH SEINEN TOD
IN ERSTEN BUCH DER
CAPITEL ZU LESEN
NACH REICHS THAL
FÜNFF, UND ZWÄNZIG
HUNDERT TONNEN GOLD
ZEHN TAUSEND TONNEN
WELCHES ZUSAMEN IN AL
VIERZIG TAUSEND SECHS HUNDERT
ALSO MIT DIESEN UNSCHÄTZBAHREN

(D. FAUST)
(AUS KUNDLING)
(IN GERMANIA)

SOLCHES AUS DER ARCAN BIBEL MOSIS GEZOGEN, WIE HIER MIT IHRER AN
WEISUNG, UND UNTERRICHT ZU SEHEN, (SCHÄTZE) OHNE CITATION ZU HEBN

(M. D. X X.)
R. P. HOFF MANNI &
MISCHINSKY REGULATIO
SINGULARI EFFECTU EXPERIA RAABÆ.

traditions. Christianity at first hardly changed this situation. Although the *Canon Episcopi*, written and circulated around AD 900, regarded witchcraft as one of the tricks by which Satan tried to seduce those of weak faith, it did not condemn sorcery as a crime. From the eleventh century onward, however, conjurers were increasingly branded as heretics, and conversely those adhering to unorthodox Christian sects were automatically accused of witchcraft. This gave rise to the systematic prosecution of witches, which reached a climax after the Middle Ages had already given way to the troubled era of the Reformation and Counter-Reformation, a period during which any aberrant philosophy or way of life was instantly condemned and punished. Even the completely innocuous herb doctors, who for generations had helped their fellow villagers with their knowledge of medicinal plants, were now burned at the stake. Such is the toll of progress.

During the heyday of the witch trials, between 1560 and 1660, the Middle Ages were already over. The cultural phenomenon now known as the Renaissance had made people realize that classical antiquity also lay behind them. Gradually modern scientific concepts began to gain ground. This led to the inevitable conclusion that the age-old notions regarding the sympathetic bonds between 'above' and 'below'—between stars and minerals, plants and animals, human beings and gods—were drawn from thin air. Even today, some people find this hard to accept, and the belief in alternative methods of healing, astrology, and palmistry is still flourishing.

Since Christianity plays a less dominant role in many people's lives today, most people would not call such beliefs heresy, but might term them 'folklore' or 'superstition'. Other convictions rather focus on

supernatural or cosmic wisdom, and are therefore believed to be of a 'superior' class. This has helped the adherents of such beliefs to be registered among the officially accepted religious denominations.

The believers of some of these cults pretend that their convictions are directly rooted in the occult wisdom of the ancient Egyptians. Although we have seen that such claims are justified with regard to the magical traditions predating the rise of modern science—medieval witch doctors were drawing from the cauldron of traditions from late antiquity, in which Egyptian ingredients were still brewing—it is quite a different matter for 'modern' religious movements. The contemporary order of Wicca likes to believe in the continuous survival of pagan traditions in Europe, but this is a notable delusion. The medieval witches did not belong to a secret cultic community, despite what was claimed by their persecutors. Other esoteric movements such as those of the Freemasons or the Rosicrucians likewise cannot be detected before the official year in which they were founded. The allegedly 'Egyptian' elements in such convictions generally conform to the state of knowledge of the period in which they were founded. Certainly, they betray a very European reinterpretation of ancient themes, and thereby belie the existence of a continuous tradition. Indeed, one may regard such convictions as expressions of Egyptomania: the phenomenon of the continuous fascination for Egyptian civilization in our own culture. Magical concepts still play a major part in these traditions.

MOSES AND THE STING-FISH

One of the links between ancient Egyptian sorcery and the magical traditions of the Middle Ages and later exists in the figure of Moses (fig. 149). As the New Testament formulates it: *Moses became expert in all the wisdom of the Egyptians and was mighty both in words and in deeds*

FIG. 149. Seal of Moses as a magic means to find treasure (German, eighteenth century). It features a number of divine names and pseudo-Hebrew texts. Photograph: RMO (coll. Bibliotheca Philosophica Hermetica, Amsterdam).

From the Sixth Book of Moses

Hear also the voice of God with which I give you the seven seals and the twelve tables. Shem, Shel, Hamforach, may the angels and the spirits serve you obediently forever, when you summon them and call their names by means of these seven seals and these twelve tables of my omnipotence. And from now onward you will also obtain knowledge of the supreme mysteries.

Therefore, my faithful friend, dear Moses, accept the strength and the superior power of your God. Aclon, Ysheye, Shannanyah, Yeshayah, E El, Elyon, Rachmiel, Ariel, Eheye, Aysher, Eheye, Elyon. By means of my seals and my tables.

The First Mystery.
Sigillum chori servilium archangelorum of the acting archangel. Conjuration.

I, N.N., a servant of God, desire and appeal to the OCH, and conjure you by means of water, fire, air, and earth, and everything which lives and moves therein, and by the most sacred names of God, Agios, Tehirios, Perailtus, Apha and Omega, Beginning and End, God and Man-Sabaoth, Adanai, Agla, Tetragrammaton, Emanuel, Abua, Ceus, Elioa, Torna, Deus Salvator, Aramma, Messiah, Clerob, Michael, Abreil, Achleof, Gachenas et Peraim, Eei Patris et Peraim Eei filii, et Peraim Dei spiritus Teti, and the words by which Solomon and Manasse, Cripinus and Agrippa conjured the spirits, and by everything else which can conjure you, that you may be obedient to me, N.N., as Isaac was to Abraham, and that you may manifest yourself at this moment before me, N.N., in the beautiful, kind and human appearance of a youth, and that you may bring me what I desire (to be specified by the performer).

The Seal.
The most effective acting archangels of this seal are the following with their Hebrew verbis revelatis citatiori divinitus coactivis: Uriel, Arael, Zacharael, Gabriel, Raphael, Theoska, Zywolech, Hemohon, Yhahel, Tuwahel, Donahan, Sywaro, Samohayl, Zowanus, Ruweno Ymoeloh, Hahowel, Tywael.

The Mystery of Mysteries.
This extremely great, secret and special use of this seal is also ex Bible, arca. Thoro. I. If this seal is buried in the ground where treasures lay hidden, those will come to the surface of their own accord, without any presence in plane lunio. [then follows the second seal, etc.]

(14-1-2010: WWW.ASIYA.ORG/ATHENEUM/SIXTH_BOOK_OF_MOSES.PDF)

MOSES AND THE STING-FISH

(Acts 7:22). At the time when these lines were written, people knew exactly what was meant thereby: this was about magical power, based on a thorough knowledge of the occult traditions of ancient Egypt. The inclusion of the five books of Moses (the Pentateuch or Torah) in the Old Testament therefore makes it an important book of magic. In the same way that Muslims use sections of the Qur'an as amulets, Christians throughout the centuries have always regarded the Bible or portions thereof as a strong defense against evil (figs. 137–38).

According to the Orisha of Trinidad, the Bible originated in Egypt but has been edited by Catholics, who added or removed parts for their own purposes. It is a universal belief that more biblical books exist than just the generally accepted ones, and that those which are kept secret are also the most effective. This includes not only those compositions which have been condemned as apocryphal, but also others of a much more poignant character. Above, we have already seen that an Eighth Book of Moses was known in Egypt from the Roman imperial period onward (fig. 68). This implies the existence of a sixth and a seventh book. Even the existence of a tenth book was already rumored at that time, whereas Moses himself was stated to be an Egyptian by birth.

A magical text entitled *The Sword of Moses* circulated in Europe from the eleventh century onward, written in a mixture of Hebrew, Aramaic, and abracadabra, and even containing a spell for walking on water! In 1725 a printer at Cologne issued an edition of 'newly discovered books with the secrets of Moses,' and before long the *Sixth and Seventh Books of Moses* were for sale across Germany. From there, these pamphlets spread to Scandinavia, also to the German-speaking communities of colonists in America. Dozens of pulp editions full of mock-Hebrew magical symbols, spells, and exorcisms for everyday use were printed until well into the twentieth century, especially in Germany, Mexico, and the United States. A new publication called *Mystery of the Long Lost 8th, 9th and 10th Books of Moses* appeared in New York in 1948. It has proved to be impossible to stop the spread of such works, despite years of eager prosecution and book burning by the Church, as well as manifold court cases dealing with reputed ritual murders. Nowadays these texts can easily be downloaded from the Internet.

In Italy around 1488, the artist Giovanni di Maestro Stefano finished a beautifully inlaid floor in the Cathedral of Siena. Occupying a place of honor directly behind the entrance, where he is the first to be seen by people entering the church, there is yet another important figure of magical tradition. He is identified by a panel of Latin text as *Hermes Trismegistus, contemporary of Moses* (fig. 150). Hermes Trismegistus has been represented in oriental garb, crowned by some kind of tiara and sporting a long beard. He hands an open book to two other persons, one of whom is also dressed as an oriental while the other wears 'Greek' clothing. Obviously they are meant to represent the two segments of the population of Hellenistic Egypt, for the book is inscribed with the text: *O Egyptians, accept the teachings and the laws!* In the context of a Christian cathedral this is a truly unexpected encounter!

To understand what was going on we must go back in time to the year 1460, when the monk Leonardo of Pistoia returned from a trip to Macedonia carrying a Greek manuscript in his luggage. Back in Florence he donated it to Cosimo de' Medici, who had it translated by his court scholar Marsilio Ficino. The latter was exhilarated to find that the manuscript held the text of the long-lost treatises of Hermes Trismegistus, which no European scholar of that time had seen with his own eyes, and which were known only from quotations by other classical authors. As soon as the texts were printed in 1471 (fig. 151), they created a sensation in the scholarly world. The treatises blended perfectly with the Neoplatonic theories propounded by these learned courtiers, and they would have an enormous impact on Renaissance philosophy, religion, and art.

Hermes Trismegistus was not considered to be a god,

FIG. 150. Hermes Trismegistus hands his teachings and laws to the Egyptians. Inlaid floor in the Cathedral of Siena, Italy. Photograph: Bibliotheca Philosophica Hermetica, Amsterdam.

but a human prophet and the teacher of Moses. This suggested that Moses's knowledge of magic in fact derived from the teachings of his Egyptian master, whose status—according to the Florentine scholars—surpassed that of all Hebrew prophets and was comparable only to the four Evangelists. Because the humanists in question continued to support the doctrines of the Catholic Church, their fascination for ancient Egypt was beyond suspicion. After all, even Jesus was believed to have owed his magical abilities to his childhood in Egypt.

Books of magic (also known as 'grimoires' at the time) whose authorship was attributed to Hermes Trismegistus, Thoth, or 'Toz the Greek' were already circulating in medieval Europe. This sorcerer was allegedly a pupil of the wise King Solomon, who was credited with the composition of several other magical texts, including The Testament of Solomon and The Key of Solomon, some of which show Islamic influences. During the major part of the twentieth century, theses pamphlets continued to be reprinted in Chicago in cheap pulp editions, and huge numbers were exported to the Caribbean, where it seems that no household could manage without them. Jewish books of magic, some of them displaying a marked Hermetic character, were also very popular during the Middle Ages and Renaissance. Certain eighteenth-century French grimoires even included copies of another old favorite: the apocryphal letter to Abgar (fig. 137).

During the twelfth century, a new interpretation of the Torah was developed by Jewish communities living in Provence, France. This became known as the *Kabbala* and emphasizes that all letters of the Hebrew alphabet are considered to be sacred and at the same time represent a numerical value. From that period on, all European grimoires comprised illustrations with pseudo-Hebrew signs and mock-hieroglyphic emblems (fig. 152), allegedly representing the secret names of God and a multitude of angels and demons. As we have seen previously, this kind of sorcery involving symbols and numbers ultimately

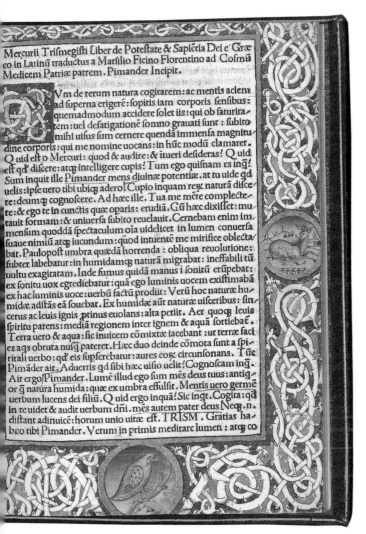

FIG. 151. Frontispiece of Hermes Trismegistus, from M. de Butricis, *About the Power and Wisdom of God* (Venice, 1491), 4th ed. Photograph: Bibliotheca Philosophica Hermetica, Amsterdam.

originated in principles formulated in ancient Egypt.

Moses and Hermes Trismegistus were not the only champions of European magic to be firmly rooted in Egyptian soil. Very popular grimoires were The Book of St. Cyprian, a third-century martyr from Antioch who studied magic in Egypt and Babylonia, and The Book of Pope Honorius, which in fact has no connection with the pope in question but was written by a namesake, a fourth-century scholar from Alexandria. Both texts were widely distributed, mainly in the United States and South America, until well into the twentieth century. It is remarkable that the chief interest of all these books lies again in love and sex, money and treasure (fig. 149), power and status: the same typically European fixations which already characterized their precursors in Greco-Roman Egypt. Even the texts and the methods used (including knotted cords and wax images) had hardly changed over the millennia.

These particular books were never popular in the Netherlands (fig. 153), but local folklore does include many elements characteristic of the same frame of mind. These concern the belief in witchcraft, spirits and poltergeists, palmistry and magnetism, the use of mascots, the popularity of horoscopes and almanacs, and manifold practices of popular medicine. An example of the latter is the use of powdered stone as a drug, as betrayed by the characteristic hollows left in the masonry of numerous medieval churches, altars, and funerary monuments in Eastern Holland and Germany. As we have seen above, this is a custom with an ancient oriental pedigree (fig. 76).

Another illustration is provided by an eyewitness account of a healing that occurred in 1942 in Katwijk, a traditional fishing community on the North Sea coast near Leiden. When a man was wounded by the poisonous spine of a sting-fish, the fish in question was thrown into the fire or hung in the chimney, and if the culprit could not be identified the whole basket of fish had to be burnt. At the same time, the following spell was read over the victim:

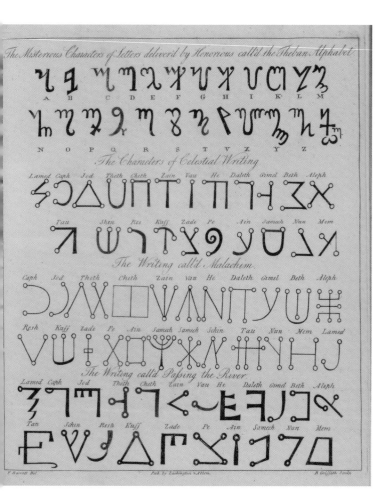

Beautiful and glorious,
God victorious,
Father, Son, and Holy Ghost.
As King Varo drowned with all his host,
And Israel crossed the Red Sea on foot,
This wound will again be good.
Amen.

Once again this procedure shows the classical trinity of text, object (in this case the sting-fish itself or the whole basketful of fish), and magical act (burning). The victim's fate is identified with that of a figure from history who was likewise exposed to the dangers of the sea. As the tribes of Israel were saved by God, so the unfortunate fisherman will also be preserved. It is almost like reading a spell from one of the ancient Egyptian books of magic. The mythical parallel in this case refers to pharaoh (or Varo in the Katwijk dialect), and to the most spectacular achievement of the sorcerer Moses, which corroborates our strong feeling that most magical traditions of ancient Egypt have survived to the present day.

GOOD CHEMISTRY

Alongside folklore, Europe also developed a number of 'higher' traditions rooted in oriental wisdom. To study these, we must first return to the fourth-century papyrus archive from Thebes. This contained two treatises dealing with alchemy (fig. 69): books that served primarily as manuals for preparing textile dyes (especially the rare purple), pigments (including substitutes for gold and silver), and inlays. The recipes in question instruct how to manufacture cheap imitations of precious metals, semi-precious stones, or the rare product of the murex or purple snail. They do not, however, distinguish between real and fake, and the craftsmen seem to have lived under the illusion that they were really making gold and silver from base products.

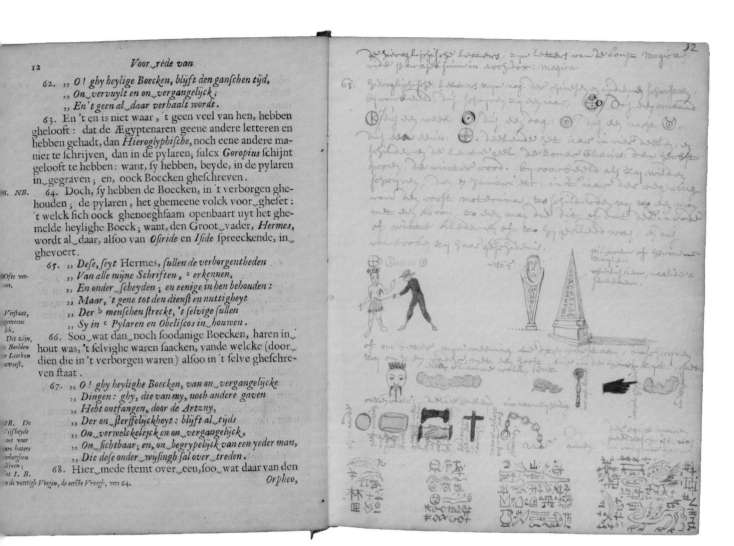

12   *Voor rède van*

62. „ *O ! ghy heylige Boecken, blijft den ganfchen tijd,*
   „ *On vervuylt en on vergangelijck ;*
   „ *En 't geen al daar verhaalt wordt.*

63. En 't en is niet waar , 't geen veel van hen, hebben
ghelooft : dat de Ægyptenaren geene andere letteren en
hebben gehadt, dan *Hieroglyphifche*, noch eene andere ma-
nier te fchrijven, dan in de pylaren; fulcx *Goropius* fchijnt
geloofd te hebben : want, fy hebben, beyde, in de pylaren
in gegraven ; en, oock Boecken ghefchreven.

6. NB.   64. Doch, fy hebben de Boecken, in 't verborgen ghe-
houden ; de pylaren, het ghemeene volck voor ghefet :
't welck fich oock ghenoeghfaam openbaart uyt het ghe-
melde heylighe Boeck ; want, den Groot vader, *Hermes*,
wordt al daar, alfoo van *Ofiride* en *Ifide* fpreeckende, in
ghevoert.

Ofte ver-   65. „ *Defe, feyt Hermes, fullen de verborgentheden*
an.   „ *Van alle mijne Schriften,* [a] *erkennen,*
   „ *En onder fcheyden ; en eenige in hen behouden :*
Verftaat,   „ *Maar, 't gene tot den dienft en nuttigheyt*
gemeene   „ *Der* [b] *menfchen ftreckt, 't felvige fullen*
lck.   „ *Sy in* [c] *Pylaren en Obelifcos in houwen .*
Dit zijn,
Beelden   66. Soo wat dan, noch foodanige Boecken, haren in
r Leecken hout was, 't felvighe waren faacken, vande welcke (door
weeft. dien die in 't verborgen waren) alfoo in 't felve ghefchreven ftaat.

67. „ *O ! ghy heylighe Boecken, van on vergangelijcke*
   „ *Dingen : ghy, die van my, noch andere gaven*
JB. De   „ *Hebt ontfangen, door de Artzny.*
Wijfheydt   „ *Der on fterffelijckheyt : blijft al tijds*
oet voor   „ *On verwelckelijck en on vergangelijck,*
re haters   „ *On fichtbaar ; en, on begrypelijck van een yeder man,*
rborghen   „ *Die defe onder wijfingh fal over treden .*
lijven ;
et I. B.   68. Hier mede ftemt over een, foo wat daar van den
n de veertigh Vragen, de eerfte Vraagh, vers 64.   *Orpheo,*

FIG. 153. Page from *Sesthien boecken van den voor-treffelijcken ouden Philosooph
Hermes Tris-megistus* (Amsterdam, 1643). The annotations have been added by
Reinier de Graaff Jr., who thereby links the text with a study of Egyptian hieroglyphs.
Photograph: RMO (coll. Bibliotheca Philosophica Hermetica, Amsterdam).

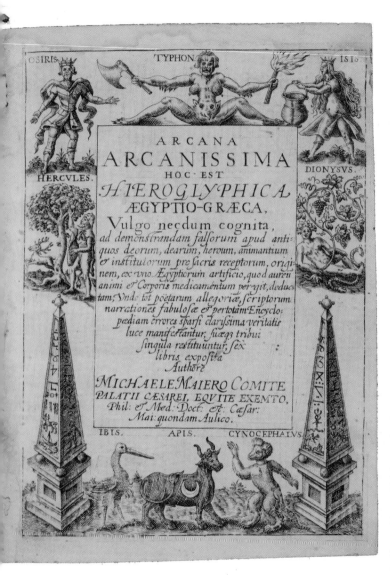

Three centuries later, the Arabs adopted this particular type of witchcraft, together with other ancient Egyptian traditions. As 'the Egyptian science' (*al-kimiya*, the precursor to chemistry), it spread all over the Islamic world, notably to centers of science such as Baghdad, Damascus, Cordoba, and Toledo. There, alchemy became part of a complex tradition based on the writings of Hermes Trismegistus and the theory of the four elements (earth, water, fire, and air), which ultimately derived from the teachings of Aristotle and other Greek scholars.

Almost literal copies of some of the prescriptions from the Theban papyri occur in eighth- to ninth-century codices now kept in Lucca and Madrid, proving that this technological heritage survived the fall of the Roman Empire and became an unbroken tradition in Christian Europe. As soon as the Arabic texts were translated into Latin, sometime in the twelfth century, alchemy became much more than just a lucrative trade. From then on, it was primarily seen as a quest for mystical knowledge. As the alchemist tries to create gold from base materials, so man must define the perfect balance between body, soul, and spirit in order to find Christ (the philosophical gold, or the Stone of Wisdom). As the elixir of life (a solution containing real or mock gold) is ingested in the hope of healing the body from all ailments, so immersing oneself in esoteric wisdom will grant the soul immortality. Such concepts explain why even the greatest scholars and the most powerful monarchs occupied themselves with what we now generally regard as fraud and superstition (fig. 154).

The epitome of the mystical interpretation of alchemy may be found in the mysterious book *Chymische Hochzeit Christiani Rosenkreuz Anno 1459*, published in Strasburg in 1616. Allegedly, Rosenkreuz was a monk who at the end of the fourteenth century left his monastery to study magic and science in Fez, Damascus, Egypt, and Spain. Upon his return to Germany, he is said to have founded an occult brotherhood for stimulating the soul. No longer were the alchemical processes actually performed

FIG. 155. Façade of the Rosicrucian Museum in San José, built in the Egyptian style in 1967. Photograph: Rosicrucian Museum.

in a laboratory; they were regarded merely as symbols referring to mystical experiences. The 'chemical wedding' of the book title did not only signify the amalgamation of two different metals but also the symbolic death and resurrection of the initiated.

Whether Christian Rosenkreuz ever existed is highly doubtful, and the 1616 text is rather a typical byproduct of the Reformation. After a brief period of prosperity during the seventeenth century, the mystical society began to decline, only to be reborn in the nineteenth and twentieth centuries. Today the ideas of the Rosicrucians are very much alive and provide inspiration for more than one hundred different religious sects and church communities. Their ideas are distinguished by a peculiar mixture of Gnosticism, esotery, and magic, Hermetism and Kabbala, whereas some societies rather stress their alleged Egyptian roots. An example of the latter is the Rosicrucian Egyptian Museum in San José, California, which is a beautiful construction in the Egyptian Revival style (fig. 155). The captions to the pharaonic objects on display focus on their symbolic meaning and refer to their relevance for Christianity.

Another occult society became public for the first time in 1717, when the earliest Masonic lodge was founded in London. Freemasons themselves state that their traditions stem from the builders of the medieval cathedrals, or even earlier. That is why the lodge is also referred to as the Grand Orient: in their quest for personal enlightenment and the improvement of society, Freemasons derive their inspiration from the wisdom of the ancient Middle East. Thus the construction of Solomon's temple is used as an allegory for the initiates' quest for inner perfection. Freemasons like to stress that their religious movement possesses ancient Egyptian roots, a conviction that found a sublime expression in Mozart's opera *The Magic Flute* of 1791 (fig. 156). A lodge of 'Egyptian Freemasons' said to stem from the time of the pyramid builders was founded by Count Cagliostro in 1777. Among the dozens

FIG. 156. Piece of scenery by Friedrich Schinkel for a performance of *The Magic Flute* in Berlin in 1816. Photograph: RMO.

of different rites for the conventions of the various lodges, the Rite of Memphis and the Rite of Misraim (the Hebrew name of Egypt) deserve special mention here. Many Masonic lodges have been built in a mock-Egyptian style. In spite of the Freemasons' fascination with Egyptian symbolism, however, the magical aspect is less pronounced with Freemasons than with Rosicrucians.

On the other hand, magic takes a central position in the movement founded by the American Joseph Smith (1805–44). Smith personally practiced magic in his youth, drawing inspiration from the cheap grimoires that enjoyed such popularity in certain colonist circles in the United States. Thus he applied himself to finding treasures by means of crystal balls, to the preparation of amulets, and to tracing magical circles as a defense against demons. After having received a number of visions, in 1830 he founded the Church of Jesus Christ of the Latter-Day Saints, better known as Mormons. Alongside the Bible, this Church acknowledges the existence of several other sacred books that are said to have been revealed to Smith by the angel Moroni. The first is the Book of Mormon (Moroni's father), which Smith allegedly found engraved on two gold tablets, written in a 'reformed Egyptian' script and describing how the ancestors of the American Indians originally came from Israel. Unfortunately, the gold plates had to be returned to the angel, but not before Smith had copied them. These copies, preserved in the Mormons' extensive archives, show that the script is distinctly un-Egyptian and was obviously a product of Smith's own fantastic inventions.

This is not quite the case with the Book of Abraham, based on a number of papyrus fragments acquired by Smith's followers in 1835. For a long time it rather looked as if the original papyri had been lost upon Joseph Smith's death in 1844, but they were retrieved in 1966. Upon reading the originals, it becomes clear that the fragments do not contain a description of Abraham's travels from Ur to Egypt (as asserted by the Mormons), but that they

ABRAHAM 1

EEN FACSIMILE
UIT HET BOEK VAN ABRAHAM
No. 1

Verklaring van bovenstaande houtsnede.

Fig. 1: de Engel des Heren. Fig. 2: Abraham op een altaar gebonden. Fig. 3: de afgodspriester van Elkenah die Abraham wil offeren. Fig. 4: het offeraltaar van de afgodspriesters dat voor de goden van Elkenah, Libnah, Mamakrah, Korasj en Farao staat. Fig. 5: de afgod van Elkenah. Fig. 6: de afgod van Libnah. Fig. 7: de afgod van Mamakrah. Fig. 8: de afgod van Korasj. Fig. 9: de afgod van Farao. Fig. 10: Abraham in Egypte. Fig. 11: getekend om de hemelzuilen voor te stellen, zoals die door de Egyptenaren begrepen werden. Fig. 12: *rakîjang*, dat uitspansel betekent, ofwel het firmament boven ons hoofd, maar in dit geval, met betrekking tot dit onderwerp, bedoelden de Egyptenaren er *sjama* mee, hoog zijn, of de hemelen, wat overeenkomt met het Hebreeuwse woord *sjamajim*.

FIG. 157. Explanation by Joseph Smith of a vignette from the Book of Breathing, based on the author's erroneous reconstruction of the original. Photograph: RMO.

Fig. 158. Glass pyramid, 'beamed in' by the Dutch healer Jomanda.
Photograph: RMO (private collection).

belong to a second-century manuscript of the Book of Breathing. Smith's fictitious 'translation' of this text and his interpretation of the vignettes of this funerary papyrus are utterly ridiculous and based entirely on his fertile imagination (fig. 157). His edition of the manuscript would never have been accepted as truth if Champollion's decipherment of hieroglyphs had not been so slow to reach certain circles in the United States. Even today, however, the greatest nonsense about ancient Egypt is still readily believed, especially if magical or supernatural aspects are involved. By way of example we can mention the ineradicable ideas about pyramid power (fig. 158) and the curse of the pharaohs.

THOTH'S BOOK OF MAGIC REDISCOVERED!

In 2004 the British journalist Jon Ronson published his book *The Men Who Stare at Goats*, which was made into a movie in 2009. It describes how in the 1980s the CIA launched a long-term research project exploring ways to eliminate the enemy through magic. This doubtless costly investigation concluded that it does not seem to be possible. The experiment is only mentioned here to underline just how common the belief in paranormal phenomena was during the 1970s and 1980s; the CIA project was a typical product of this period of flower power and New Age. In a way, it formed the apex of a century during which the belief in (Egyptian) magic became increasingly popular. Ironically, this coincided with the development of Egyptology as a scientific discipline.

It was Napoleon's Egyptian campaign of 1798–1801 that seriously opened up the Nilotic countries for archaeological research. At first it was no more than systematic treasure hunting, but a more scientific archaeological method was introduced in about 1850. In the meantime, western museums had already been filled with Egyptian antiquities, and by 1822 hieroglyphs

had also been deciphered. This meant that the voice of the ancient Egyptians could finally be heard again. One might imagine that this would put an end to the common misconceptions about pharaonic culture. Strangely enough, however, the spread of new information had the opposite effect. Immediately new grimoires began to be published in France, Germany, and America, such as *Napoleon Bonaparte's Book of Fate*, allegedly based on papyri or pyramid texts discovered by the French expedition. During the second half of the nineteenth century, spiritualists and theosophists discovered ancient Egyptian heritage and adapted it to conform to their theories. Magic played a major part in this, as illustrated by the famous book *Isis Unveiled*, written in 1877 by the founder of the Theosophic Movement, Madame Blavatsky.

In 1884 the American Peter Davidson started a mail-order company called the Hermetic Brotherhood of Luxor, which sold magic mirrors, crystal balls, and grimoires. Four years later the Hermetic Order of the Golden Dawn was founded in Britain, a society explicitly devoted to the practice of ritual magic. To this end, a number of temples were set up, such as a shrine to Isis-Urania in London, one for Osiris in Weston-super-Mare, a Horus temple in Bradford, and a sanctuary to Amun-Re in Edinburgh. The concomitant 'rituals of Isis' were designed by their pastor Samuel Mathers, who together with his wife Mina donned Egyptian vestments to perform these rites. The Irish poet W.B. Yeats and the author of *Dracula*, Bram Stoker, counted among the distinguished followers of the Order. In fact, the Order was not much different from the Rosicrucians and Freemasons, although it had a stronger focus on contemporary information as distributed by the popular books of Wallis Budge, Keeper of Oriental Antiquities at the British Museum. Initiates of the Order liked to suggest that Budge himself was secretly one of their company.

Another member of this sect was Aleister Crowley, who would become the most notorious black magician of the twentieth century. It is largely due to his influence that the Order developed satanic traits. Crowley styled himself 'the Great Beast' and the Antichrist. He worshiped the pagan god Pan, with his goat's legs, and was very interested in sexual magic. In the end, he left the Hermetic Order after a tremendous quarrel with Mathers, during which they launched vampires and demons against each other. Together with another member of the Order, Gerald Gardner, Crowley became a founding father of the modern order of Wicca, an intentionally neo-pagan religious society of witches and sorcerers that originated in the 1950s. Although the witches primarily worship the 'great goddess' (usually regarded as an aspect of the moon goddess Diana) they are broad-minded. Thus these circles, which have a prosperous existence especially in Britain and the United States, are equally interested in Celts, Egyptians and Greeks, King Arthur and fantasy, the works of J.R.R. Tolkien and Gothic fashion, Maori tattoos and Indian music, feminism and wellness. Together, these ingredients provide an even richer fill for the magic cauldron than in Roman times.

Another offshoot of the same family is the modern satanic movement, which owes much to the writings of Anton Szandor LaVey from San Francisco. In 1970, this goatee-bedecked posturer and showman published *The Satanic Bible*, to the dismay of well-meaning Christian families who happened to spot the book in the bedrooms of their adolescent sons! In fact, this pamphlet is no more than a diluted concoction of the well-known grimoires of preceding centuries, including the *Sixth and Seventh Books of Moses*, which even after two millennia still seem to find admirers. The Satanic Church founded by LaVey (there is even a Temple of Seth) is also not as wild as it sounds, and the magical rituals practiced there hardly differ from performances in the average sex theater. LaVey knew perfectly well that he was just an impostor, writing about his own Bible: *This book was written because, with very few exceptions, every tract and paper, every 'secret' grimoire, all*

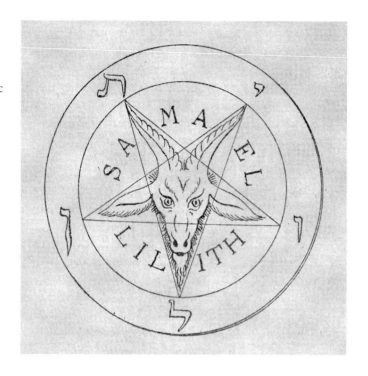

FIG. 159. Seal of Baphomet, a pseudo-Egyptian fantasy god with satanic aspects only known of since the nineteenth century. Photograph: RMO.

the 'great works' on the subject of magic, are nothing more than sanctimonious fraud—guilt-ridden ramblings and esoteric gibberish by chroniclers of magical lore unable or unwilling to present an objective view of the subject. In spite of LaVey's pretensions—his book's cover shows the seal of Baphomet (fig. 159), a non-existent ram-headed deity allegedly derived from the ancient Egyptian ram god of Mendes—this sentence is an apposite description of his own work.

Even so, many people continue to believe in the possibility of establishing contact with a supernatural world and to exert personal influence on the course of

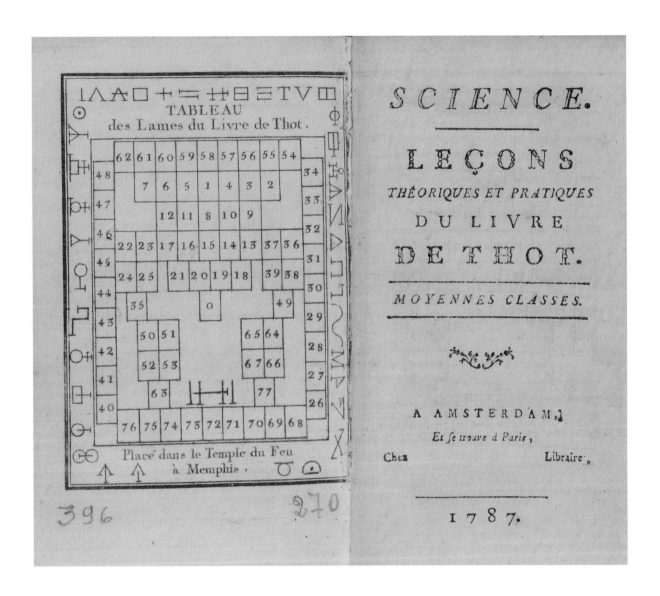

FIG. 160. Frontispiece of Etteilla, *Livre de Thot* (Paris, 1787), including a
plan showing how the cards were arranged in the Memphite temple of Ptah.
Photograph: RMO (coll. Bibliotheca Philosophica Hermetica, Amsterdam).

events. Obviously, the use of prophylactic stones and medicinal herbs, the aid of healers and magnetizers, the consultation of horoscopes or the ghosts of the dead, the wearing of amulets and the recitation of protective charms are all constants throughout history—even though the underlying principles stem from a 'sympathetic' world view which does not conform to modern science. Apparently humans need the conviction that they can affect their own fate, and the ancient Egyptians would certainly nod approvingly if they could see our present-day expressions of that feeling.

Although contemporary believers of these concepts like to claim the existence of a direct and unbroken chain of traditions linking us to the time of the pyramids, this can be ruled out in most cases. At the same time, it is fascinating to observe how many people are convinced of such a direct link. Movies such as *The Mummy Returns* (2001), television series such as *The House of Anubis* (2006), computer games such as *Tomb Raider* (2008), and comics such as *Asterix and Cleopatra* (1965) owe their popularity in part to the 'magic' attraction of ancient Egyptian sorcery. Even the best-selling Harry Potter books have many themes in common with the stories about the magicians of the pharaohs.

Does all this imply that Thoth's magic book has finally been discovered? According to certain people it does. In the fifteenth century a new card game was introduced in Europe under the name of *tarot*. Though originally a game for pure diversion, the cards were soon employed to predict the future as well. During the eighteenth century tarot became increasingly associated with the occult domain. It was even said, incorrectly, that the game originated in the Kabbala and the wisdom of the ancient Egyptians. Thus as early as 1781 the French Freemason Antoine Court de Gebelin declared that the innocent pack of cards was nothing less than the magic book of Thoth itself, and that it contained the mysteries of Isis. He asserted that the game had originally been introduced by the gypsies—who were Egyptians themselves, according to the common belief of the period—and that the name *tar-ro* meant 'royal road' in the Egyptian language (which is wrong, unfortunately).

Some years later the occultist Jean-Baptiste Alliette (alias Etteilla) became the first to publish a pack of cards decorated with Egyptian motifs (fig. 160). He also founded a *Society of Interpreters of the Book of Thoth*. An Egyptian tarot was also distributed by the magician Aleister Crowley; this edition was designed by the artist Frieda Harris, another associate of the Order of the Golden Dawn (1938–43, reprinted 1986). All cards display symbols derived from the Kabbala, alchemy, and astrology. Crowley himself wrote the accompanying pamphlet with instructions for use, which is entitled . . . *The Book of Thoth*.

And thus we return to the beginning of the present book. The quest for the principles of the cosmos proves to be just one of those indestructible cycles which are so characteristic of Egyptian magic. The greatest minds of ancient Egypt were convinced that the laws of nature were written down by the god of wisdom, Thoth, in a book for his own use. Though today very few people still take this in a literal sense, the quest for the magic book of Thoth is not so different after all from the dreams of our modern scientists who hope one day to understand the universe.

CHRONOLOGY

The names are those of the pharaohs and other rulers mentioned in this book; names in italics are those of the sorcerers. Year dates conform to those given by J. Baines and J. Malek, *Atlas of Ancient Egypt* (New York, 1993), although several corrections have been proposed since that publication came out.

PREHISTORY	(before 3000 BC)	
ARCHAIC PERIOD	(3000–2575)	
First Dynasty	(3000–2770)	
Narmer	(c. 3000)	
Second Dynasty	(2770–2649)	
Third Dynasty	(2649–2575)	
Djoser	(2630–2611)	*Imhotep*
OLD KINGDOM	(2575–2134)	
Fourth Dynasty	(2575–2465)	
Snefru	(2575–2551)	*Djadjaemanch*
Khufu	(2551–2528)	*Djedi*
Khafra	(2520–2494)	
Menkaura	(2490–2472)	*Hordedef*
Fifth Dynasty	(2465–2323)	
Unas	(2356–2323)	
Sixth Dynasty	(2323–2150)	
Seventh to Eighth Dynasty	(2150–2134)	
FIRST INTERMEDIATE PERIOD	(2134–2040)	
Ninth to Tenth Dynasty	(2134–2040)	
MIDDLE KINGDOM	(2040–1640)	
Eleventh Dynasty	(2040–1991)	
Twelfth Dynasty	(1991–1783)	
Senwosret I	(1971–1926)	
Thirteenth to Fourteenth Dynasty	(1783–1640)	
SECOND INTERMEDIATE PERIOD	(1640–1550)	
Fifteenth to Seventeenth Dynasty	(1640–1550)	

NEW KINGDOM	(1550–1070)	
Eighteenth Dynasty	(1550–1307)	
Amenhotep III	(1391–1353)	
Tutankhamun	(1333–1323)	
Nineteenth Dynasty	(1307–1196)	
Seti I	(1306–1290)	
Ramesses II	(1290–1224)	*Khaemwas*
Seti II	(1214–1204)	
Twentieth Dynasty	(1196–1070)	
Ramesses III	(1194–1163)	
Ramesses IX	(1131–1112)	
THIRD INTERMEDIATE PERIOD	(1070–712)	
Twenty-first to Twenty-fourth Dynasty	(1070–712)	
LATE PERIOD	(712–332)	
Twenty-fifth to Twenty-Sixth Dynasty	(712–525)	
Twenty-seventh Dynasty (Persians)	(525–404)	
Darius I	(521–486)	*Wedjahorresnet*
Twenty-eighth to Twenty-ninth Dynasty	(404–380)	
Thirtieth Dynasty	(380–343)	
Nectanebo II	(360–343)	
Thirty-first Dynasty (Persians)	(343–332)	
GREEK PERIOD	(332–31)	
Alexander the Great	(332–323)	
Ptolemy I	(304–284)	
Cleopatra VII	(51–31)	
ROMAN PERIOD	(31 BC–AD 395)	
Constantine	(AD 306–337)	
Theodosius	(379–395)	
BYZANTINE PERIOD	(395–640)	
ISLAMIC PERIOD	(640–present)	
Amr ibn al-'As	(640–663)	

CONCISE BIBLIOGRAPHY

GENERAL

- Borghouts, J.F. *Ancient Egyptian Magical Texts*. Leiden, 1978.
- Étienne, M. *Heka, magie et envoûtement dans l'Egypte ancienne*. Paris, 2000.
- Kákosy, L. *Zauberei im alten Ägypten*. Leipzig, 1989.
- Lexa, F. *La magie dans l'Égypte antique*. Paris, 1925.
- Pinch, G. *Magic in Ancient Egypt*. London, 1994.

CHAPTER 1

- Hart, G. *Egyptian Myths*. London, 1990.
- Ions, V. *Egyptian Mythology*. Feltham, 1968.
- Lurker, M. *The Gods and Symbols of Ancient Egypt*. London, 1980.
- Meeks, D., and C. Favard-Meeks. *Daily Life of the Egyptian Gods*. London, 1997.

CHAPTER 2

- Ghalioungui, P. *The House of Life (Per Ankh), Magic and Medical Science in Ancient Egypt*. Amsterdam, 1973.
- Gomaà, F. *Chaemwese, Sohn Ramses' II. und Hoherpriester von Memphis*. Wiesbaden, 1973.
- Griffith, F.Ll. *Stories of the High Priests of Memphis: The Sethon of Herodotus and the Demotic Tales of Khamuas*. London, 1900.

- von Känel, F. *Les prêtres-ouâb de Sekhmet et les conjurateurs de Serket*. Paris, 1984.
- Raven, M.J. *Schrift en schrijvers in het Oude Egypte*. Amsterdam, 1996.

CHAPTER 3

- Eschweiler, P. *Bildzauber im alten Ägypten*. Freiburg/Göttingen, 1994.
- Otto, E. *Das ägyptische Mundöffnungsritual*. Wiesbaden, 1960.

CHAPTER 4

- Raven, M.J. "Resin in Egyptian Magic and Symbolism," *Oudheidkundige mededelingen uit het Rijksmuseum van Oudheden* 70 (1990): 7–22.
- Raven, M. *Symbols of Resurrection: Three Studies in Ancient Egyptian Iconography*. Leiden, 1984.
- Ritner, R.K. *The Mechanics of Ancient Egyptian Magical Practices*. Chicago, 1993.

CHAPTER 5

- Betz, H.D. *The Greek Magical Papyri*. Chicago, 1986.
- Bommas, M. *Die Mythisierung der Zeit: die beiden Bücher über die altägyptischen Schalttage des magischen pLeiden I 346*. Wiesbaden, 1999.
- Borghouts, J.F. *The Magical Texts of Papyrus Leiden I 348*. Leiden, 1970.

- de Buck, A., and B.H. Stricker. "Teksten tegen schorpioenen naar papyrus I 349," *Oudheidkundige mededelingen uit het Rijksmuseum van Oudheden* 21 (1940): 53–62.
- Caffaro, A., and G. Falanga. *Il papiro di Leida*. Salerno, 2004.
- Dieleman, J. *Priests, Tongues, and Rites: The London–Leiden Magical Manuscripts and Translation in Egyptian Ritual (100–300 CE)*. Leiden, 2005.
- Gardiner, A.H. *The Ramesseum Papyri*. Oxford, 1955.
- Griffith F.Ll., and H. Thompson. *The Demotic Magical Papyrus of London and Leiden*. London, 1904–1909.
- Massart, A. *The Leiden Magical Papyrus I 343 + I 345*. Leiden, 1954.
- Massy, A. *Le papyrus de Leyde I 347*. Ghent, 1887.
- Quibell, J.E. *The Ramesseum*. London, 1898.

CHAPTER 6

- Altenmüller, H. *Die Apotropaia und die Götter Mittelägyptens*. Munich, 1965.
- Edwards, I.E.S. *Oracular Amuletic Decrees of the Late New Kingdom*. London, 1960.
- Erman, A. *Zaubersprüche für Mutter und Kind*. Berlin, 1901.
- Leitz, C. *Tagewählerei*. Wiesbaden, 1994.

- Pinch, G. *Votive Offerings to Hathor.* Oxford, 1993.
- Sternberg-El Hotabi, H. *Untersuchungen zur Überlieferungsgeschichte der Horusstelen.* Wiesbaden, 1999.
- Westendorf, W. *Erwachen der Heilkunst: die Medizin im alten Ägypten.* Zurich, 1992.

CHAPTER 7

- Derchain, P. *Le papyrus Salt 825 (B.M.10051), rituel pour la conservation de la vie en Égypte.* Brussels, 1965.
- Fairman, H.W. *The Triumph of Horus: An Ancient Egyptian Sacred Drama.* London, 1974.
- Germond, P. *Sekhmet et la protection du monde.* Basel, 1982.
- Raven, M.J. *Symbols of Resurrection: Three Studies in Ancient Egyptian Iconography.* Leiden, 1984.
- Van de Walle, B. *Princes et pays d'Asie et de Nubie: Textes hiératiques sur des figurines d'envoutement du Moyen Empire.* Brussels, 1940.

CHAPTER 8

- Faulkner, R.O. *The Ancient Egyptian Book of the Dead.* London, 1985.
- Gardiner A.H., and K. Sethe. *Egyptian Letters to the Dead, Mainly from the Old and Middle Kingdoms.* London, 1928.
- Ikram, S., and A. Dodson. *The Mummy in Ancient Egypt.* London, 1998.

- Raven, M.J. "Egyptian Concepts on the Orientation of the Human Body," *Journal of Egyptian Archaeology* 91 (2005): 37–53.
- Schneider, H.D. *Shabtis.* Leiden, 1977.

CHAPTER 9

- Abitz, F. *Statuetten in Schreinen als Grabbeigaben in den ägyptischen Königsgräbern der 18. und 19. Dynastie.* Wiesbaden, 1979.
- Andrews, C. *Amulets of Ancient Egypt.* London, 1994.
- Malaise, M. *Les scarabées de cœur dans l'Égypte ancienne.* Brussels, 1978.
- Mekis, T. "Données nouvelles sur les hypocéphales," *Kút (Quarterly of the Doctoral School of History Eötvös Loránd University)* 7 (2008): 34–80.
- Raven, M.J. *Symbols of Resurrection: Three Studies in Ancient Egyptian Iconography.* Leiden, 1984.
- Raven M.J., and R.J. Demarée. "Ceramic Dishes Used in the Preparation of Kyphi," *Jaarbericht Ex Oriente Lux* 39 (2005): 39–94.
- Strauss, E.-C. *Die Nunschale: eine Gefässgruppe des Neuen Reiches.* Munich, 1974.

CHAPTER 10

- Blackman, W.S. *The Fellahīn of Upper Egypt.* London, 1927. (Repr. Cairo, 2000).

- Fowden, G. *The Egyptian Hermes: A Historical Approach to the Late Pagan Mind.* Princeton, 1986.
- Iversen, E. *The Myth of Egypt and its Hieroglyphs in European Tradition.* Copenhagen, 1961.
- Kropp, A.M. *Ausgewählte Koptische Zaubertexte.* Brussels, 1931.

CHAPTER 11

- Burckhardt, T. *Alchemy.* Longmead, 1986.
- Coenen, M., and V. Couckuyt. "Over Mormonen en Oudegyptische dodenteksten," *Phoenix* 45:1 (1999): 7–20.
- Davies, O. *Grimoires: A History of Magic Books.* Oxford, 2009.
- van der Molen, S.J. *Vrijdag de dertiende: Bijgeloof en wat erachter zit.* Utrecht and Antwerp, 1979.
- Russell, J.B. *A History of Witchcraft.* London, 1980.

INDEX